Securing Your Business with Cisco ASA and PIX Firewalls

Greg Abelar

D1262439

Cisco Press

800 East 96th Street
Indianapolis, Indiana 46240 USA

Securing Your Business with Cisco ASA and PIX Firewalls

Greg Abelar

Copyright © 2005 Cisco Systems, Inc.

Published by:
Cisco Press
800 East 96th Street
Indianapolis, IN 46240 USA

Printed in the United States of America 1 2 3 4 5 6 7 8 9 0

First Printing June 2005

Library of Congress Cataloging-in-Publication Number: 2004111842

ISBN: 1-58705-214-8

Warning and Disclaimer

This book is designed to provide information about how to deploy the ASA/PIX version 7 operating system using the Adaptive Security Device Manager (ASDM). Every effort has been made to make this book as complete and as accurate as possible, but no warranty or fitness is implied.

The information is provided on an "as is" basis. The authors, Cisco Press, and Cisco Systems, Inc. shall have neither liability nor responsibility to any person or entity with respect to any loss or damages arising from the information contained in this book or from the use of the discs or programs that may accompany it.

The opinions expressed in this book belong to the author and are not necessarily those of Cisco Systems, Inc.

Trademark Acknowledgments

All terms mentioned in this book that are known to be trademarks or service marks have been appropriately capitalized. Cisco Press or Cisco Systems, Inc. cannot attest to the accuracy of this information. Use of a term in this book should not be regarded as affecting the validity of any trademark or service mark.

Corporate and Government Sales

Cisco Press offers excellent discounts on this book when ordered in quantity for bulk purchases or special sales.

For more information please contact: **U.S. Corporate and Government Sales** 1-800-382-3419
corpsales@pearsontechgroup.com

For sales outside the U.S. please contact: **International Sales** international@pearsoned.com

Feedback Information

At Cisco Press, our goal is to create in-depth technical books of the highest quality and value. Each book is crafted with care and precision, undergoing rigorous development that involves the unique expertise of members from the professional technical community.

Readers' feedback is a natural continuation of this process. If you have any comments regarding how we could improve the quality of this book, or otherwise alter it to better suit your needs, you can contact us through email at feedback@ciscopress.com. Please make sure to include the book title and ISBN in your message.

We greatly appreciate your assistance.

Publisher	John Wait
Editor-in-Chief	John Kane
Cisco Representative	Anthony Wolfenden
Cisco Press Program Manager	Jeff Brady
Executive Editor	Brett Bartow
Acquisitions Editor	Michelle Grandin
Production Manager	Patrick Kanouse
Senior Development Editor	Christopher Cleveland
Development Editor	Allison Beaumont Johnson
Senior Project Editor	San Dee Phillips
Copy Editor	Keith Cline
Technical Editors	Andy Huey, Tom Hunter, Darrin Miller
Editorial Assistant	Tammi Barnett
Book and Cover Designer	Louisa Adair
Composition	Interactive Composition Corporation
Indexer	Tim Wright

CISCO SYSTEMS

Corporate Headquarters
Cisco Systems, Inc.
170 West Tasman Drive
San Jose, CA 95134-1706
USA
www.cisco.com
Tel: 408 526-4000
    800 553-NETS (6387)
Fax: 408 526-4100

European Headquarters
Cisco Systems International BV
Haarlerbergpark
Haarlerbergweg 13-19
1101 CH Amsterdam
The Netherlands
www-europe.cisco.com
Tel: 31 0 20 357 1000
Fax: 31 0 20 357 1100

Americas Headquarters
Cisco Systems, Inc.
170 West Tasman Drive
San Jose, CA 95134-1706
USA
www.cisco.com
Tel: 408 526-7660
Fax: 408 527-0883

Asia Pacific Headquarters
Cisco Systems, Inc.
Capital Tower
168 Robinson Road
#22-01 to #29-01
Singapore 068912
www.cisco.com
Tel: +65 6317 7777
Fax: +65 6317 7799

Cisco Systems has more than 200 offices in the following countries and regions. Addresses, phone numbers, and fax numbers are listed on the
Cisco.com Web site at www.cisco.com/go/offices.

Argentina • Australia • Austria • Belgium • Brazil • Bulgaria • Canada • Chile • China PRC • Colombia • Costa Rica • Croatia • Czech Republic
Denmark • Dubai, UAE • Finland • France • Germany • Greece • Hong Kong SAR • Hungary • India • Indonesia • Ireland • Israel • Italy
Japan • Korea • Luxembourg • Malaysia • Mexico • The Netherlands • New Zealand • Norway • Peru • Philippines • Poland • Portugal
Puerto Rico • Romania • Russia • Saudi Arabia • Scotland • Singapore • Slovakia • Slovenia • South Africa • Spain • Sweden
Switzerland • Taiwan • Thailand • Turkey • Ukraine • United Kingdom • United States • Venezuela • Vietnam • Zimbabwe

About the Author

Greg Abelar has been an employee of Cisco Systems, Inc., since December 1996. He was an original member of the Cisco Technical Assistance Security Team, helping to hire and train many of the engineers. He has held various positions in both the Security Architecture and Security Technical Marketing Engineering Teams at Cisco. Greg is the primary founder and project manager of the Cisco Written CCIE Security exam. Prior to his employment at Cisco, Greg worked at Apple Computer, Inc., for eight years as a TCP/IP, IPX, and AppleTalk cross-platform escalation engineer. At Apple, he also served as a project leader in the technical platform deployment for the Apple worldwide network. From 1991 to 1996, Greg worked as both a systems programmer and an IT manager for Plantronics, Inc. From 1985 to 1991, Greg was employed by the County Bank of Santa Cruz, working as an applications programmer. Greg lives with his wife, Ellen, and three children, Jesse, Ethan and Ryan, in Aptos, California.

About the Technical Reviewers

Steve DeJarnett is a senior manager in the Cisco Systems Security Technology Group, where he leads the team that developed ASDM 5.0 and the Cisco IPS Device Manager (IDM 5.0). Prior to his work in security management, Steve held various leadership positions in the Cisco Integrated Communications and Managed Appliances and Services Groups. Prior to his employment at Cisco, Steve led development teams at Origin Technology, Philips Electronics, and IBM. Steve's interest in security started in college, where he spent many late nights trying to keep hackers out of computer systems at Cal Poly San Luis Obispo.

Andy T. Huey is currently a technical leader with the VPN and Security Business Unit at Cisco Systems, Inc. He has been working at Cisco since 1997 and has more than 13 years of experience in computer networking. Prior to his development work on ASDM, he developed ease-of-use configuration and management solutions for Cisco IP telephony and access routing platforms. Andy holds a Bachelor of Arts degree in computer science from the University of California, Berkeley.

Darrin Miller is an engineer in the Cisco Security Technology Group. For the past two years, Darrin has conducted security research in the areas of IPv6, SCADA, incident response, and network device hardening. This work has included protocol security analysis and security architectures for next-generation networks. Darrin has authored and contributed to several books and white papers on the subject of network security. Prior to his six years at Cisco, Darrin held various positions in the network security community.

Dedications

This book is dedicated to the hundreds of Cisco customers who were the early adopters of security technology. You put your trust in me and my co-workers at the Cisco Technical Assistance Center, calling in search of advice and help to deploy security solutions to protect your network resources. Your passion and understanding of the importance of security technology provided the inspiration to write this book. I hope that this book can reach out and help others in their efforts to secure their network assets.

Acknowledgments

I want to give special recognition to Michelle Grandin for making me a believer in myself and giving me the confidence to write this book. Also, very special thanks to Brett Bartow, Chris Cleveland, Allison Johnson, and the Cisco Press production team for their support and commitment. They took this book from just another engineering idea to a comprehensive book that will hopefully help many people to understand and implement network and host security.

When this book was started, ASA and the PIX version 7 operating system were in pre-beta stage; there was little information available about the product. Because of this, I needed to lean heavily on my technical editors, who are key individuals in delivering this product to the market. A very, very special thanks to the technical editors—Steve DeJarnett, Andy Huey, and Darrin Miller—for their incredible efforts to ensure the accuracy of the technical information of this book. You guys are the best!

Also a very special thanks to Steve DeJarnett, the engineering manager for ASDM, for his trust and support in allowing me to represent the hard work of his team by bringing this book to press. In addition, I want to thank the ASDM and 7.0 software development team, who did such an incredible job delivering this product. The book scratches only the surface of the effort and sweat that you folks put into the development of this product. I want to formally acknowledge the superhuman feat you guys and gals pulled off bringing Cisco into the twenty-first century with this product.

A big "thank you" goes out to Cisco managers Mike Jones, Dan Angst, Mark Doering, and Larry Battle for allowing me the opportunity to complete this project. Also a thank you to Ido Dubrawsky, a good friend and Cisco Press author, who helped build the foundation of this book with his contributions to the original outline and table of contents. I also want to recognize the efforts of my friends Tom Hunter, Matt Kaneko, and Cihan Yazicioglu, all ASA/PIX technical marketing engineers, who helped in many different ways, but mostly provided me with early technical material that enabled me to make early headway in this book.

I want to thank my cousin Gary Chavez, who is also a published author, for helping to set my expectations before, after, and during the delivery of this book. Through his success as an author, he has motivated me to move forward with this project.

There are also five individuals who have been professional and life mentors, without whom I wouldn't even have been in the position to write this book. Cisco managers and friends Lorne Braddock and Kevin Lueders, who helped me to shape my career, as well as helping me to understand the importance of a strong foundation and the importance of integrity. My friend Joe Riera, who believed in and who helped me get started on my career path. And finally, thanks to my father and mother, Pete and Betty Abelar, for being who they are and helping me through life's lessons and supporting me unconditionally.

Finally, and most importantly, I want to thank my family. My wife, Ellen, who not only encouraged me to work weekends for three months while she took care of our three young sons, but who also stood behind me and supported me through the year-long process of bringing this book to market. In addition, she spent countless hours editing my grammar and flow so I wouldn't look too silly when I delivered my final draft. Also, thanks to my boys, Jesse, Ethan and Ryan, who patiently waited for Daddy to come home late at night and on weekends, still greeting me with warm and open arms.

This Book Is Safari Enabled

The Safari® Enabled icon on the cover of your favorite technology book means the book is available through Safari Bookshelf. When you buy this book, you get free access to the online edition for 45 days.

Safari Bookshelf is an electronic reference library that lets you easily search thousands of technical books, find code samples, download chapters, and access technical information whenever and wherever you need it.

To gain 45-day Safari Enabled access to this book:

- Go to http://www.ciscopress.com/safarienabled
- Complete the brief registration form
- Enter the coupon code YLFA-JIAG-SZK5-XMGD-LHHR

If you have difficulty registering on Safari Bookshelf or accessing the online edition, please e-mail customer-service@safaribooksonline.com.

Contents at a Glance

Table of Contents

Icons Used in This Book

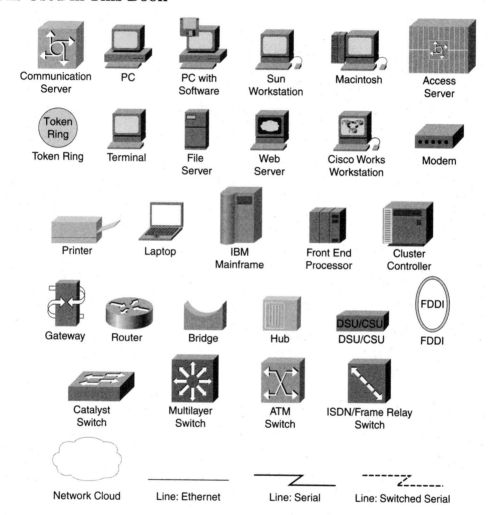

Command Syntax Conventions

The conventions used to present command syntax in this book are the same conventions used in the IOS Command Reference. The Command Reference describes these conventions as follows:

- **Boldface** indicates commands and keywords that are entered literally as shown. In actual configuration examples and output (not general command syntax), boldface indicates commands that are manually input by the user (such as a **show** command).
- *Italics* indicate arguments for which you supply actual values.
- Vertical bars (I) separate alternative, mutually exclusive elements.
- Square brackets [ ] indicate optional elements.
- Braces { } indicate a required choice.
- Braces within brackets [{ }] indicate a required choice within an optional element.

Foreword

About twenty years ago, IEEE Spectrum called me for input on their year-end technology review and asked, "What is the biggest unsolved problem in computer security?" My immediate answer was, "lack of user awareness." Unfortunately, with the exception of spam and viruses, which are already wreaking havoc, my answer would probably be the same today.

While it is a dream that is unlikely to come true, when a system has just two possibilities—being secure or insecure—I would like to see vendors include the appropriate modifier in their sales pitches. Imagine the response if, when cell phones first came out, the banners in electronics stores had read, "Buy your insecure cell phone here!" Had this type of candor been a requirement rather than a voluntary disclosure, vendors would certainly have taken security more seriously.

In the same way, the fact that the Internet is inherently insecure needs to be recognized and dealt with. We need more forward-looking attempts to bring security to our electronic communications and I welcome Greg Abelar's effort in that direction. Firewalls are a critical part of any integrated network security strategy, and books such as this help raise awareness of the threats inherent in today's open, heterogeneous internetworking environments and the solutions that can be applied to make the Internet a safer place.

Martin E. Hellman
Professor Emeritus of Electrical Engineering
Stanford University
Co-inventor of public key cryptography

Introduction

Understanding and deploying network security is a key factor in determining whether your business, which relies on the Internet, will succeed. The costs that businesses have incurred over the past few years because of security vulnerabilities are staggering. Losses are estimated to be in the billions of dollars. In addition to the direct costs to your business if you suffer a network security compromise, you can also put other businesses or Internet users at risk because the compromise you suffered can be leveraged to attack against other network devices. This problem has become so serious that in some areas of government there are discussions on whether a business or individual can be held liable in this situation.

This book provides you with complete step-by-step processes using the Cisco Adaptive Security Device Manager (ASDM) in conjunction with Cisco Security Agent (CSA) host intrusion prevention software to ensure that your security posture is strong enough to stand up against any network or host attack, whether sourced from the Internet or from inside your own network.

Goals and Methods

The primary objective of this book is to provide you with the following:

- An understanding of network and host security
- The risk involved with deploying your network on the Internet
- Step-by-step instructions on how to mitigate Internet security risks

The key mitigation technique or methodology used in this book is a structured approach to security called *defense in depth*. Defense in depth is a method using several layers of network and host defenses to protect your infrastructure. These security layers are deployed using ASDM and the ASA/PIX Security Appliance. However, because a security appliance alone can't protect against all network attacks, CSA host intrusion prevention software is recommended as a mandatory security deployment. CSA is capable of stopping any attacks launched against a Microsoft Windows (and some Solaris and Linux) host or server environment connected to the Internet.

Who Should Read This Book?

Many people view security as a "black-box voodoo" technology that is sophisticated and intimidating. Although that might have been true a few years ago, vendors have been successful in reducing the complexity and bringing security to a point where most anyone with a good understanding of technology can deploy network security.

This book is an extension of the work to simplify security deployment. It's designed to help the following classes of technical and business professionals:

- Business owners
- Network administrators
- Network engineers
- Operating systems administrators
- Security engineers
- Current ASA/PIX security appliance users

- Current PIX Firewall users
- Application developers
- IT, network, and development managers
- Managers responsible for evaluating corporate risk

People with all levels of experience might benefit from this book. Every attempt has been made to explain security technology in such a way that individuals will be able to grasp the basic concepts and deploy an ASA/PIX Security Appliance and host security.

Even if you are an experienced security engineer, you will still find value in this book because it encompasses new mitigation technologies not possible before the ASA/PIX version 7 operating system and the CSA were brought to market.

How This Book Is Organized

The book is divided into three distinct parts. Part I is dedicated to helping you understand security and the technology used to mitigate security risks. Part II guides you through step-by-step procedures of how to deploy ASDM, ASA/PIX version 7, and CSA, which mitigate those security risks. The appendixes in Part III help you to understand the new features of the ASA/PIX version 7 operating system along with some best practices for deploying those features.

The book is intended to be read cover to cover but is flexible enough that if you have experience with security, the PIX Firewall, or the ASA/PIX Security Appliance, you can use a specific chapter as a reference for deploying specific security mitigation technology.

The book is formatted according to the following list of sections and chapters.

- **Part I, "Network Security and the ASA/PIX Security Appliance"** — This section establishes a foundation of security, firewall, and ASDM knowledge:

  - **Chapter 1, "Internet Security 101"** — This chapter explains the risks associated with doing business on the Internet. It covers how a security attack can impact you or your business and outlines the different ways that an attack can occur.

  - **Chapter 2, "Principles of Network Defense"** — This chapter covers a security defense method called defense in depth, which is the model used in this book for deploying security appliance and host protection.

  - **Chapter 3, "Getting Started with the ASA/PIX Security Appliance"** — This chapter walks you through setting up ASA/PIX Security Appliance and ASDM hardware and software.

  - **Chapter 4, "Exploring the Adaptive Security Device Manager"** — This chapter is an in-depth discussion of the navigation methods and features of ASDM.

- **Part II: "Securing Network Infrastructures with ASDM"** — This section is a step-by-step deployment guide for deploying defense in depth by using a combination of ASA/PIX version 7 and ASDM.

  - **Chapter 5, "Deploying Secure Internet Connectivity"** — This chapter is a step-by-step deployment guide explaining how to use the ASDM Startup Wizard to connect your business securely to the Internet.

- — **Chapter 6, "Deploying Web and Mail Services"**—This chapter is a step-by-step deployment guide explaining how to use the ASDM Startup Wizard to securely add public devices such as mail or web servers to your network.

- — **Chapter 7, "Deploying Authentication"**—This chapter is a step-by-step deployment guide explaining how to use ASDM to authenticate users of the ASA/PIX Security Appliance and how to authenticate users of public web services.

- — **Chapter 8, "Deploying Perimeter Protection"**—This chapter is a step-by-step deployment guide explaining how to use ASDM to filter only wanted traffic and protect your network from perimeter attacks.

- — **Chapter 9, "Deploying Network Intrusion Prevention"**—This chapter is a step-by-step deployment guide explaining how to use ASDM to deploy intrusion prevention software (IPS). IPS examines the traffic you let into you network in Chapter 8 and ensures that attack traffic is not buried inside the packets.

- — **Chapter 10: "Deploying Host Intrusion Prevention"**—This chapter examines CSA host intrusion prevention software, which is a key element in defense in depth. It covers in detail how CSA works and provides some suggestions for deployment in your environment.

- — **Chapter 11: "Deploying VPNs"**—This chapter provides a step-by-step guide for configuring and monitoring network remote access using the IPSec VPN technology.

- **Part III, "Appendixes"**— This section outlines the new features of the ASA/PIX version 7 operating system and includes some best practices for deploying those features:

  - — **Appendix A, "Deploying Effective Security Management"**—This appendix covers security management best practices to help increase the security posture and effectiveness of your security system.

  - — **Appendix B, "ASA/PIX Version 7 Advanced Features"**—This appendix covers the new advanced features available with the ASA/PIX version 7 operating system.

  - — **Appendix C, "ASA/PIX Version 7 and ASDM Software Recovery"**—This appendix is a step-by-step procedure of how to recover your security appliance in the event of failure.

+ Ethernet - Base system by which the ......
....
...... the .... from your .... have to ......
....

    Protocols ....

10. ....
7. .... (........ ....)
y 92. .... 92.168 ....
* SMTP Protocols defines how mail messages are sent
between hosts
* POP3 & IMAP4 (retrieval) these two protocols
are mechanisms for downloading ....
....
IMAP ....

    ....
        IMAP ....
....
tracert - used to trace a route to the host ....
ping - used to test connectivity ....
.... with ....
.... your connection ....
nslookup - used to perform ....

PART I

Network Security and the ASA/PIX Security Appliance

This chapter addresses the following topics:

- **Network Attacks: A Serious Problem**—Understand the seriousness of network threats, the current statistical trends, and the availability and sophistication of attack tools.

- **Assessing Your Vulnerability to Network Attacks**—Learn what makes you or your company vulnerable to a network or computer attack.

- **Attack Impact**—Discover the real and hidden costs that a company can incur if attacked, as well as government regulations and liabilities that can be incurred for violation of those regulations.

- **Attackers**—Understand the various reasons why hackers attack systems, how they launch their attacks, and how they choose their victims.

- **Protecting Yourself and Your Business**—Explore solutions that you can deploy to protect computers and networks.

CHAPTER 1

Internet Security 101

One of the main ideas you should walk away with after reading this book is that implementing Internet access and doing it securely is neither difficult nor intimidating. In this book, you learn in a straightforward way what threats exist and how to defend against those threats. No one can guarantee an absolutely risk-free Internet experience, but if you follow the recommendations in this book, you will have protection against *almost* all known and unknown attacks.

Network Attacks: A Serious Problem

Every device that connects to the Internet is subject to security threats. The risk of network and host attacks not only affects businesses that sell goods via the Internet but also any computer that connects to the Internet at any time. Internet-connected hosts can be attacked from many different sources and in many different ways. A host can be infected with worms and viruses through e-mail, web pages, or almost any network service.

The impact on computers that have been attacked can be as benign as a pop-up message that does no harm to as harmful as the removal of critical files causing computers to crash, consequently destroying critical data. The attack that most people fear the most is the theft of confidential data.

CAUTION   Don't be fooled into thinking that because you have a personal firewall and antivirus software that you are protected from attacks. Antivirus software can stop only known attacks, and personal firewalls generally limit traffic but stop few attacks. Personal firewalls need to let valid traffic into a host, and hackers generally attack a network or a device using the valid traffic passed by firewalls. Chapter 2, "Principles of Network Defense," covers this issue in greater detail.

The average user often overlooks the fact that not only PCs are subject to attacks. The network devices that support the network connectivity of PCs, such as routers, switches, and firewalls, can also be attacked and used for malicious activity that can compromise the network.

Rising Security Incidents

One thing that is clear is that security incidents are on the rise and that the trend is concerning. Several of the worms that have hit the Internet since 2001 have affected in excess of one million computers. In several cases, such as the Slammer attack in January 2003 and the Blaster attack in August 2003, disruptions included services such as airline reservation systems going down and the interruption of bank machine operation.

Accurately measuring the problem of computer and network exploits is not an easy task. Most security professionals today refer to data from an organization called the Computer Emergency Response Team (CERT), run by the U.S. government, and the CERT/ Coordination Center (CERT/CC), run out of the Carnegie Mellon Software Engineering Institute. Another good source for attack trends and statistics is the attack survey published jointly each year by the FBI and the Computer Security Institute (CSI) (the latter of which holds conferences attended by business owners, engineers, and administrators to help them understand Internet security risks). In addition, nongovernmental (and sometimes nonprofit) organizations—such as the SysAdmin, Audit, Network, Security (SANS) Institute—track computer security incidents and publish "vendor-impartial" best practices for dealing with network and host security issues.

NOTE   You can find more information about the CERT organizations at http://www.cert.org. The CSI website at http://www.gocsi.com prominently features a link to the results of the most recent Computer Crime and Security Survey.

This book uses the statistics collected by CERT/CC. According to their survey, there has been almost a 100 percent increase in computer-related incidents year over year since 1998. Table 1-1 lists the number of security incidents reported to CERT/CC for the past four years. The data for 2003 is only four months into the year, so you can see the number will likely be doubled by the end of the year.

Table 1-1   *CERT/CC Security Incidents*

Year	1998	1999	2000	2001	2002	2003
Incidents	3734	9859	21,756	52,658	82,094	137,529

When looking at the data in Table 1-1, you also need to consider that many companies don't report incidents because they are afraid of the intangible costs they might incur if the market finds out they have been compromised. With this in mind, the numbers might be, and probably are, much higher than reported.

According to the CERT/CC, because of widespread use of attack tools, they have changed their reporting metrics and no longer publish the number of incidents reported. However, the number of incidents is still on the rise and is not abating, which underscores the basic message that security incidents are a concern that must be addressed.

Hacking Tools

The number of security incidents is high for many reasons. Probably the two most common reasons are as follows:

- The ease of obtaining attack tools
- The simplicity of using those tools

A search on Google using the search criteria "hacker tool download" nets a result of 26,000 websites. If you take out the quotes and use the words separately (hacker, tool, download), the result is more than 800,000 sites. Not to be all doom and gloom: The actual number of hacker download sites is probably fewer than the 26,000 reported in the first Google query, because many of the sites refer to a download site more than once. However, the fact is that there are many, many sites and many, many tools available to anyone who wants to search and download.

NOTE   The number of Google hits actually increases on a weekly basis. Before this chapter was completed, the number of hits using the separated words increased to more than 826,000.

Many hacker tools have the lethal combination of being sophisticated and easy to use. Many of these tools enable a hacker to gain administrative or root access to your systems. After hackers have gained root access, they have a remote shell to their computer, the equivalent of your DOS prompt or UNIX shell, which enables them to perform a wide range of malicious activities, including the following:

- Reading your e-mail.
- Sending e-mail from your account.
- Copying files to the hacker's own machine.
- Creating usernames and passwords.
- Deleting key files.
- Scanning keyboards to steal passwords.
- Sniffing the network to steal other passwords or sensitive data.
- Accessing customer or engineering databases.
- Using any application stored on the machine.

- Stealing credit card numbers or web password information.
- Accessing personal files, such as addresses books or password lists.
- Planting programs that will crash your computer.
- Installing software that will allow other hackers full access to your system.
- Crippling your network by using all of your available network bandwidth.
- Accessing other computer or network devices.
- Launching an attack from your computer.
- With tools such as BO2K, when used as a malicious tool, an attacker can even randomly eject your CD-ROM drive; so, don't set a full cup of coffee in front of your CD-ROM if you don't have security deployed in your network.

The preceding list is just a small sample of damage that can be done with these tools. The limit is really the imagination of the hacker. After hackers have privileged access to your system, no limit applies to what they can do except what you have imposed by the security that you have deployed.

Not all tools used for attacks are designed to gain privileged access and cause damage to a computer. Some tools focus more on specific malicious activity such as sniffing data on your network and stealing usernames and passwords. These more-focused tools even create a helpful, easy-to-read formatted report for the attacker, showing the site name along with the stolen username and password. Note that the authors of these tools did not intend for them to be attack tools used by hackers. The intent was to provide proof-of-concept tools to show that certain vulnerabilities existed and to encourage vendors to fix vulnerabilities. Even with this in mind, remember that these tools *can* be used for malicious purposes.

CAUTION   The sniffing tools previously mentioned also work on encrypted Secure Sockets Layer (SSL) and Secure Shell (SSH) connections. SSL and SSH are often thought of by common users as secure methods to protect logon credentials, but not so with the sophistication of some easy-to-obtain, easy-to-use tools such as ettercap or dsniff. Although threats clearly exist, don't panic. As indicated in Appendix A, "Deploying Effective Security Management," you can mitigate these types of attacks by deploying the Layer 2 best practices as outlined on the Cisco SAFE web page at http://www.cisco.com/go/safe. For more information on how dsniff and ettercap work, refer to their respective web pages at http://www.monkey.org/~dugsong/dsniff/ and http://ettercap.sourceforge.net/.

Many of the tools hackers use in attack kits were originally designed to help security administrators track vulnerabilities in their systems and are freely available on the Internet. An example of one such tool is Nessus, which enables you to scan a network, find all of the devices on the network, and then generate an informative and easy-to-read report that provides the following information:

- The IP addresses of all devices
- The operating systems of each device
- The version of the operating system
- The applications that have network ports open
- The version of those applications
- A full list of vulnerabilities present in each device

If you want to see a description of Nessus to get an understanding of these types of tools, take a look at the http://www.nessus.org web page.

The ease of use, availability, and sophistication of the tools add up to fun for hackers and a challenge for businesses.

Assessing Your Vulnerability to Network Attacks

Who's next? Although no one can predict with complete accuracy the chances of you personally or your business being attacked, the bottom line is that you do need to look at the security you currently have in place. If you have no security, the likelihood of an attack, and most likely a successful attack, is close to 100 percent. If you deploy the layer security, also known as *defense in depth* (the foundational concept of this book), hackers might still try to attack you, but their chances of success fall substantially.

As mentioned previously, every computer is subject to attack when connected to the Internet. Reports indicate that hackers scan the average home computer connected to the Internet by a cable modem between 10 and 25 times per day. Of course, these numbers could be higher or lower depending on many circumstances, and just because a machine is scanned doesn't mean the machine will be attacked. When you consider that security incidents are on the rise at a rate of about 100 percent year over year, the chances of your computer being attacked while on the Internet is steadily increasing.

When hackers scan networks, they are looking for networked devices (such as PCs) that are exposed to the Internet and have software or applications that have known problems that the hacker can exploit. Firewall hardware and software will considerably reduce the amount of information a hacker can gain by a scan and will encourage the hacker to move on to the next victim.

Although all systems should have antivirus software, don't be fooled into thinking that antivirus software will protect you from all attacks. Antivirus software can stop only known attacks, because it based on signatures derived from known attacks or known vulnerabilities. Because of this, the software is unlikely to thwart any new attacks launched against your system. The only way to "stop" new attacks is to use layered defense as described in this book.

NOTE   Although this is beyond the scope of this book, if you are curious to see whether anyone is trying to probe your system for information, try acquiring some freeware intrusion detection software, or a Cisco intrusion detection or prevention appliance, and put it on the outside of your network. This software generates a report if it detects any malicious activity on the front door of your network. The amount of detected activity might surprise you.

The reports generated by intrusion detection on the outside of your network might be sobering and are often effective in persuading management to make the investment in adequate security.

Attack Impact

In the world of modern business, owners walk a fine line between profitability and loss. Margins are being squeezed, and expenses are increasing. The last thing business owners want to worry about is additional losses caused by network security problems. It's beyond the scope of this book to conduct security expenditure versus threat risk analysis, but it is appropriate to point out that the cost of an attack can affect the profit and loss of a business. This section helps business owners understand what the impact of a security incident in their company might entail.

The impact on a business of being attacked could be manifold; such impact includes not only the obvious loss of revenue and cost of cleaning up after an attack, but also several hidden implications and considerations.

Tangible Costs

Tangible costs include things such as loss of revenue and the administrative costs to recover from an attack. The web is ripe with information surrounding tangible costs. Instead of focusing on a single report in this book, you are encouraged to use the web to research the different sites and decide which surveys and studies apply to your business.

The general guideline for figuring out the tangible costs of computer security in an enterprise is to assume that an administrator or IT engineer spends approximately fifteen hours per year per desktop on security related issues. This estimate includes operations such as attack forensics, attack clean-up, patch application, operating system upgrade, network device upgrades, syslog processing, event log processing, and antivirus maintenance.

Table 1-2 is a simple calculation to show your average expected security costs based on your number of desktops in combination with a range of the average pay for a desktop or security administrator and assumes that you have an average security policy and that you won't be hit with a major attack.

Table 1-2   *Yearly Average Tangible Costs*

Maintenance Hours	Desktops	Wages	Tangible Costs
15	25	$15.00	$5,625.00
15	100	$15.00	$22,500.00
15	1000	$15.00	$225,000.00
15	2500	$15.00	$562,500.00
15	25	$25.00	$9,375.00
15	100	$25.00	$37,500.00
15	1000	$25.00	$375,000.00
15	2500	$25.00	$937,500.00
15	25	$50.00	$18,750.00
15	100	$50.00	$75,000.00
15	1000	$50.00	$750,000.00
15	2500	$50.00	$1,875,000.00

The numbers in this table for the average number of hours per years spent on desktop security was derived from informal surveys with IT and security executives conducted over the entire year 2004.

The overall monetary cost to a small or medium-size business (SMB) will vary depending on how well your current security is deployed and the attacks that are successful within your environment. However, remember that when intangible costs are taken into consideration, an attack can cost much more than described in the previous table, which is discussed in the next section. Table 1-2 illustrates that an attack can be costly and that generally the cost of purchasing security hardware and software to prevent such attacks is justified.

The following are some suggested websites that are considered to be objective sources for attack and security-relevant information including attack costs:

- The Computer Security Institute   http://www.gocsi.com/
- The SANS Institute   http://www.sans.org/
- Federal Bureau of Investigation   http://www.fbi.gov/

Intangible Costs

In addition to the traditional and obvious costs incurred during an attack, a business must consider the intangible costs. Intangible costs are those that can't be easily calculated but could represent a significant impact on a company. Some of the common intangible costs include the following:

- Possible liability if an attack is launched against another business from inside your network.

- Possible liability if an attack is successful against your network and sensitive data belonging to partners, end users, or customers is compromised.

- Productivity loss—the cost of lost business when your network and hosts are down.

- The credibility of your company as viewed by customers, end-users and the market. No one wants to do business with a company that can't secure customer, user, and partner information.

- Loss of shareholder confidence.

- Negative publicity for competitors to use against a company.

- Legal liability if you are a health provider or have customer financial data on your network that is lost due to a network attack.

- Legal liability if you are a health provider and your network is compromised and patient data is stolen or, worse yet, modified.

CAUTION   Keep in mind that many business owners see a list like this and respond with, "This can't happen to us, we have a firewall in place." The truth is, a firewall alone cannot stop all attacks sourced from outside or many attacks launched from inside your network!

Government Network Security Regulations

Businesses *must* understand the legal exposure and liabilities as outlined by some recent government regulations. If you don't have the proper level of security built in to your network and host devices, you might face liability with the U.S. government based on regulations dating from 2003. Governments in Europe and other parts of the world have also recently proposed or approved laws to regulate host and network security for financial and health-care organizations.

Currently in the United States, three sets of regulations outline guidelines and liabilities for businesses. The first two regulations apply only if the business is involved in health care or handles financial data for customers. The third regulation was authored by the Office of Homeland Security. This third regulation doesn't involve any legal liability, but all companies should be aware of it.

U.S. businesses must adhere to the following regulations:

- **Sarbanes Oxley Act and Gramm-Leach Bailey Act, collectively known as the Gramm-Leach-Bailey Act (GLBA)** — Requires U.S. financial institutions to ensure the security and confidentiality of financial customer records and information.

- **Health Insurance Portability and Accountability Act (HIPAA)** — Includes regulations to protect networks and hosts that contain patient health information.

- **The Office of Homeland Security** — Published a document that encourages businesses to put security in place to protect themselves and others from computer attacks. This document also has some broad recommendations for how to implement security. The main focus of this document is to protect businesses from potential terrorist activities.

CAUTION   Don't make the mistake of thinking that just because you run a small business that a terrorist would have no interest in gaining access to your computer or a computer in your network. The most common method for an attack is for a hacker to first take over a host in a small network or university and then launch the main attack from that host. This scenario benefits hackers because no forensic data points back at them.

The principles of defense in depth (or layer security) described in Chapter 2 help to ensure that a company is compliant with many of the regulations previously described. Some of these regulations might require other technologies not described in this book, such as (but not limited to) server data encryption or audit functions. If you are responsible for finance or patient health data, recommended practice is that you have a specialist in these areas determine your compliance posture.

Attackers

A wise and prudent course of action is to become familiar with the people who pose a threat to you and your business and not underestimate them.

Those who are responsible for network attacks are known by several different names. The most common are hackers, crackers, phreaks, or attackers. This book uses the term *hacker* and *attacker* interchangeably. Attackers are those who attempt to run software with malicious intent on or against a network device that doesn't belong to them.

The sophistication of attackers ranges from people who are elite programmers to people who download and run well-documented scripts. Script downloaders are often referred to as *script kiddies*. Don't make the mistake of thinking that a script kiddie, who is not as experienced or knowledgeable as an elite hacker, can't break into your system. Scripted tools on the Internet are advanced and can break into almost any system with the same ease as an elite hacker. The predominant notion is that most security attacks are carried out by script kiddies.

Never underestimate attackers. Most of them are highly intelligent people and know their way around a computer or a network as well as or better than many network or computer professionals. Attackers can be creative in ways they choose to compromise computers. For this reason, you should strongly consider using the previously mentioned layered security architecture (defense in depth) to counter their exploit attempts. The good news is that most attackers look to exploit networks that are marginally secured. If you implement defense in depth and subvert initial attacks, most hackers who are randomly looking for networks to attack will give up and start looking for the next victim. Although firewall deployment is the main focus of this book, you also learn how to deploy defense in depth all the way to your hosts and servers, providing a solid security platform that will deter or stop attackers.

Motivation for Attacks

Some people might be surprised that hackers aren't all evil and don't attack sites just to cause harm. Many attackers believe that because of their efforts to subvert security, they are making the industry stronger; after all, they reason, vendors are forced to provide more sophisticated and effective security. Many times, an attacker targets operating system vendors, application vendors, or network equipment makers so that they will clean up their security flaws, resulting in tighter security for everyone.

Of course, many attackers exploit systems for fun, fame, bragging rights, profit, revenge, or just to be destructive.

Whatever the motive of the attacker, the approach to defend a network is the same. Build layers of defense to ensure that if an attacker gets past the first layer, the next layer catches the attack. Chapter 2 covers this network defense strategy in detail.

Anatomy of a Computer Attack

To know what security is required to stop an attack, you must understand how hackers launch an attack. This understanding also helps you to recognize whether networks or hosts within your network have come under attack.

The first thing to know is that there are three "basic" types of attacks, as follows:

- **Worm**—Propagates itself across a network and begins its malicious activity.

- **Virus**—Requires that a user take an action such as opening an e-mail attachment before it starts its malicious behavior. Sometimes, if a virus spreads itself outside of the infected host, it will start to propagate itself similar to a worm. Viruses that exhibit this behavior are sometimes referred to as *virms* (virus-borne worm), a named derived by morphing the words *virus* and *worm* together.

- **Directed attack**—This is when a hacker decides that he wants to attack a specific device or network. This is not a random attack. A certain device is the focus of an attack, and the hacker manually tries to exploit its vulnerabilities. This type of attack is generally done for a specific reason (for example, financial gain, revenge, or bragging rights).

Any attack against a network host or server comprises five basic parts, as illustrated in Figure 1-1.

Figure 1-1   *Worm/Virus Attack Model*

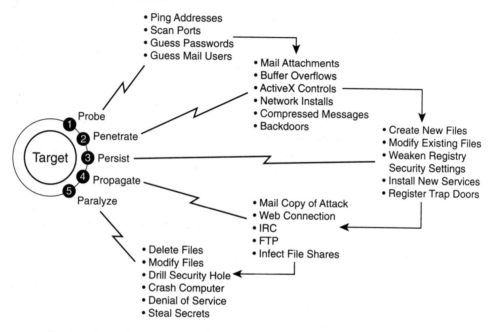

The list that follows provides detailed information about the five different stages of the worm/virus/directed attack model illustrated in Figure 1-1. This is a general list. All attacks fall within this attack paradigm. For example, an e-mail virus might or might not do a probe, but its insertion point is still done in the penetrate or persistence phase:

1 **Probe**—Hackers must learn certain basic things about your network or host before they know what attacks to run. This is called the probe phase. Normally, hackers want to know what type of traffic is allowed into a network, what servers are accessible from the outside, the operating system of the exposed servers, and the applications running on the exposed servers.

2 **Penetrate**—After attackers have discovered the information from the probe phase, they can check one of many databases on the Internet to find out how to exploit the exposed servers. The weaknesses in these systems are also called *security vulnerabilities*. In the penetrate phase, hackers run scripts or programs against the

servers to put themselves into a position where they can gain access to the system. In many of the popular worms of the past few years, attackers looked to cause buffer overflows (which allow a hacker to overwrite memory with their own code) and then executed a shell script from the buffer, gaining Shell mode access with administrative rights to the exploited machine. In many cases, hackers literally have a DOS prompt from an exploited machine displayed on the device they are using to launch the attack.

3 **Persist**—After attackers have control of a machine they must download their malicious software and perhaps install it to the system directory or put it into the startup of the exploited machines so that even if the machine reboots the hacker can still have control of the machine. During this phase, attackers can also add usernames and passwords so that they can easily get back into the machine whenever they want. Attackers at this point have control over the device, and because the device is on the network, they could choose to exploit other devices or use a network sniffer to steal usernames and passwords from other devices.

4 **Propagate**—In this phase, the malicious code run in the persist stage looks for other machines with the same vulnerability to attack and infect using the same process and same malicious code. The worm called Slammer did this extremely effectively, infecting 1.4 million hosts in a short period of time. Almost all the publicized attacks in the past few years (including worms such as Slammer, Code Red, Nimda, Sasser, and Blaster) have had an efficient propagation phase.

5 **Paralyze**—This is potentially the most damaging stage of an attack. The objective or side effect of many worms is to use up all the network bandwidth and render entire networks unusable. However, other worms are more destructive and remove key files (causing systems to crash), create back doors, or steal customer information, such as credit card numbers, customer lists, or financial information. Imagine for a second the damage that could have been done by a worm such as Slammer. If the author had chosen to search a disk drive and steal credit card numbers on all the compromised hosts, instead of just flooding the network, there could potentially have been tens of thousands of credit cards that could have been used for fraudulent activity. In turn, that could have cost businesses and consumers untold millions of dollars.

This attack model was used in the first network attack (the Morris worm, 1988) and is still used today. This model is a classic worm attack. E-mail viruses and directed attacks use basically the same methods, except the probe phase isn't generally necessary before a virus attack.

For more in-depth information on host mitigation, see Chapter 10, "Deploying Host Intrusion Prevention."

Choosing Victims

In many cases, except for revenge or fame, hackers randomly choose their victims, looking for easily exploitable systems. If they find a network that is easy to get into, they take advantage of that and start trying to exploit that network. If hackers try to penetrate a system and can't get the basic information, in many cases, they give up after a few tries. However, don't count on this to protect your network. It is important to put pervasive end-to-end security in place to defend against an attack in case hackers don't give up and do find a vulnerability.

Hackers run network vulnerability scans for days on end using many different IP addresses. When the software reports a vulnerability that they can exploit, their target is identified. The scripted scanning software provides them the following information:

- A report of which services or ports are being passed through the firewalls on the networks they have scanned

- A report on the operating systems used on the open ports

- A report on the applications used on the open port

- (Most alarmingly) A report on which security vulnerabilities are known for that combination of operating system and application

- The data they need to discover how to exploit the vulnerability and break into the system

The bottom line is that any company that is connected to the Internet can be a victim of a random hacker attack.

Protecting Yourself and Your Business

The question begging to be answered is, "How do I protect myself and my business from an Internet attack?" The protection is not as difficult as you might imagine. Fortunately, the anatomy of an attack hasn't changed since the original Morris worm in 1998. Defense in depth has proven to be an effective, proactive technique. Generally speaking, companies that have deployed defense in depth have not been affected by the successful attacks of the past several years. The attacks might have circumvented some layer of defense in depth, but they were eventually stopped before they did damage, even if the attack needed to be stopped at the host targeted by the attack. Chapter 2 explains how to deploy defense in depth.

Developing a Security Policy

Because almost every company has unique networking requirements, the way you deploy defense in depth needs to be defined by means of a document called a *security policy*.

A security policy defines what services (network traffic) you are going to let into and out of your network and the ways that your users are allowed to use these services. This information serves as the foundation for your security policy.

A small, high-level sample of information that you should include in your security policy is as follows:

- Policies to define network services
- Policies to define how user may use network services
- Policies to define who can access your network

For an excellent in-depth discussion of the elements of and ideas for a security policy, refer to the SANS website at http://www.sans.org. You can find various papers on this site about security policies. Just search for "security policy" and determine which guidelines make sense for you and your network.

The examples in this book make various policy assumptions. The assumptions are only to help you understand the fundamental steps of deploying defense in depth. You are given enough information about how to configure your firewall that you should be able to apply your individual policy easily.

Summary

The main messages of this chapter are as follows:

- The Internet security threat is real.
- Attacks are on the increase.
- Attack tools are easy to acquire and are sophisticated.
- Being attacked is costly.
- Never underestimate the intelligence or resolve of a hacker.
- You can defend against attacks.

Based on CERT/CC, hundreds of security incidents occur every day. Depending on the severity of the attack, an attack on a business might cost a substantial amount of money in lost revenue and recovery operations, in addition to intangible costs such as losing customers, partners, and investor confidence.

CERT/CC also indicates that security incidents are on the rise. The increase year over year for the past five years is approximately 100 percent. This increase indicates that if you have devices connected to the Internet, your chances of being attacked are increasing each year.

Attack tools are available on several hundred sites on the Internet. To obtain tools, someone just needs to go to one of these sites and download the tool, just like you would any freely available piece of software.

These downloadable tools are sophisticated. With these tools, hackers can gain administrative access to your system, enabling them to do anything on a system that you would be able to do as a local administrator. This access includes reading e-mail, sending e-mail, looking at or stealing important data, copying files to their own machine, setting usernames and passwords, deleting files, scanning keyboards, and many other malicious activities. In addition, more-focused tools might be used to sniff your network looking for usernames and passwords for websites or local network resources. Remember that these tools can also steal usernames and passwords (even SSL-protected usernames and passwords).

The cost of being attacked can be high. Some costs can be readily valued; these are called *tangible costs*. Other costs are difficult to value but could be devastating to a business; these are called *intangible costs*. Tangible costs include things such as loss of revenue and the administrative cost to recover from an attack. Intangible costs include the loss of business you might incur if customers find out that their information such as credit card numbers or social security numbers have fallen into dangerous hands, or shareholders who are no longer willing to own your stock because an attacker compromised your engineering secrets and sold them to a competitor.

Although some hackers attack for profit and fun, others do it to further the security awareness in the industry. Either way, they are capable individuals—don't underestimate their knowledge or resolve. You only need to attend a security conference and see firsthand that these people are highly intelligent and motivated. The one thing a business has going for them is that many hackers, generally speaking, look for easy-to-exploit systems, and with millions of computers on the Internet, hackers have an easy job finding vulnerable systems. Deploying effective security reduces your chances of attack.

The most important thing to remember from this chapter is that you can defend against Internet attacks. The ASA/PIX Security Appliance, the Adaptive Security Device Manager (ASDM), and the Cisco Security Agent make it possible to build a security system that is difficult, if not impossible, for the average hacker to exploit. You will read more about these technologies in the subsequent chapters of this book.

Defense in depth is a technique that uses many layers of network defense to secure a network and all devices connected to that network. The theory behind defense in depth is to deploy different layers of security in key parts of the network to detect, contain, and ultimately stop an attack. This book explains how you can use the ASA/PIX Security Appliance and Adaptive Security Device Manager (ASDM) together to protect a network using this methodology.

This chapter addresses the following topics:

- **Understanding Defense in Depth**—This section helps you to understand how defense in depth works to mitigate attacks against networks, network devices, and PCs connected to the network.

- **Deploying Defense in Depth**—This section explains the technology used in a defense-in-depth model to secure your network environment.

- **Security Best Practices**—This section highlights additional steps, beyond technology, that you should take to help ensure your network security.

CHAPTER 2

Principles of Network Defense

Understanding Defense in Depth

Defense in depth is the key to stopping most network and computer-related attacks. It's a concept of deploying several layers of defense that mitigate security threats. As discussed in Chapter 1, "Internet Security 101," many hackers look for what is called "low-hanging fruit" (that is, easy targets to attack). With defense applied, attackers usually either become frustrated and move on to the next target or stop the attacks altogether, deterred by the security you've put in place.

Stopping a Computer Attack

Although security experts debate the different methods to deploy defense in depth, each method involves the same technologies. The deployment of defense in depth used throughout this book involves four main layers of defense and some device-hardening best practices. You use the ASA/PIX Security Appliance and ASDM to address the first three layers, and host intrusion prevention addresses the fourth layer. The layers are as follows:

- Authentication layer
- Perimeter layer
- Network intrusion prevention layer
- Host intrusion prevention layer
- Security best practices

Authentication Layer

Authentication validates username and password credentials before allowing a user or a device to access your network or devices in your network. Authentication is only possible if a protocol is designed to accept and track usernames or passwords. Protocols that can be authenticated include File Transfer Protocol (FTP), e-mail protocols, Hypertext Transfer Protocol (HTTP), IPSec VPN access, Telnet, Secure Shell (SSH) access, and Secure Sockets Layer (SSL) (Hypertext Transfer Protocol Secure, HTTPS).

In this book, the authentication example you use protects access to the ASA/PIX Security Appliance at the edge of the network. You also use the local username and password database on the security appliance to authenticate the following network and remote-access protocols:

- **IPSec**—For remote network and remote management access
- **SSH**—For remote management access
- **HTTPS**—For remote management access
- **HTTP**—For inbound and outbound web connections

IPSec, HTTPS, and SSH encrypt traffic, including passwords. This encryption mitigates against attackers who might be sniffing your network to glean these important bits of information.

A network deployment with a small number of users could use passwords that are stored locally on the ASA/PIX Security Appliance. A larger user base would deploy a central authentication server, such as the Cisco Secure Access Control Server (Cisco Secure ACS), so that authentication can be done using Active Directory, the user domain database, TACACS+, and RADIUS. In addition, Cisco Secure ACS facilitates easy password maintenance, user maintenance, password timeouts, password expirations, and auditing from a single location.

Perimeter Layer

After users have been authenticated (or not authenticated as is the case for most web traffic), the next step is to determine what these users can or cannot do after they access the network.

The perimeter layer has two main functions:

- Traffic filtering
- Network perimeter attack protection

The first function, traffic filtering, enforces rules that define what traffic is allowed into the network as defined by your security policy. This ensures that outside users have access only to devices and services that you have defined.

The second function, network perimeter attack protection, provides protection against attacks on the perimeter of your network, such as the following:

- Denial-of-service attacks
- Session hijacking
- Unauthorized perimeter device access

You can configure the ASA/PIX Security Appliance to lock down access to the inside network as well as defend against traditional perimeter attacks. In this book, you will complete exercises enforcing user access and defending against perimeter attacks.

Network Intrusion Prevention

Up to this point, with the first two layers (authentication, perimeter) of defense in depth, you have effectively

- Granted access only to desired users
- Enforced rules specifying what those users can do
- Provided protection for perimeter attacks

The next step is to deploy network intrusion prevention systems (NIPSs). The purpose of this layer is to look inside the traffic that you have allowed into the network and determine whether that traffic is valid or whether the traffic might be a network or host attack. The ASA/PIX Security Appliance operating system relies on attack signatures to recognize an attack in progress.

NOTE   A *signature* is a definition of a sequence of data that might indicate an attack.

If an attack is identified by the ASA/PIX Security Appliance, you can configure the security appliance to either drop the packets to protect the inside resource or report the possible attack to an event logger. Users who elect to drop the packet must make sure that they are not dropping valid packets; therefore, the signatures shipped with the security appliance are well-known attacks and leave little chance of valid traffic being dropped.

The main problem with signature-based network intrusion prevention is that it's only as good as the last attack. That means that signatures can stop only known attacks. Day-zero attacks, or new attacks, pose the greatest threat to network and host security. Because of this, the ASA/PIX version 7 operating system has some new features called service policy rules that analyze the behavior of network traffic based on protocol rules and custom rules configured by you, the network, or security administrator. This layer of protection goes a long way toward providing day-zero protection.

Host Intrusion Prevention Layer

Even though the ASA/PIX Security Appliance has deployed signature-based and some behavior-based protection, there is still the possibility that attack traffic not matching these signatures or behavior can be passing through to the inside of the network. Because of this, host intrusion prevention is required as a final layer of defense in depth.

CAUTION   *Required* is a key word. Day-zero attacks are among the most costly and difficult attacks to defend against. If you deploy host intrusion prevention, the impact of these attacks is a nonissue.

By the time traffic reaches this layer, the data has been authenticated, perimeter attacks have been mitigated, traffic has been filtered, and intrusion prevention has used signatures and protocol-based rules to block any known attacks. The purpose of host intrusion prevention is to stop any remaining threats, such as the following:

- Any attack that doesn't traverse the security appliance, such as those sourced by inside users

- Any attack that was sourced from the outside of the security appliance but wasn't stopped by the security appliance filters or the application firewall

The Cisco solution for host intrusion prevention is a product called the *Cisco Security Agent* (CSA). CSA triggers on the behavior of the host or server to decide whether an attack is in progress. If it detects an attack in progress, it stops the attack by killing the infected process running on the host or by stopping the malicious behavior. Because CSA doesn't rely on attack signatures, updates are not required when new attacks (day-zero attacks) circulate on the Internet.

All attacks must display some common behaviors to exploit a host. CSA knows what those behaviors are and stops an attack before it can damage a machine. It's imperative that antivirus software be run in conjunction with CSA. Antivirus software cleans up damage caused by the attacks (as well as stopping known attacks), which provides an addition layer of host defense.

Security Best Practices

Even if defense in depth has been applied in your network, you should still follow certain network, host, and server security best practices to ensure additional protection. By implementing the technology previously described in this chapter, you can build the foundation for defense in depth. Be aware, however, that there is more to it than just putting a few building blocks into place and then walking away. As a business owner, administrator, or security engineer, you need to always ensure that you have made it as difficult as possible for someone to get into your hosts as well as any device on the network. In many cases, people secure hosts and servers but ignore network devices. This security posture has inherent risks: If attackers compromise a network device, they might find it relatively easy to build back doors or exploit access lists or routing protocols to give them unlimited access to your network. Security best practices are discussed here at an overview level only because a detailed discussion of such is beyond the scope of this book.

NOTE   For a detailed discussion on network device best practices, refer to the "SAFE Enterprise Architecture" white paper on the Cisco website at http://www.cisco.com/go/safe.

As a matter of common security practice, you should harden every device on your network. The devices that you should harden include the following:

- Firewalls (ASA/PIX Security Appliance)
- Switches
- Routers
- Hosts
- Servers

Hardening includes tasks to secure devices, such as the following:

- Applying current operating system patches
- Applying current host and server hot fixes
- Applying current application patches
- Enforcing secure usernames and passwords
- Deploying configuration best practices as recommended by the vendor
- Deploying current antivirus or intrusion prevention system signatures

---

CAUTION   Operating system upgrades and patches must be considered for all network devices, including routers, switches, and firewall security appliances, not just hosts and servers.

Cisco Network Device Hardening

Network device hardening is important and should not be overlooked. Because this book focuses on the ASA/PIX Security Appliance, however, the discussion on network device hardening is kept to a minimum here.

Cisco Router Hardening

You need to effectively lock down Cisco routers in your network. Cisco Router and Security Device Manager (SDM) is a tool to help you with this process. SDM has an easy-to-use GUI that enables you to connect to a router and run a wizard that will

- Log on to the router
- Analyze the configuration
- Look for vulnerable services enabled in the configuration
- Reconfigure the router to eliminate those vulnerabilities

NOTE	You can find extensive information about SDM on the Cisco website at http://www.cisco.com/go/sdm.

SDM identifies running processes that that hackers might exploit. It also analyzes passwords to makes sure that they are not easily cracked by guessing or dictionary attacks.

Cisco Switch Hardening

If you are using switches in your network infrastructure, you risk the launching of many possible serious attacks. Examples of such attacks are ettercap and dsniff (discussed in Chapter 1). These tools are easy-to-acquire, easy-to-use, man-in-the-middle attacks that can steal clear text and SSL-encrypted usernames and passwords. How to mitigate these attacks is beyond the scope of this book, but you should deploy the recommendations found in the white paper titled "SAFE L2 Application Note" on the Cisco SAFE website at http://www.cisco.com/go/safe.

ASA/PIX Security Appliance Hardening

The hardening of the ASA/PIX Security Appliance discussed in this book includes the following:

- Turning off clear text management services to the security appliance
- Correctly applying access control lists limiting connectivity to the inside of your network
- Turning on auditing functions
- Auditing passwords

Hardening Hosts and Servers

Because hosts and servers are usually the focus of attacks, they are the last line of defense. It's especially critical to harden these devices. Six major recommendations apply to hardening your hosts and servers, as follows:

- Install the current operating system and application security patches.
- Enforce difficult-to-guess username and password schemes.
- Deploy administrative rights only on a *required* basis.
- Apply registry and file-sharing security as recommended by the operating system vendor.
- Install antivirus software from a leading vendor.
- Install Cisco Security Agent.

Recommended practice is that you install current operating system and application patches. By doing so, you keep your operating system security posture at it highest possible level.

Cisco Security Agent (CSA) is a host intrusion prevention system that stops unknown attacks. This means that on the first day an attack comes out, even though a signature has not yet been defined, CSA will stop it. CSA also performs operating system hardening upon installation. It modifies system registries to turn off unneeded services and ensures that basic administration functions are operative.

CAUTION   Defense in depth is a layered defense system. Security appliance alone or security appliance in conjunction with network intrusion prevention will not stop all computer attacks. This point cannot be stressed enough: Host prevention *must* be applied to deploy a fully functional security system.

Defense-in-Depth Implementation Details

The ASA/PIX Security Appliance is a multifunctional device that includes the following:

- Stateful firewall services
- Network intrusion prevention
- Encryption services (VPN/IPSec)
- Auditing and reporting functions
- Authentication capabilities
- Application firewalling (protocol compliance enforcement)

These services make the Cisco ASA/PIX Security Appliance an excellent solution for defense-in-depth deployment in any network environment.

Authentication, Authorization, and Accounting

For simplicity within this book, you use the ASA/PIX Security Appliance local database to implement authentication. Because the local database is used, this type of username password verification is called *local authentication*.

Although not used in this book, the ASA/PIX Security Appliance is capable of an authentication method called *authentication, authorization, and accounting* (AAA). The security appliance, used in conjunction with the Cisco ACS, performs AAA. The ASA/PIX Security Appliance forwards username password requests to the ACS server to be accepted or rejected. If a request is accepted by the authentication server, the user is granted the request. If a request is rejected, the user is denied access to the command or access to the device.

Authentication is the process of confirming (before allowing access) usernames and passwords to ensure that the person who is logging on to a network device has the correct credentials. The common methods that the ASA/PIX Security Appliance supports for authentication are as follows:

* Simple username and password authentication using the local device database
* One-time password authentication (use with smart cards)
* Username and password authentication using credentials from domain controllers
* Username and password authentication using credentials from Lightweight Directory Access Protocol servers

Authorization is a method of controlling what users can do after they have been authenticated. Authorization can control specific events, including commands that are entered or services that are requested by a user.

Accounting is reporting provided by the ACS server and tracks user logins to the ASA/PIX Security Appliance or other devices protected by the ACS server. Accounting records include fields such as the time a user logs on, the username and the IP address from which the user logged on, and the command a user executed (or attempted) while on a device.

Two main protocols are used within AAA: RADIUS and TACACS+. Both protocols are excellent for simple username and password authentication. TACACS+ is the protocol of choice if you plan to use authorization. It enables an administrator to control down to a command level what a user can do when logged on to a device protected by an AAA server.

Perimeter Security

The perimeter of the ASA/PIX Security Appliance is the outside interface. The outside interface is the side of the security appliance that is connected to the Internet, and it is considered insecure because you have no control over traffic or events on the outside. The inside of the security appliance is the side connected to your network and is considered the secure interface.

Perimeter security entails four main functions:

* Filters traffic so that only wanted traffic is let into the inside of the network. The goal is to allow only desired traffic into the network.
* Controls denial-of-service (DoS) attacks. DoS attacks try to use up all the bandwidth of a network or a network device. The ASA/PIX Security Appliance has defenses built in to it to limit the number of connections that can use the security appliance resources.
* Ensures that the outside interface cannot be exploited to gain access to the security appliance itself (access that might allow an a hacker to make changes to the security appliance configuration).

- Allows exposure of Internet services to the outside world.
- Ensures against attacks that misuse HTTP for malicious purposes.

NOTE   You will deploy all of these perimeter defenses when you configure the ASA/PIX Security Appliance with ASDM.

Traffic Filtering

Traffic filtering on the ASA/PIX Security Appliance is done using access control lists.

NOTE   ASDM combines access control lists and the associated interface and calls them *access rules*.

These lists are applied to the security appliance network interfaces and define what traffic is allowed to traverse the security appliance. By default, all traffic is allowed from the inside of the security appliance to all the other interfaces. The security appliance recognizes a flow originated by an inside host and lets return traffic back through; the concept is sometime referred to as *stateful firewalling*. If a new connection is attempted from the outside of your security appliance to the inside, however, two things must happen:

- The traffic must be destined to an address advertised by the security appliance as a public Internet service.
- An access list must be applied defining exactly what traffic will be allowed to and from that public address.

Denial-of-Service Mitigation

DoS or distributed denial-of-service (DDoS) attacks at one time were the most popular and easiest attacks to launch on the Internet. DoS attacks overload a network to a point where the network becomes unusable. Recently, the number of DoS attacks has subsided, partly because more effective technology now stops these attacks but also partly because hackers now consider DoS attacks as being poor form and only done by those who cannot do something more sophisticated. However, DoS attacks can still be crippling. The ASA/PIX Security Appliance mitigates against various types of DoS attacks by deploying different technologies:

- **DNSGuard**—Protects against DoS attacks aimed at DNS servers. Allows only a single response to multiple DNS queries, preventing DNS storms.

- **FloodGuard**—Prevents DoS attacks caused by multiple AAA authentication attempts.

- **FragGuard**—Prevents a class of attacks based on sending parts of the attack in fragmented packets to try to circumvent the security of the ASA/PIX Security Appliance.

- **IPVerify**—Most DoS attacks use invalid or spoofed addresses so that the attack cannot be traced back to the attacker. IPVerify ensures that the source traffic is valid before the security appliance will respond to the request, effectively mitigating spoofing DoS attacks.

- **TCP Intercept**—Protects against the most popular DoS attack, called a *TCP SYN flood*. In this attack, a hacker sends thousands of requests to open a connection through the security appliance. TCP Intercept recognizes these packets as being an attack and cleans up the resources, allowing only valid traffic to go through the security appliance.

In general, these technologies use various techniques to recognize whether traffic is valid and silently drop invalid traffic to free up internal resources before the attack traffic can bring the network down. You use these techniques later in the step-by-step portion of this book.

Security Appliance Device Access Protection

If attackers obtain management access to your security appliance, they can do several things to weaken your protection:

- Configure the security appliance to allow themselves access to the inside of your network

- View the configuration of your network, making it easier for them to exploit network devices

- View traffic going through the security appliance and steal critical information such as usernames and passwords

Locking down your security appliance from attackers is a critical part of securing your network. You use ASDM to perform the following lockdown steps:

- Turn off all services where the username and password might be passed in the clear

- Disallow management access to the outside interface of the security appliance

- Configure IP addresses that are allowed to manage the security appliance

Limit Access to Network Devices

One of the fundamental and most valuable uses of a security appliance is to ensure that traffic sourced from the outside is allowed only to the devices that you've defined for public access. These services are defined on the ASA/PIX Security Appliance using a combination of functions called *static network access translation* (NAT) and *access control*.

NAT defines a link between a device on the inside of your network and an Internet address that you advertise on the outside of your security appliance. You should use NAT in combination with an access list defining what traffic is allowed to this public address. Some services that you might want to advertise are as follows:

- Web server

- DNS server

- Mail server

In Chapter 5, "Deploying Secure Internet Connectivity," you configure web and mail servers to be exposed on the Internet and filter appropriate traffic using access rules.

Note that these devices with public addresses are the network assets that attackers will scan and attack. Generally, attacks launched from the outside can target only Internet devices such as those described previously. However, after hackers have control of one of your public servers, they've established a presence on your network. Their next step is to try to exploit other nonpublic devices inside your network. It is considered best practice to place your public servers on an interface other than your inside interface. This ensures that if hackers compromise a public server, they are not yet on the inside of your network and still have a considerable amount of work to do to get there. These interfaces are often called *demilitarized zone* (DMZ) interfaces.

CAUTION   If you are exposing resources such as web servers or mail servers from your network, you *must not* use a security appliance that has only two interfaces. If you do, you must put your public servers on the inside network, which in turn exposes your internal network to an unreasonably high risk of attack.

Network Intrusion Prevention

Network-based intrusion prevention is a key component of defense in depth and the ASA/PIX Security Appliance. The purpose of this technology is to recognize and stop attacks when they flow through the appliance. The ASA/PIX version 7 operating system implements two basic forms of network intrusion prevention; one is signature-based, and the other is behavior-based and is called *application firewall features*.

Signature-based intrusion prevention is similar to the way that antivirus software works on a host. The prevention device looks for a sequence of bytes on the network that matches an attack string; if the string matches, the device can either drop the traffic or report the attack to a logging server. Using the application firewall features, the ASA/PIX version 7 operating system can enforce strict protocol usage, which will protect you against unwanted software such as unencrypted personal messenger services, peer-to-peer file sharing, or software that might tunnel traffic other than web traffic through the HTTP protocol. You can determine the action the security appliance should take if this traffic is encountered. You have the following options:

- Drop traffic.
- Report the event to syslog.
- Drop traffic and report the event to syslog.
- Reset the connection.
- Reset the connection and report the event to syslog.
- Take no action.

Part of the application-based firewall includes user-defined rules. For example, if you know that the longest URL on your web server is 50 bytes, you might want to create a rule that tells the security appliance that any request coming in greater that 50 bytes might be an attack. When the security appliance enforces this rule, it will drop or report traffic that violates this rule depending on how you set it up. You have the same choice of event actions in the previous list if a user-defined rule is triggered.

The ASA/PIX Security Appliance uses signature-based prevention. It's up to the discretion of the security administrator whether traffic will be dropped or only reported.

The signatures used in the ASA/PIX Security Appliance are common attacks and relatively easy to identify, so in this book, we are dropping traffic. In some NIPS implementations where more complex signatures are used, you might not want to drop traffic, because an alarm might not represent an actual attack. We might not want to drop attacks at the security appliance for two reasons:

- If the security appliance has a heavy traffic load, intrusion prevention might take up additional cycles and slow down network throughput.
- If there is a chance that the security appliance might drop valid traffic. (This is called a *false positive*.)

Host Intrusion Prevention

Host intrusion prevention is the final layer of defense in depth. Simply stated, attacks (usually day-zero attacks) might get past the other defensive layers; therefore, an agent on the host must stop the attack on the host or server. CSA is designed for this type of use.

CSA is security software that can recognize when software is acting badly on a host and stop that software from doing damage and stop the host from getting infected with the malicious software.

Automated Host Hardening

CSA modifies system registries to turn off unneeded services and ensures that basic administration functions are operative.

System Behavior Rules Engine

The behavior rules engine stops bad behavior on the system. This behavior includes code being executed from the stack, which is one of the main ways that hackers break into systems. This behavior engine also stops writes to the registry and to key directories on a system. Hackers use all of these methods when attempting to run or install their software on a victim's system, and so CSA can stop many common attacks just with this rule.

Chapter 10, "Deploying Host Intrusion Prevention," discusses the rules engines in greater detail.

Firewall Rules Engine

CSA has a fully functional firewall engine that behaves similarly to a personal firewall (but is more powerful). It can filter unwanted traffic and ensure that the host running the agent can't start an outbound connection, which might indicate that an attack is in process.

The CSA firewall capability includes a rule called *Net Shield*, which is capable of fooling traditional scanning tools that determine the operating system of a host or server. These scanning tools rely on certain header bits and the timing of packets to determine whether the host they are scanning is a Linux host or Microsoft Windows host. Net Shield randomly alters these bits, returning false information to those tools so that they give the attacker false information about the makeup of the network.

Application Rules Engine

The CSA application rules engine enforces proper behavior for applications to mitigate any attacks against application vulnerabilities. For example, a browser has a fairly narrow range of functions, such as the following:

- Browse and update websites using HTTP
- Browse and update using SSL or HTTPS
- Write logs to certain directories
- Run ActiveX and Java in certain contexts

Several actions, if taken by a web browser, indicate that a vulnerability of a browser is being exploited. A well-behaving browser would never do any of the following:

- Copy cmd.exe to a different name or different location
- Execute any applications
- Install applications
- Write to the registry
- Write to the system directory

When CSA detects this type of behavior, it kills the process and stops the attack that is in process.

NOTE	For system protection, CSA is one of the most powerful security applications on the market. Note, however, that CSA is designed to work in conjunction with antivirus software. CSA stops attacks, known and unknown, but it does not clean up malicious software. Antivirus protection should be viewed at as a critical additional level of defense in depth on the host.

Global Correlation Engine

CSA also has a powerful feature that can identify attacking machines that might be trying to scan or attack your hosts and stop traffic from those machines. This feature is called the *global event correlation engine*.

The global event correlation engine is effective in stopping what has become known as the *low and slow scan*. Global correlation is also effective in stopping virus or worm propagation.

Each time an event is generated by the CSA agent, the agent sends the information to the CSA Management Console (CSA MC). The CSA MC can then make decisions based on repeated attack or malicious behavior events (such as a scan present on the network). After the malicious behavior is recognized, CSA creates a rule to defend against this behavior and makes the new rule available for all the host in the network that are running CSA.

CSA in Action

Take a practical look at how CSA stops attacks. (As mentioned previously, Chapter 10 examines in more detail how CSA mitigates attacks.) Use the attack paradigm discussed in Chapter 1 that illustrates how attackers break into a host or server. Table 2-1 maps the attack phase, attack action, and CSA mitigation engine.

NOTE	Some of these attack actions have "not applicable" (n/a) under the mitigation engine. That's because the action can't be stopped, but it doesn't matter. If hackers gain access through that action, CSA stops them when they try to run malicious code.

Table 2-1   *CSA in Action*

Attack Phase	Attack Action	CSA Mitigation Engine
Probe	Scan ports	Global event correlation, firewall engine
	Guess passwords	n/a
	Ping addresses	Global event correlation, firewall engine
	Guess mail users	n/a

Table 2-1   *CSA in Action (Continued)*

Attack Phase	Attack Action	CSA Mitigation Engine
Penetrate	Mail attachments	Application engine
	Buffer overflows	Behavior engine
	ActiveX controls	Application engine, behavior engine
	Network installs	Application engine, behavior engine
	Compressed messages	Application engine, behavior engine
	Back doors	Application engine, behavior engine
Persist	Create new files	Application engine, behavior engine
	Modify existing files	Application engine, behavior engine
	Weaken registry settings	Application engine, behavior engine
	Install new services	Application engine, behavior engine
	Register trap doors	Application engine, behavior engine
Propagate	Mail copy of attack	Application engine, behavior engine
	Web connection	Application engine, firewall engine
	IRC	Firewall engine
	FTP	Firewall engine
	Infect file shares	Behavior engine, firewall engine
Paralyze	Delete files	Application engine, behavior engine
	Modify files	Application engine, behavior engine
	Denial of service	Application engine, behavior engine, firewall engine
	Crash computer	Application engine, behavior engine, firewall engine
	Steal secrets	Application engine, behavior engine, firewall engine

Additional Security Best Practices

Along with defense in depth, you need to put some additional best practices into practice to ensure that network security is achieved in your business.

Specific issues that you need to address include the following:

- VPN users are at higher risk of software infection because their environment isn't controlled by a corporate security policy.

- Security management functions such as logging, reading, and responding to syslog messages and events need to be deployed.

The bulk of the best practices described throughout the book are summarized in Appendix A, "Deploying Effective Security Management."

Remote-Access Defense

Remote access is a staple of many businesses in today's Internet environment. Increasingly, companies are finding that by allowing employees to telecommute from home or remote offices that productivity increases and expenses and overhead decrease. From a business perspective, it's a win-win situation; from a network security perspective, however, it has its challenges.

Telecommuters often connect to different Internet security providers (ISPs) that don't provide a secure environment and from wireless hotspots that are inherently insecure. Because of that, telecommuter hosts often have a higher exposure to viruses, worms, Trojans, adware, spyware, and direct attacks. This exposure becomes a problem when the telecommuter connects to the main business network. If proper security isn't in place, those hosts can spread viruses and worms to other devices inside the network. Another problem associated with telecommuting is the threat of proprietary data being sent over the Internet. Fortunately, you can mitigate both of these problems with a virtual private network (VPN) and the principles of defense in depth in the ASA/PIX Security Appliance.

The ASA/PIX Security Appliance allows businesses to set up private encrypted tunnels for people who need access to the inside network from the Internet. This group might include employees, partners, and even customers. This solution is called *virtual private networking*, and the ASA/PIX Security Appliance uses technology called IPSec to achieve the secure and encrypted communication. If you use IPSec/VPN, users who connect to your security appliance from the Internet essentially become part of a virtual network and have access to network services just as if they were inside the network.

VPN tunnels require authentication to allow only valid users access to the network. To mitigate the malicious software that can spread from these remote machines, you can use the VPN client "are you there" function to ensure that these users are running firewalls or CSA before they are allowed to connect to your network. After the VPN tunnel is terminated on the ASA/PIX Security Appliance, the security appliance then applies all its security functions to ensure that an attack isn't embedded within the VPN tunnel.

Security Management of the ASA/PIX Security Appliance

You should look at security management as a serious issue. The bottom line is that the security of your network is only as good as the management policies that have been deployed.

NOTE   For an in-depth discussion of security management, refer to the "Cisco SAFE Enterprise" white paper at http://www.cisco.com/go/safe.

Ensure at minimum that you enforce the following from a security management perspective:

- Use username and password best practices.

- Use syslog to recognize possible security appliance or attack issues.

- Perform attack forensics, follow up on attacks, and take any required action if you think an attack has been successful on one of your network devices.

- Use CSA logs to recognize possible day-zero attacks and modify your perimeter rules to help mitigate those attacks.

Securing ASA/PIX Security Appliance Usernames and Passwords

You should develop a password policy that helps to ensure that attackers cannot obtain access to your security appliance. In this book, the ASA/PIX Security Appliance is the most critical device in the network, and password protection is stressed in many different parts of this book.

Passwords should be at least eight characters and should have upper- and lowercase characters as well as special characters (numerals and +_)(*&^%$#@!). The password should never be a word that can be found in a dictionary. Many password-cracking programs available on the Internet assist hackers in breaking into password-protected devices or parsing and decrypting password files or password hashes. Because an eight-character password is difficult to remember, you might want to match your password to an easy-to-remember phrase. For example, the password Slatfatf42 could be matched to the phrase "so long and thanks for all the fish 42." Many administrators take it a step further and use obscure usernames as well as passwords. Instead of using admin or root, they use the same guidelines as passwords—a minimum of eight characters that should have upper- and lowercase characters as well as special characters (numerals and +_)(*&^%$#@!). The downside, of course, is that these names and passwords might be hard to remember. The upside is that it becomes exponentially difficult for a hacker to break into the security appliance with a brute-force password attack.

NOTE   Unless it's absolutely necessary, you would never allow management access to your security appliance from the outside. This would open the door for one of the oldest attacks on record, a brute-force password attack from the Internet. Not allowing management access from the outside also ensures that if a hacker wants to break into your security appliance, the hacker must first compromise a system on the inside. With defense in depth applied, this is a difficult, if not impossible, task. If you *must* allow management from the outside, you should use IPSec/VPN as the secure management connection.

Using the ASA/PIX Security Appliance Reporting System

The ASA/PIX Security Appliance uses the syslog protocol for reporting error messages and alerts. Syslog data can be sent to the device running the ASDM software for troubleshooting purposes, but normally, the security appliance is configured to write syslog data to a remote machine.

Syslog will contain messages that will help you to troubleshoot your environment. For example, if customers can't get to a web server and you know the web server is up and running, check the syslog; you will likely have an error message that will help you to solve the problem. Cisco.com has all the ASA/PIX Security Appliance syslog messages documented at http://www.cisco.com/go/pix in the Technical Documentation section. If you need help analyzing a message, the Cisco Technical Assistance Center is there to help every day of the year on a 24/7 schedule.

Syslog might also contain messages if you are under attack. Those message will be indicated by an intrusion detection system (IDS) prefix. If you are dropping attack packets, this indicates that the security appliance blocked a potential attack. If you are not dropping packets, you will want to go to the machine that the attack was destined for and ensure that CSA caught the attack before it was successful.

If you find that you have hundreds of IDS messages and you don't have a security manager or engineer within your business, you might want to call Cisco Technical Assistance Center to discuss what steps you should take next.

One of the most important usages of syslog is that it will tell you when someone logs on to the ASA/PIX Security Appliance, and it will show any changes made. Therefore, you should view the syslog frequently to ensure that only administrators have access to the security appliance and that there are not commands being issued that might disrupt or cause security concerns for your network.

Summary

This chapter presented defense in depth as a solution to secure a business network. Defense in depth is a concept using layers of defense to mitigate computer and network attacks. Those who fully deployed defense in depth were protected from the major worms and viruses that hit the Internet in recent years.

The basic building blocks of defense in depth are as follows:

- **Authentication**—Control who gains access to your network by deploying username and password authentication along with access control.

- **Perimeter security**—Expose only Internet addresses that you choose and control access to those services (usually public servers such and web and DNS servers). Perimeter security also provides DDoS protection for your security appliance.

- **Network intrusion prevention**—The valid traffic that is let into your network is inspected by security appliance intrusion prevention and service policy rules to ensure that there isn't known attack traffic within the data. This traffic can be dropped or reported depending on the available bandwidth of your security appliance.

- **Host intrusion prevention**—The last stop for attack prevention. This software runs on the host and provides protection for both known and unknown (day-zero) attacks. Host intrusion prevention software looks at the behavior of the operating system, the network stack, and the applications to determine whether an attack is happening. If an attack is detected, the software kills the process responsible for the attack. This technology is critical to a complete defense-in-depth implementation.

This book shows how to implement defense in depth on the ASA/PIX Security Appliance using ASDM. The following technologies and best practices are used to deploy defense in depth.

Local device authentication (usernames and passwords) verifies management access to the security appliance.

Perimeter security is implemented via the ASA/PIX Security Appliance using NAT for publishing Internet-reachable addresses; these are typically your web servers, mail servers, and DNS servers. Access to this exposed address is granted based on inbound access lists. Internet users cannot use your public services unless there is a specific access list allowing them to access these services. The ASA/PIX Security Appliance uses the technology listed in Table 2-2 to mitigate against various DoS attacks that can be expected from the Internet.

Table 2-2   *Technologies Used by the ASA/PIX Security Appliance to Mitigate Against DoS Attacks*

Protection Feature	Attack Mitigated
DNSGuard	Protects against DoS attacks aimed at DNS servers
FloodGuard	Prevents DoS attacks caused by multiple AAA authentication attempts
FragGuard	Prevents attacks based on fragmented packets
IPVerify	Prevents attacks using invalid or spoofed addresses
TCP Intercept	Protects against the most popular DoS attack (SYN flood attacks)

Host intrusion prevention is used as the critical last line of threat defense. It is the only portion of defense in depth that you cannot achieve using the ASA/PIX Security Appliance. CSA stops attacks based on the behavior of operating systems, network stacks, and applications.

Additional best practices that are discussed in this chapter include remotes-access and security management. The ASA/PIX Security Appliance implements remote access using a combination of IPSec and authentication. In addition to these technologies, CSA is required on the hosts that will connect to the network remotely, thus ensuring that the unregulated computers that might connect via IPSec won't spread viruses or worms to the internal network.

Security management best practices suggest choosing difficult-to-guess usernames and passwords for access to your security appliance and recommend that a remote syslog server be used to capture error messages for troubleshooting and security purposes.

This chapter examines the following introductory aspects of the ASA/PIX Security Appliance:

- **Cisco ASA/PIX Security Appliance Overview**—This section provides you with general information regarding the ASA/PIX Security Appliance. It explains the specific security features of the product and the protection that it offers.

- **ASA/PIX Security Appliance Models**—This section introduces the entire ASA/PIX Security Appliance family line that is capable of running the ASA/PIX version 7 operating system.

- **Installing the ASA/PIX Security Appliance Hardware**—This section provides a step-by-step guide for powering and connecting the ASA/PIX Security Appliance.

- **Installing the ASA/PIX Version 7 Operating System Software**—This section provides a step-by-step guide to install the ASA/PIX version 7 operating system and the Adaptive Security Device Manager (ASDM) 5.0.

CHAPTER 3

Getting Started with the ASA/PIX Security Appliance

This chapter covers ASA/PIX Security Appliance hardware and software information. The PIX Firewall is the industry leading firewall device as measured by the Gartner Group and many other organizations that track market share for security devices. The ASA Security Appliance nicely complements and also extends the PIX Firewall functionality with attractive speeds, features, and functions.

Cisco offers ASA/PIX Security Appliance models varying from the PIX 515/E and ASA 5500 for small to medium businesses to the PIX 535 designed for large enterprise and service provider class networks.

Cisco ASA/PIX Security Appliance Overview

The ASA/PIX Security Appliance is a multipurpose security device designed to provide protection against many different security threats. The ASA/PIX Security Appliance is unique in that you can use it as a perimeter device, and it can handle many of the layers of the tradition defense-in-depth model.

The ASA/PIX Security Appliance has many functions that protect your network. This book addresses the following specific functions:

- Denial-of-service protection
- Traffic filtering
- Interface isolation (DMZ deployment)
- Stateful traffic inspection
- Application inspection
- User authentication
- Intrusion prevention
- Secure management
- Event logging

Denial-of-Service Protection

The ASA/PIX Security Appliance uses various technologies to determine whether a distributed denial-of-service/denial-of service (DDoS/Dos) attack is launched against the security appliance. In general, it determines whether invalid data flows are being sent to the ASA/PIX Security Appliance leaving half-open connects. If so, the security appliance determines which attempted flows are invalid and cleans them up so that the appliance hardware resources are available to do the intended job of securing the network.

Traffic Filtering

The ASA/PIX Security Appliance uses access control lists (ACLs) to determine which protocols should be let into and out of the security appliance. The ACLs ensure that users on your inside network can access the Internet while keeping Internet traffic from entering into your network unless you explicitly allow access.

Interface Isolation (DMZ Deployment)

The ASA/PIX Security Appliances have multiple interfaces that you can dedicate to isolating Internet servers. This topology is often referred to as a *demilitarized zone* (DMZ). This feature is significant because, as discussed in earlier chapters, Internet servers are often the devices that hackers attack. If hackers want to get to hosts or devices on the inside of the network, and they compromise a host on the DMZ, they still face getting through the security appliance to get to the inside devices.

Stateful Traffic Inspection

Stateful inspection means that the security appliance keeps track of connections going in and out. This monitoring capability is significant because it enforces the concept that only traffic sourced from the inside of a security appliance or explicitly allowed with an ACL will be let back through the appliance. Stateful inspection keeps possible malicious traffic sourced from the Internet from traversing the security appliance and helps secure your inside network from application-level attacks.

Application Inspection

Application inspection has two functions in the ASA/PIX security appliance, as follows:

- **Protocol-compliance enforcement**—Ensures that network traffic adheres to the protocol specifications, which helps to protect against applications that might be using protocols such as HTTP to do other functions. For example, programs such as point-to-point file-sharing applications and messaging applications that tunnel traffic through HTTP are recognized and their network traffic is blocked.

- **Modify certain packets to ensure that this traffic can properly traverse the network**—Sometimes, traffic that transverses an ASA/PIX Security Appliance to the Internet causes problems because the inside address of a source machine is embedded deep within a packet and the source IP address of the packet changes before it is sent to the Internet. Application inspection monitors for this scenario and inserts the correct return traffic into the TCP packet. Without inspection capabilities, traffic such as voice traffic, FTP, SQL, and some video-streaming protocols might not find its way back to its source device.

User Authentication

The ASA/PIX Security Appliance can authenticate protocols that are let through the security appliance such as Telnet, FTP, and HTTP. If you elect to authenticate users using these protocols, they must enter a username and password before traffic can cross the security appliance. If users enter the correct set of authentication credentials, they are allowed to access the requested service. If the username and password are not entered or entered incorrectly, users are denied access and the access attempt is logged to your security appliance syslog server. The ASA/PIX Security Appliance also offers several options for authenticating users who are managing the security appliance.

Intrusion Prevention

The Cisco ASA/PIX Security Appliance uses a set of well-known attack signatures to determine whether attack traffic is attempting to traverse the security appliance. You can configure the security appliance to either drop the attack traffic it finds or report the traffic to a syslog server. In addition, the security appliance enables you to write custom access service policy that enforces protocol compliance on certain traffic traversing the appliance.

Secure Management

The ASA/PIX Security Appliance uses two secure methods to manage the appliance from the network: Secure Shell (SSH) or Hypertext Transport Protocol Secure (HTTPS). Although you do learn in this book how to configure SSH, all the configurations herein use ASDM, which uses HTTPS to secure its connection to the device. The ASA/PIX Security Appliance also has built-in management support for Telnet and HTTP. Because these protocols pass traffic, including usernames and passwords, in clear text, which makes it easy for someone to steal access credentials, these methods are not recommended.

Event Logging

Many different levels of logging are available on the ASA/PIX Security Appliance. This book uses syslog with the output destined for the ASDM application. Along with providing vital information regarding the status of your appliance, syslog makes troubleshooting the security appliance much more user friendly. ASA/PIX Security Appliance syslog enables you to identify possible network attacks and helps you perform attack analysis.

Models

The PIX Firewall has several different models, each intended to address the needs of a different portion of the firewall market. Because this book is targeted to small businesses and medium-to-small enterprises, the PIX 515E is the hardware that is used to do all the configurations herein.

The following models of the ASA/PIX Security Appliance can run the ASA/PIX version 7 operating system:

- Cisco PIX Security Appliance 515E
- Cisco PIX Security Appliance 525
- Cisco PIX Security Appliance 535
- Cisco ASA Security Appliance 5510
- Cisco ASA Security Appliance 5520
- Cisco ASA Security Appliance 5540

PIX 515E

The target market for the PIX 515E is the small business and low- to medium-end enterprise customers. The PIX 515E can handle 130,000 simultaneous connections. The theoretical limit for throughput on the 515E is 190 Mbps.

The PIX 515E can support multiple hardware interfaces, which makes the PIX 515E the lowest model Cisco PIX Firewall to support interface isolation (DMZ functionality). Unlike the smaller firewalls, the PIX 515E represents an ideal machine for companies that want to use public servers from the inside of their company network. With this firewall, you no longer have to worry that if hackers exploit one of your public servers that they might be able to exploit devices on the inside of your network.

Depending on licensing, the PIX 515E can support up to six different hardware interfaces. The PIX 515E is also the lowest PIX model that supports failover, which is a technology that allows a secondary PIX Firewall to take over operation if your primary firewall fails. The secondary PIX becomes a fully functional firewall in as little as 1.5 seconds.

PIX 525

The PIX 525 is a large enterprise or small service provider class machine. The 525 can handle 280,000 connections and can pass 330 Mbps. It can also support up to eight physical interfaces. All the concepts discussed and the configuration performed in this book using the ASDM apply to the PIX 525, too; because the target market for this book is smaller enterprises, however, the examples in this book focus on PIX 515E.

PIX 535

The PIX 535 is a large enterprise (with high-traffic requirements) service provider class machine. The 535 can handle 500,000 connections and can pass 1.7 Gbps. It can also support up to ten physical interfaces. The concepts discussed and the configurations performed in this book using the ASDM apply to the PIX 535, too.

Cisco ASA 5510 Security Appliance

The Cisco ASA 5510 Security Appliance is targeted to the small- to medium-size business/small enterprise market. Its estimated throughput is 300 Mbps, with 32,000 maximum connections with a base license and 64,000 with a security-plus license. The ASA Security Appliance optionally comes with an add-on security module that can accelerate the network intrusion prevention features.

Cisco ASA 5520 Security Appliance

The Cisco ASA 5520 Security Appliance is targeted to the medium-size business/small- to medium-size enterprise market. Its estimated throughput is 450 Mbps, with 130,000 maximum connections. The ASA Security Appliance optionally comes with an add-on security module that can accelerate the network intrusion prevention features.

Cisco ASA 5540 Security Appliance

The Cisco ASA 5540 Security Appliance is targeted to the larger enterprise/small service provider market. Its estimated throughput is 650 Mbps, with 280,000 maximum connections. The ASA Security Appliance optionally comes with an add-on security module that can accelerate the network intrusion prevention features.

NOTE   All references to *target market* are generalized based on average business requirements. A small business might have enough traffic to justify a Cisco ASA 5540 Security Appliance or a small service provider might have only enough traffic to justify a Cisco ASA 5510 Security Appliance. Talk to your local Cisco representative to determine the correct hardware to support your network.

Installing the ASA/PIX Security Appliance

Installing the ASA/PIX Security Appliance is a straightforward and easy procedure. Regardless of the security appliance model, all its components are shipped in the same box. The contents of the box include the following:

- Security appliance chassis
- Power supply
- Power cord

Most ASA/PIX Security Appliances are installed directly, as is, out of the box. This discussion does not cover memory upgrades or power requirements for special-case installations, but does cover the basics required to get your security appliance up and running, including the following:

- Understanding the ports
- Installing power
- Failover
- Booting

Because PIX/ASA Security Appliances are not yet on the market, installation instructions and back-panel diagrams are not published in this book. If you purchase one of these devices, the diagrams and instructions come with the device.

Understanding the ASA/PIX Hardware Ports

Before discussing installation of the ASA/PIX Security Appliance, this chapter briefly introduces you to the interfaces. This interface information will establish a foundation of knowledge you might find necessary as you work through this book. The PIX 515E has several different types of ports on its backplane, as follows:

- Ethernet ports
- Console port
- Failover port

Ethernet Ports

The PIX 515E can have up to six 10/100-bps Ethernet ports. This book covers with three Ethernet ports: an inside port, where your protected user network will be located; an outside port, which will be connected to the Internet; and if you plan to house a web server or a mail server, you will have a third port, referred to as a DMZ port. The ASA 5500 Security Appliance is capable of 10/100/1000-bps Ethernet speeds.

Console Port

The console port isn't used in this book except to install the initial ASA/PIX version 7 operating system. For reference, however, it is a management serial port where you can plug in a PC using terminal emulation and enter or view commands on the ASA/PIX Security Appliance.

Failover Port

The failover port is a specialized port that connects two security appliances together and is used to keep the configuration in sync between the primary and secondary appliance. This book does not cover failover technology.

Installing Power

To apply power to the PIX 515E, PIX 525, and PIX 535, it's simply a matter of plugging the power cable into the back of the units. Notice that the PIX 535 has dual power supplies. To enable power-supply failover, you can plug two cables into the back of the PIX 535.

See Figures 3-1 through 3-3 for backplane layout and power-receptacle locations for the various models of the ASA/PIX Security Appliance.

Figure 3-1 *PIX 515E Back Panel*

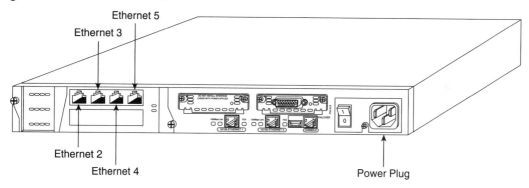

Figure 3-2 *PIX 525 Back Panel*

Figure 3-3 *PIX 535 Back Panel*

Power Plug

Booting the ASA/PIX Security Appliance

This book addresses booting the ASA/PIX Security Appliance in two different ways. Although it's not generally recommended, you can boot the security appliance just by turning the power supply off on the back of the unit, waiting 15 seconds, and then turning the switch back on. If you boot a security appliance this way, changes made to the configuration are not saved unless you do a **write memory** command before you turn off the device. The second option for restarting the ASA/PIX Security Appliance is to enter the **reload** command in the Enable mode of the command-line interpreter. This boot method gives you a chance, before your device reboots, to save any configuration changes you have made.

Troubleshooting

Although not likely, if you power up your ASA/PIX security appliance for the first time and it hangs and reports an error that hardware cards were not found, follow these steps:

Step 1 Power down your ASA/PIX Security Appliance.

Step 2 Remove the cover as instructed by the hardware installation instructions. Remember to use ESD grounding before you handle the internal cards.

Step 3 Reseat any removable network interface cards or memory cards.

Step 4 Replace the cover as instructed by the hardware installation instructions.

Step 5 Turn the power back on the ASA/PIX Security Appliance.

If the problem persists, contact the Cisco Technical Assistance Center. They can instruct you on further troubleshooting or arrange for a new unit to be sent to your location.

Installing the ASA/PIX Software

The ASA/PIX operating system software comes installed on the security appliances. If you purchased your hardware before 2005, it will not have the version 7 operating system.

Version 7 will be shipped on all ASA/PIX Security Appliances larger than a PIX 515E after the first part of 2005. ASDM runs only on ASA/PIX version 7. If you have a version of the PIX operating system prior to 7, you must manually install ASA/PIX version 7 before you can complete the step-by-step instructions outlined in this book.

Manual ASA/PIX Version 7 Installation

You must do seven things before you can upgrade the security appliance, as follows:

- Ensure that your PIX operating system is at minimum version 6.3(x).

- Obtain a valid ASA/PIX version 7 license.

- Obtain a version of the ASA/PIX version 7 operating system and ASDM from the download area of Cisco.com.

- Prepare your PC for the version 7 upgrade. Install a TFTP server on your PC and configure your PC so that you can upgrade the ASA/PIX operating system.

- Prepare your ASA/PIX Security Appliance to download the version 7 operating system.

- Download ASA/PIX version 7 to your security appliance.

- Download ASDM 5.0 to your security appliance.

Ensure That PIX 6.3(x) Is Installed

It's a simple task to ensure that PIX version 6.3 is running on your ASA/PIX Security Appliance. Connect to the console port and reboot the device; the version numbers display just before the security appliance prompt displays. Alternatively, manually log in to your appliance and enter the **show version** command in Privileged or Nonprivileged mode. The Security Appliance will display the following output in the first few lines, revealing the current version of the operating system:

```
Cisco PIX Firewall Version 6.3(4)
Cisco PIX Device Manager Version 3.0(2)
Compiled on Fri 02-Jul-04 00:07 by CiscoSystems
CiscoPix up 7 days 18 hours
```

If you are on a version of the PIX operating system lower than 6.3, you must go to the Cisco website and upgrade to 6.3 before proceeding to the following steps. You can find all software versions and instructions on the website download pages.

Obtain a Valid ASA/PIX Version 7 License

Before you can use the full functionality offered in ASA/PIX version 7, you must ensure that you have a valid ASA/PIX version 7 license. You have two options for obtaining a license. One is to call Cisco customer support and ask for the license. They will provide you with step-by-step instructions. If you currently have a SmartNet contract, you should be eligible for a no-cost upgrade to the ASA/PIX version 7 operating system.

The second option is to go to Cisco.com and search for the "Licensing and Activation Keys [Cisco PIX Firewall Software]" document. This document describes how you can obtain an ASA/PIX license from Cisco.

Obtain the ASA/PIX Version 7 Operating System and ASDM 5.0 Software

To obtain a version of the ASA/PIX version 7 operating system, you must log on to the Cisco website with a valid username and password. Navigate to Technical Support and then to Downloads. When you are on the download pages, navigate to Cisco Secure Software and then to Cisco Secure PIX Firewall Software.

NOTE	Occasionally, Cisco changes the look of its website, so these steps might vary depending on when you download the software.

Proceed to the location marked Download PIX Firewall Software. On this page, you will see the binary image for the ASA/PIX version 7 operating system. Click the image name, and you will be prompted to open or save the image. Click **Save** and put the image in a safe location on your PC; later, you will transfer the file to the home directory of your TFTP server. If you have a TFTP server on your system already, you can save the file directly into the home directory of the TFTP server.

Repeat this procedure for the ASDM 5.0 software.

Preparing Your PC for an ASA/PIX Security Appliance Upgrade

To upgrade your ASA/PIX Security Appliance to version 7, you must have a PC with a TFTP server, and you must configure your network interface card to allow connectivity to the security appliance.

NOTE	If you already have a TFTP server on your network, you can skip the section that describes how to configure a PC as a TFTP server.

You can install any number of free TFTP servers from the Internet on your PC. Any implementation of TFTP should work for this download.

NOTE	When this text refers to a *PC*, the reference can apply to either a Windows- or a Linux-based machine. However, the examples in this book use Windows as the primary operating system.

Before you can transfer the software from your PC to the ASA/PIX device, you must establish a network connection between the two. This connection requires configuration on the PC as well as configuration on the security appliance.

If you already know how to connect the two machines, use the following steps as a reference only. If you have no experience in doing this, however, you can follow the step-by-step instructions to successfully move the file from the TFTP server to the ASA/PIX Security Appliance:

Step 1   Install the TFTP software on your PC and ensure that the ASA/PIX version 7 binary and ASDM file are in the TFTP default directory. This procedure was previously described.

Step 2   Configure the properties of the network card on your PC so that it can communicate with the ASA/PIX Security Appliance. Configure the following parameters: IP address **192.168.1.2**, subnet mask **255.255.255.0** and default gateway **192.168.1.1**. (See Figure 3-4.)

Figure 3-4   *Windows IP Configuration*

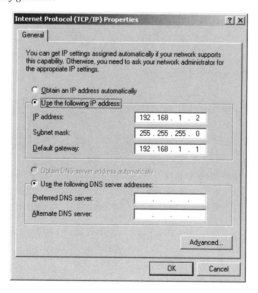

Step 3   Ensure that the ASA/PIX version 7 operating system and the ASDM 5.0 software are in the download directory of your TFTP server, and then launch the server.

Your PC should now be prepared to copy the ASA/PIX operating system and ASDM software.

Preparing the ASA/PIX Security Appliance for the Upgrade

You must now put the ASA/PIX Security Appliance in a mode in which you can configure it to use its TFTP download functions:

Step 1   You must first be connected to the ASA/PIX via the console port. This is done using a serial cable from your PC to the security appliance console port and using a terminal emulator such as HyperTerminal. Set the HyperTerminal properties to use your PC serial port with the parameters shown in Figure 3-5: speed at 9600 bps, 8 data bits, no parity checking, and 1 stop bit.

Figure 3-5   *HyperTerminal Settings*

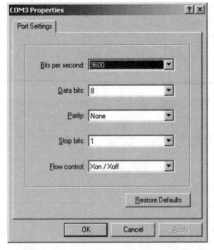

Step 2   After you establish console connectivity, you are ready to upgrade your ASA/PIX appliance to the ASA/PIX version 7 image. Enter the **enable** command followed by the **conf t** command to get into Command mode.

Step 3   Plug a crossover Ethernet cable between an Ethernet 1 port on your security appliance and the networking card on your PC.

Upgrading the ASA/PIX Security Appliance to Version 7

The following tasks have been completed:

- Your PC has the ASA/PIX and ASDM software.
- TFTP is running on your PC.
- Your PC is connected physically to the ASA/PIX Security Appliance.
- The ASA/PIX Security Appliance is configured to access the TFTP server of the PC.

You are ready to start the download procedure. A word of caution: All steps are critical in this process. If these steps are not followed, you might have to restart the download process from the beginning.

Enter the following commands on you security appliance:

Step 1   Initialize Ethernet 1 to prepare for the download:

```
pixfirewall(config)# ip address inside 192.168.1.1 255.255.255.0
```

Step 2   Ping your TFTP server to ensure connectivity. If you don't have connectivity (if your pings are not successful), go back to the previous section and ensure that you have performed all the required steps:

```
pixfirewall(config)# ping 192.168.1.2
        192.168.1.2 response received -- 0ms
        192.168.1.2 response received -- 0ms
        192.168.1.2 response received -- 0ms
```

Step 3   Enter the commands and the appropriate responses to copy the ASA/PIX version 7 operating system image to your security appliance:

```
pixfirewall(config)# copy tftp://192.168.1.2/asapix70.bin flash:
copying tftp://192.168.1.2/asapix70.bin to flash:image !!!!!!
Image installed
```

Step 4   Reload your security appliance to start the ASA/PIX version 7 operating system:

```
pixfirewall(config)# reload
Proceed with reload? [confirm]
```

Step 5   Your security appliance might display the expected benign messages letting you know that it is reformatting the Flash file system and that some old commands are being converted to new commands:

```
Old file system detected. Attempting to save data in flash
Initializing flashfs...
flashfs[7]: Checking block 0...block number was (-23149)
flashfs[7]: erasing block 0...done.
flashfs[7]: Checking block 1...block number was (-20086)
flashfs[7]: erasing block 1...done.
INFO: converting 'inspectionprotocol ftp 21' to MPF commands
```

Step 6   After your security appliance has rebooted, you need to show the version to verify that the ASA/PIX version 7 operating system is now running:

```
pixfirewall> show version
Cisco PIX Security Appliance Software Version 7.0
```

Congratulations. At this point, you should have a fully functioning ASA/PIX version 7 image loaded and running on your security appliance.

Upgrading the ASA/PIX Security Appliance to ASDM 5.0

After installing the ASA/PIX version 7 operating system, you need to complete the following steps from Configuration mode (enter the two commands **enable** and then **conf t** to get into this mode) to install ASDM 5.0:

Step 1 Configure your ASA/PIX appliance interface with the following commands:

```
pixfirewall(config)# interface Ethernet1
pixfirewall(config)# nameif inside
pixfirewall(config)# security-level 100
pixfirewall(config)# ip address 192.168.1.1 255.255.255.0
```

Step 2 Use the **ping** command to ensure that you still have connectivity between your PC and the security appliance:

```
pixfirewall(config)# ping 192.168.1.2
```

If you don't have connectivity, you might need to reconfigure your PC and your security appliance to establish a communication path. But if you have followed this procedure step by step, you should be okay.

Step 3 Now, you are ready to download the ASDM software. Enter the following command on the ASA/PIX Security Appliance in Enable mode:

```
pixfirewall(config)# copy tftp://192.168.1.2/asdm50.bin flash
```

Note The filename for the ASDM software might differ from the preceding command.

When prompted for the output filename, use **asdm.bin** to be consistent with the rest of this book.

You should see exclamation marks displayed on your screen indicating that the file is in the process of downloading.

Step 4 After the ASDM download has completed, you must configure the ASA/PIX Security Appliance to identify the image name for ASDM. In Enable mode on the security appliance, enter the following command:

```
pixfirewall(config)# asdm image asdm.bin
```

Step 5 To enable ASDM to run, you must first enable the web server with the following command:

```
pixfirewall(config)# http server enable
```

Step 6 After the HTTP server has started, you must add a command that tells the ASA/PIX Security Appliance what IP address it can access an ASDM session from. To enable your PC to administer your security appliance, enter the following command:

```
pixfirewall(config)# http 192.168.1.2 255.255.255.255 inside
```

Note	This command allows access *only* for the PC with the IP address 192.168.1.2.

ASA/PIX Licenses

Before you can use the full functionality of your ASA/PIX Security Appliance, you must ensure that you have a valid license key.

ASA/PIX licenses come in the following basic flavors:

- Restricted license
- Unrestricted license
- 3G Mobile Wireless security services
- Active/active failover
- Specialized ASA licenses

Restricted License

The licensing structure on the ASA/PIX Security Appliance is such that you get different functionality with different types of licenses. If you purchase a restricted license, you are limited as to the number of users who can use the security appliance at any one time. When a user goes outbound through the appliance, a table is built called an *xlate*. The licenses use the number of xlates to enforce the number of users allowed on the PIX. A limited license does not include support for failover. (See Table 3-1 in the next section.)

Unrestricted License

An unrestricted license allows you to pass as many users as you want to the Internet; it also allows failover connectivity to an ASA/PIX Security Appliance with a failover license. This license also allows you to use the maximum number of interfaces and memory available in the security appliance. With more memory, you can support more VPN users.

3G Mobile Wireless Security Services

The 3G Mobile Wireless security services license is a license for security services covering 3G Mobile Wireless deployments that use the General Packet Radio Service (GPRS) Tunneling Protocol standard (GTP). This license also includes advanced GTP inspection services that provide mobile wireless users secure interaction with roaming partners. Refer to the ASA/PIX Security Appliance 7 software description at Cisco.com for more information.

Active/Active Failover

The active/active failover license supports bidirectional state sharing between active/active failover pair members for network environments with asymmetric routing topologies, allowing flows to enter through one Cisco ASA/PIX Security Appliance and exit through the other.

Specialized ASA Licensing

This is a class of licenses to be used specifically for ASA Security Appliance hardware. Refer to the ASA/PIX Security Appliance 7 software description at Cisco.com for more information.

Installing the PIX License Key

Installing an ASA/PIX license key is straightforward. To upgrade a license on PIX 6.3 and above, just follow these steps:

Step 1   Obtain a valid license that is generated for the serial number of your ASA/PIX Security Appliance.

Caution   If the license is not generated using the serial number on your ASA/PIX Security Appliance, it will not activate the device.

Execute a **show version** command on your ASA/PIX Security Appliance, and a serial number will be printed in the following format:

```
Serial Number: 818273311
```

Step 2   Follow instructions for obtaining a license key from the previous section "Obtain a Valid ASA/PIX version 7 License."

Step 3   After you have your new key, log on to your ASA/PIX Security Appliance using Access Enable mode. (You do not have to get into Configuration mode.) Enter the following command:

```
activation-key <five-tuple license key>
```

Step 4   Enter the command **write memory** to write the new key to nonvolatile memory.

Summary

This chapter covered the basics of installing the ASA/PIX Security Appliance hardware, the ASA/PIX version 7 operating system, and the ASDM 5.0 management GUI.

The "Cisco ASA/PIX Security Appliance Overview" section covered the functions of the security appliance that are deployed in this book, including the following:

- Denial-of-service protection
- Traffic filtering
- Interface isolation (DMZ deployment)
- Stateful traffic inspection
- Application inspection
- User authentication
- Intrusion prevention
- Secure management
- Event logging

These functions are the basics that should be deployed by anyone who is using an ASA/PIX Security Appliance to secure his environment. As discussed in Appendix B, "ASA/PIX Version 7 Advanced Features," you can deploy extra functionality at your discretion depending on the security policy of your organization.

The various ASA/PIX Security Appliance models were discussed, including the PIX 515E, 525, 535, and the ASA 5500. This chapter then provided an overview of installing the ASA/PIX Security Appliance hardware and powering up the unit. This basic tutorial covered installing power cords and failover cables. (Because it's beyond of the scope of this book, this chapter did not go into detail about how to set up failover; interested readers are referred to the Cisco website for instructions.)

The chapter covered the installation of ASA/PIX version 7 and ASDM 5.0 in detail. The chapter provided step-by-step instructions on how to do the following:

- Ensure that your ASA/PIX operating system is at minimum version 6.3.
- Obtain a valid ASA/PIX version 7 license.
- Obtain a version of the ASA/PIX version 7 operating system from the download area of the Cisco website.
- Prepare your PC for the ASA/PIX version 7 upgrade.
- Install a TFTP server on your PC and configure your PC so that you can upgrade the ASA/PIX operating system.
- Prepare your security appliance to download the ASA/PIX version 7 operating system.
- Download ASA/PIX version 7 and ASDM 5.0 to your security appliance.

This chapter provides the background and information you need to easily navigate through ASDM and complete the step-by-step portions in the remaining chapters of this book.

This chapter addresses the following topics:

- **Introduction to the Adaptive Security Device Manager**—This discussion provides a brief overview of the ASDM product.

- **Exploring the ASDM Graphical User Interface**—The chapter then provides a detailed explanation of the different components of the ASDM GUI, including all menu options, navigation icons, navigation features, pull-down menus, and wizards.

CHAPTER 4

Exploring the Adaptive Security Device Manager

The Adaptive Security Device Manager (ASDM) is the primary application used to configure the ASA/PIX Security Appliance running ASA/PIX version 7 or greater. Previous versions of this management GUI were called PIX Device Manager (PDM). The ASDM has been enhanced to provide support for the new features in the ASA/PIX version 7 operating system.

This chapter is an in-depth discussion regarding all sections of the ASDM graphical user interface (GUI). Instructions on how you can do a step-by-step security deployment using ASDM are found in Chapters 5 through Chapter 11 of this book.

Exploring the GUI

ASDM has two main components, both of which are explored in this chapter:

- Pull-down menus
- Navigation bar

These two components have several subcomponents that are addressed in detail in this chapter. In many cases, subcomponents have several layers of detail.

The enable/disable state of some menu items will change depending on the current selection of the GUI and rights of the logged-on user. Because of this, the navigation bar is discussed with appropriate information interjected about the pull-down menus as the chapter progresses.

If you followed the instructions in Chapter 3, "Getting Started with the ASA/PIX Security Appliance," you should be able to access the ASDM GUI. The following is a summary of the steps you need to take to connect your PC to the ASA/PIX Security Appliance for ASDM access:

- Ensure that your PC is connected to Ethernet 1 on the ASA/PIX Security Appliance via a crossover cable or a switch.
- Ensure that your PC has the IP address 192.168.1.2.

- On the Windows operating system, launch either Internet Explorer 6.0 or greater or Netscape 7.1/7.2. Netscape 7.0 and Mozilla 1.7.3 are also supported on Sun Solaris and Linux.

- Java 1.4.2 or 1.5.0 must be installed on any browser platform that you select. (The examples in this book use Microsoft Windows.)

To start the ASDM on your Windows PC, follow these steps:

Step 1   Enter the command **https://192.168.1.1/admin**. The screen in Figure 4-1 will display.

Figure 4-1   *ASDM Start Screen*

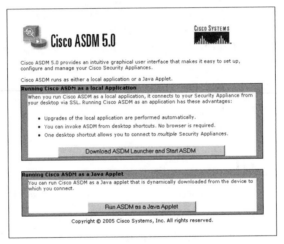

Step 2   When the screen from Figure 4-1 displays, you can select either to launch ASDM as a Java applet or as a Windows application. (This book uses the Java applet; but if you select to use the application, there will be differences in what you see on the screen.)

Step 3   Appropriately answer all the prompts for passwords and certificate acceptance. One of the advantages of using the ASDM launcher application is that you don't need to respond to the certificate dialog boxes seen when using the Java applet.

When you have successfully connected to the ASA/PIX Security Appliance, the panel shown in Figure 4-2 displays on your browser.

Figure 4-2 *ASDM Main Menu*

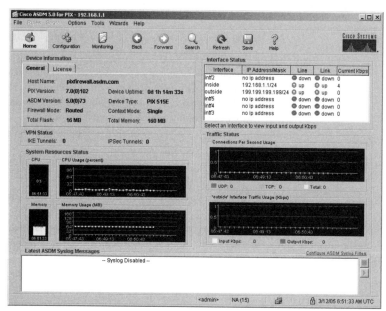

Exploring the Pull-Down Menus

Across the top of the page in the ASDM display are seven pull-down menus. The menus are labeled File, Rules, Search, Options, Tools, Wizards, and Help.

Table 4-1 provides a general overview of each pull-down menu. A more detailed explanation is provided in the section following the table.

Table 4-1 *Pull-Down Menu Command Summary*

Pull-Down Menu	Summary
File	Contains commands to save configuration files and internal log buffer to the Flash memory in the ASA/PIX Security Appliance and various other locations.
Rules	Used to insert items into a rules list. This pull-down is active only when the Configuration icon is selected in the navigation bar and the security policy or NAT panels are active. Note that functions in the Rules menu are also accessible on the toolbar, in the rules panels, and from the buttons or right-mouse click menus in the tables.
Search	Used to search items that exist in a rules list. This pull-down is active only when the Configuration icon is selected and the security policy or NAT panels are active.

continues

Table 4-1 *Pull-Down Menu Command Summary (Continued)*

Pull-Down Menu	Summary
Options	Sets global behaviors of ASDM such as previewing commands or prompting when ASDM is exited.
Tools	Contains tools for common system tasks for the ASA/PIX Security Appliance. This includes Flash, file management, image and ASDM upgrades, a CLI tool to allow direct execution of most ASA/PIX commands, and system reloads.
Wizards	Houses the two wizards that are available with ASDM: the VPN Wizard and the Startup Wizard.
Help	Provides full access to three ASDM help systems, including a table of contents and an online help search.

Many items within the pull-down menus contain submenus and information to help troubleshoot or configure the ASA/PIX Security Appliance. Detailed information about each item follows.

File Menu

The File menu contains common functions for Flash and file operations that you might need to perform on the ASA/PIX Security Appliance. The File menu pull-down contains 11 items, as shown in Figure 4-3 and described in the list that follows:

Figure 4-3 *File Menu Pull-Down*

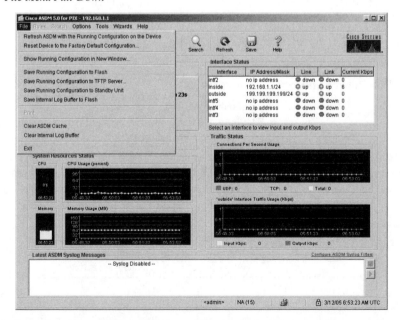

- **Refresh ASDM with Running Configuration on the Device**—This menu item enables you to ensure that the configuration you are displaying in ASDM is the current running configuration. The running configuration contains the commands that are currently active on the security appliance. This arrow turns to red when the ASDM configuration is out of sync with the ASA/PIX Security Appliance.

- **Reset Device to Factory Default Configuration**—Choosing this menu item erases the current configuration on the ASA/PIX and sets all commands back to their factory default settings.

- **Show Running Configuration in New Window**—ASDM will display the running configuration in a new browser window. This provides you with the opportunity to see the commands that are current on your security appliance in the ASA/PIX native command-line interface format.

- **Save Running Configuration to Flash**—This option saves the current running configuration to Flash. It overwrites the current startup configuration, and the next time the security appliance is booted, is the active configuration.

- **Save Running Configuration to TFTP Server**—This option enables you to save the current running configuration of your ASA/PIX to a TFTP server. This can be a valuable tool if something happens to the memory of your ASA/PIX Security Appliance and you need to do a restore from a remote source. If you select this option, you are prompted for the IP address and directory of your TFTP server.

- **Save Running Configuration to Standby Unit**—This option enables you to copy the current configuration to another ASA/PIX Security Appliance if you are using an active/standby configuration. Standby features are beyond the scope of this book; you can find further information regarding standby features on the Cisco website.

- **Save Internal Log Buffer to Flash**—This enables you to save your system log to the Flash on the ASA/PIX Security Appliance. In most cases, administrators would want to save the buffer to a syslog server, but this feature is useful if you syslog server is inaccessible or you are logging a small amount of real-time data from analysis or troubleshooting.

- **Print**—The Print option enables you to print information contained in only select pages of the ASDM GUI.

- **Clear ASDM Cache**—Like most web applications, ASDM saves reusable information in a cache file. This option enables you to clear the cache, if you want. This cached data is saved in a compressed format on your PC. If you leave the files in cache, ASDM saves reusable information in a cache file to speed up future access. The cached files are not a significant resource on your PC; the average size of the encrypted cache files is between 5.0 and 6.0 MB.

- **Clear Internal Log Buffer**—When troubleshooting an error message in a security appliance, it is often useful to clear out old messages so you can see only the sequence of messages applicable to your troubleshooting. The Clear Internal Log Buffer option accomplishes this task.

- **Exit**—This option disconnects your ASDM session from the ASA/PIX Security Appliance and shuts down the ASDM GUI. You are prompted to both save configuration changes and to verify that you really want to exit from the application.

Rules Menu

The Rules menu is activated only when the **Configuration > Security Policy** or the **Configuration > NAT** functions are chosen from the navigation bar.

The basic function of the Rules menu is to make it easier for you to place commands within long lists of items, such as the rules list and the network address translation (NAT) list.

All of the functions in the Rules menu can be done by right-clicking the display panels if you navigate into the **Configuration > Security Policy** and the **Configuration > NAT** functions. For deploying commands more quickly when using ASDM, right-clicking tends to be faster than using the pull-down menu.

Figure 4-4 shows the activated Rules menu.

Figure 4-4   *Rules Menu Pull-Down*

Each command in this menu helps you to control the order in which items appear in the list. The Configuration/Security Policy list is a compilation of all the access rules that you have configured in your security appliance. Using the Rules pull-down menu, you can easily add, copy, and paste rules as desired. It's an excellent tool to help you keep rules in an order that makes sense to you. By default, ASDM lists rules in the order in which they are entered for each interface.

An exhaustive explanation of each rule option isn't necessary because these actions are similar to commands that PC users deal with on a daily basis.

Search Menu

The Search menu is activated only when the **Configuration > Security Policy** or the **Configuration > NAT** functions are chosen from the navigation bar.

The basic functions of the Search menu are to make it easier to search the fields of the rules that might be long and to find keywords within the list.

The activated Search menu is shown in Figure 4-5, and the options are described in the list that follows:

Figure 4-5   *Search Menu Pull-Down*

- **Search by Field**—This option enables you to perform a text search within either the Security Policy or NAT list. To help you narrow your search, this option enables you to perform a search with an *any* or *all* qualifier; in addition, it displays a pick list of known values. For example, if you choose Search by Source Address, the Value field will contain a selection box in which you can click and see all known source addresses. You can then click the desired source address, expediting your search.

- **Search by Host/Network**—When this option is selected, a dialog box displays enabling you to search on one of the ASA/PIX Security Appliance interfaces. You can just highlight the network you want to search, and the resulting data displays within the ASDM active window.

- **Clear Search Selections**—This option clears any of the data that had been found and highlighted by the previous search.

Options Menu

The Options menu enables you to control how ASDM displays certain data.

Figure 4-6   *Options Menu Pull-Down*

Figure 4-6 shows the Options menu, and the list that follows describes the options available from this menu:

- **Show Commands Ignored by ASDM on Device**—The commands that show up in this list are commands that aren't supported by ASDM. To see any commands that have been ignored, choose this pull-down menu item.

- **Preferences**—Figure 4-7 illustrates the preferences controlled by this menu item.

Figure 4-7 *Preferences Options*

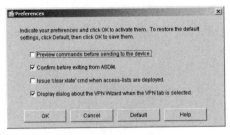

These preferences are saved in a file and applied for subsequent ASDM sessions:

- **Preview Commands Before Sending to the Device**—This preference causes ASDM to display the native ASA/PIX commands every time a change is made in ASDM. Many advanced users prefer this option so that they can see exactly which commands are being sent to the ASA/PIX Security Appliance. This option serves as an excellent way with which to become familiar with the new ASA/PIX version 7 command set.

- **Confirm Before Exiting ASDM**—When this option is enabled, ASDM prompts you before you disconnect from the security appliance and exit the application. This is on by default to help keep users from exiting ASDM unintentionally.

- **Issue "Clear Xlate" Cmd When Access-Lists Are Deployed**—The xlate table is a data structure that keeps track of connections through the security appliance. When an access list is closed, those connects are still active until the xlate table is cleared. This option clears the active connections table on the device for you, instead of you having to go to a command menu and enter the CLI command.

- **Display Dialog About the VPN Wizard When the VPN Tab Is Selected**—This option instructs ASDM to prompt you with a menu to give you the choice of whether you would like to use the VPN Wizard if you are accessing the VPN configuration. It encourages you to use the wizard because it's a step-by-step process that will ensure that you set up all commands correctly.

Tools Menu

The Tools menu enables you to control various aspects of ASDM related to file management, system reloads, manual command entry, and service group setup.

Figure 4-8 shows the Tools menu, and the list that follows describes the options available from the Tools menu:

- **Command Line Interface**—This option enables you to enter either a single native ASA/PIX version 7 command or multiple ASA/PIX version 7 commands into ASDM and have it sent to the security appliance. You can either enter the command you want or select a command from the Command drop-down. The result of the command displays in a window on the same page.

Figure 4-8   *Tools Menu Pull-Down*

- **Ping**—This option is a shortcut for the **ping** command. You just enter the IP address in the query box and then see the results in the window below.

Note   You can also enter the **ping** command in the Command Line Interface option.

- **Service Groups**—This option is used to define service groups, which is a way to group protocols for ease of use with other commands. For instance, you might want a group of users who are using file-sharing applications to be lumped together for certain types of access controls. Service groups are discussed in further detail in Appendix B, "ASA/PIX Version 7 Advanced Features."

- **File Management**—This option enables you to perform operations such as copying, deleting, moving, and viewing files in Flash. Directories can also be created in Flash, where the same operations can be performed.

- **Upload Image from Local PC**—This option enables you to upload, using HTTPS, an ASDM or ASA/PIX operating system file from your local PC to Flash on the ASA/PIX Security Appliance. Features include local PC file navigation and navigation on the Flash file system of the security appliance.

Note   If you are just doing an upload, and not doing an upgrade, be careful not to name the destination file the same as the active file on the security appliance.

- **File Transfer**—This option enables you to use HTTP/HTTPS to copy files to the ASA/PIX Security Appliance and also to use FTP and TFTP to move files back and forth between the security appliance and TFTP or FTP servers.

- **System Reload**—This option enables you to schedule a system reload or to cancel a reload currently scheduled. It also provides you with the option to save your current configuration before proceeding with the reload.

NOTE   When the ASA/PIX reloads, ASDM disconnects and you must restart ASDM if you need further access to the security appliance.

ASDM Wizards Menu

The Wizards menu enables you to launch the VPN Wizard and the Startup Wizard. Both of these wizards are covered in detail later in this book. The VPN Wizard is covered in Chapter 11, "Deploying VPNs"; the Startup Wizard is covered in Chapter 5, "Deploying Secure Internet Connectivity."

Figure 4-9   *Help Menu Pull-Down*

Help Menu

The Help menu provides you with several different layers of assistance in using ASDM. Figure 4-9 shows the Help menu pull-down, and the following list describes the available options:

- **Help Topics**—This option provides context-sensitive help, including a search page, subject index, and a glossary.

- **Help for Current Screen**—As you go from screen to screen in ASDM, you can choose Help for the Current Screen from the Help pull-down menu. A full explanation of the screen usage is presented in a browser-type display.

- **Release Notes**—This option displays the release notes for the installed version of ASDM.

- **Getting Started**—This option is a brief overview of how to use ASDM to begin configuring the ASA/PIX Security Appliance.

- **Glossary**—This option displays a link to the glossary of terms used in the Help subsystem.

- **Feature Search**—This option is used for finding panels in ASDM that match the supplied keywords.

- **Legend**—This option presents you with a screen displaying all the icons that are used in ASDM, the section in which they are used, and a definition of them.

- **About Cisco ASA/PIX Security Appliance**—This option displays the current licensing information and version of the ASA/PIX Security Appliance to which ASDM is connected.

- **About Cisco ASDM 5.0**—The following information displays if you are running ASDM from a browser:

  — Host name

  — ADSM user

  — ASDM version

  — Browser running ASDM

  — Operating system running ASDM

  — ASA/PIX device type

  — ASA/PIX operating system version

  — User privilege level

  — Java version installed

Exploring the Navigation Bar

The navigation bar provides access to the main areas of ASDM. Figure 4-10 shows the contents of the bar. The navigation bar contains three buttons that enable you to do the bulk of the work for configuring and monitoring the ASA/PIX Security Appliance:

- Home
- Configuration
- Monitoring

The remaining buttons are used for navigating ASDM, saving files, and obtaining help:

- Back
- Forward
- Search

- Refresh
- Save
- Help

Figure 4-10 *Navigation Bar*

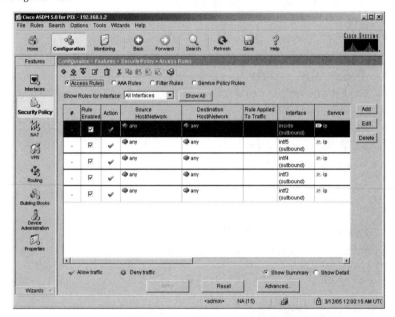

Table 4-2 provides an overview of each item on the navigation bar. A more detailed explanation is provided in the section following the table.

Table 4-2 *Navigation Bar Overview*

Navigation Icon	Summary
Home	This is the default screen seen when ASDM launches. It primarily contains status and device information of the security appliance and ASDM.
Configuration	This is the main portion of ASDM. It contains all the configuration options for the ASA/PIX Security Appliance.
Monitoring	The Monitoring icon offers options to monitor many of the security appliance features and functions. This includes graphing and table views.
Back arrow	This allows backward navigation through previously viewed ASDM screens.
Forward arrow	This allows forward navigation through previously viewed ASDM screens.

Table 4-2   *Navigation Bar Overview (Continued)*

Navigation Icon	Summary
Search	This icon finds the ASDM panel that matches user-entered search criteria.
Refresh	The Refresh icon reloads the current ASA/PIX configuration to the ASDM application. This icon turns red when ASDM is not in sync with the ASA/PIX Security Appliance configuration.
Save	This icon saves any changes made through ASDM to the ASA/PIX Security Appliance running configuration. A copy of the running-config is saved to Flash memory.
Help	This contains context-sensitive help.

Many items within these navigation bar icons contain configuration panels and information to help troubleshoot or configure the ASA/PIX Security Appliance. Detailed information about each navigation icon follows.

Home Navigation Icon

The Home navigation icon displays real-time information about the ASA/PIX Security Appliance. (See Figure 4–11.)

Figure 4-11 *Home Navigation Icon*

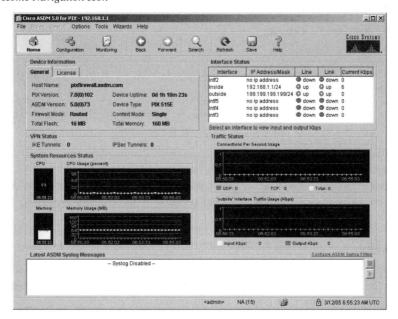

In the upper-left corner, there are two tabs under Device Information. One tab is labeled Licensing and displays pertinent information about the license that is installed in the ASA/PIX Security Appliance. The other is labeled General and displays information about the ASA/PIX Security Appliance, such as the following:

- ASA/PIX version
- Device type
- Memory information
- ASDM version

Below the Device Information section is a panel called VPN Status, which displays information about VPN tunnels.

Below the VPN Status section is a panel called System Resource Status. This panel displays information about the ASA/PIX Security Appliance CPU and memory usage.

At the bottom of the screen is a panel that displays the latest ASDM syslog messages. ASDM gives you the option on the right side of this panel to configure filters for syslog messages, enabling you to see only the messages that you consider important for your network.

In the upper-right corner of the Home navigation icon screen, the Interface Statistics panel displays. This panel shows the following:

- The ASA/PIX Security Appliance interfaces
- Interface names
- Interface status
- Interface IP address
- Interface traffic, in kilobits per second

If you click the interface, the input and output traffic statistics for that interface display just under the Interface Statistics panel.

Below the Interface Statistics panel is the Traffic Status panel. This panel displays, in graph form, the UDP, TCP, and total connections per second.

Below the Traffic Status panel is a second panel that displays traffic usage on the outside interface. This graph can prove helpful in determining whether a denial-of-service (DoS) attack is being launched against the outside interface of the security appliance or whether an excessive amount of traffic is being serviced by the security appliance.

Configuration Icon

The Configuration section of ASDM contains most of the functions needed to configure and control the features of your security appliance. Eight features are listed under the Configuration icon. (See Figure 4-12.)

Figure 4-12 *Configuration Navigation Icon*

The following features are available under the Configuration icon:

- Interfaces
- Security policies
- NAT
- VPN
- Routing
- Building blocks
- Device administration
- Properties

Although this list of features represents a comprehensive set of tasks that need to be accomplished to fully configure the ASA/PIX Security Appliance, most deployments can be done using the defaults already configured as part of ASDM. Many of these features are optional depending on your networking requirements. For instance, routing, VPN, and building blocks might not be required in many small business network deployments.

This chapter touches on each of these features so that you learn the capabilities of the ASA/PIX version 7 operating system and ASDM. However, the configurations deployed in this book follow the defense-in-depth model and are covered in the following chapters:

- Chapter 5, "Deploying Secure Internet Connectivity"
- Chapter 6, "Deploying Web and Mail Services"
- Chapter 7, "Deploying Authentication"

- Chapter 8, "Deploying Perimeter Protection"
- Chapter 9, "Deploying Network Intrusion Prevention"
- Chapter 10, "Deploying Host Intrusion Prevention"
- Chapter 11, "Deploying VPNs"

Interfaces

The Interface panel, shown in Figure 4-13, enables you to control the features of the hardware interfaces on your ASA/PIX Security Appliance.

Figure 4-13 *Interface Features Panel*

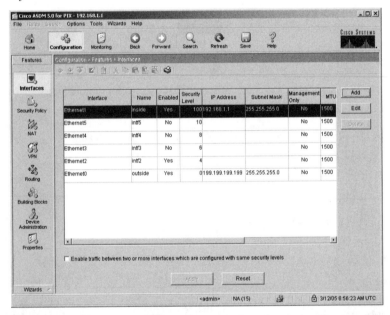

This panel enables you to configure the network and security characteristics, as well as enable or disable the hardware interfaces.

Security Policy

The Security Policy panel, shown in Figure 4-14, has four subpanels:

- Access Rules
- AAA Rules
- Filter Rules
- Service Policy Rules

To add, delete, modify, or move elements in any of the panels within the Security Policy feature (see Figure 4-14), you have three options. You can either right-click the panel and use the pop-up screen, use the icons across the top of the current panel, or use the pull-down menu labeled Rules.

Figure 4-14 *Security Policy Features Panel*

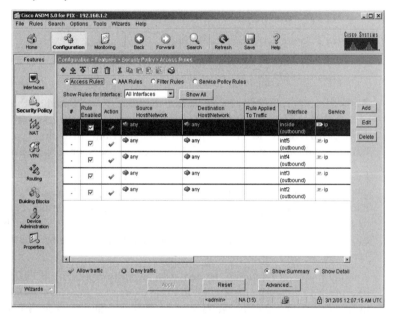

- **Access Rules**—These rules enable you to decide what traffic will be allowed to traverse your security appliance. By default, most traffic sourced from the inside interface of the security appliance is allowed to go to the outside interface and return back to the inside. By default, all traffic sourced from the outside is blocked from going to your inside network. If you are hosting any network services, such as web servers or mail servers, on the inside of your network, you must create an access list to let that traffic through the security appliance.

  The traffic flow on an ASA/PIX Security Appliance is defined by a value called a *security level*. By default, traffic flows freely from an interface with a high security level to an interface with a lower security level. For example, the inside interface has a security level of 100, and an outside interface has a security level of 0. Therefore, by default, traffic can flow from the inside to the outside without any configuration.

Note   Defining access rules is a *must* for any security appliance deployment. Configuring inbound network services is addressed in Chapter 6.

- **AAA Rules**—These rules enable you to authenticate traffic coming from the outside of your security appliance or going into your security appliance. You can define a AAA server to authenticate users, or you can use this panel to define local users. The only traffic that can be authenticated is traffic that uses a protocol that has the capability to accept a username and password. The ASA/PIX Security Appliance supports four such applications:

  - **HTTP**—Web traffic

  - **HTTPS**—Encrypted web traffic

  - **Telnet**—Text-based terminal traffic

  - **FTP**—File Transfer Protocol

  Authentication rules can also be activated or deactivated based on the time of day or day of week. For example, you can limit users to access only these services from 8 A.M. to 5 P.M., Monday through Friday. In addition, you can limit authentication rules to certain IP addresses, users, or service groups.

- **Filter Rules**—Many virus, worms, and spyware can be spread using malicious code embedded inside of web traffic. To help prevent this spread, these filter rules look deep into packets and can filter out ActiveX and Java applets that might cause malware to spread to the inside hosts on your network through day-to-day web browsing. You can use this filter panel to create an exclusion rule that allows or disallows ActiveX or Java from specific sites.

  Another powerful feature of the ASA/PIX Security Appliance is URL filtering. You can implement URL filtering using the filter rules. Using a third-party vendor such as WebSense, you have the ability to control which websites your users can access from the inside of your network. The software packages are easy to use; often with just a single click you can filter out all known porn sites, hacker sites, sport sites, or file-sharing sites. URL filtering can also catch URL attacks such as a Unicode attack which, when crafted correctly and sent to a vulnerable system, can execute the DOS command prompt.

Caution   In some of the 50 states, deploying URL filtering is a freedom of information issue versus the right of an employer to protect company assets. You might want to get legal advice if you suspect this is an issue in your state.

- **Service Policy Rules**—Like filtering rules, these rules also look deeply into packets to determine whether the packet is valid and should be passed through the security appliance. Service policy rules classify traffic by protocol or sets of protocols and then apply rules to allow or reject content based on configurations that you have previously defined. This is discussed further in Chapter 8.

The subpanels within the service policy rules enable you to classify your traffic and then apply rules to that traffic. Consider inbound web traffic as an example, but remember that this is just an example, and it is not necessarily recommended to use this policy on your security appliance. Service policy rules enable you to create a policy that resets a connection if an outside user is trying to send a URL longer then the largest URL you have on your web server. This policy could mitigate several attacks such as a hacker trying to manually send a SQL request to access unauthorized data or trying to send a large URL to overflow the buffer of your web server.

Policy rules give you several other options to mitigate attacks or recover bandwidth used by unauthorized activity, including the following:

— Stop certain types of traffic that is not adhering to the RFC specifications.

— Stop certain types of files from being transferred within a protocol such as HTTP or SMTP (mail). Often attackers send files compressed in formats such as Zip GZip to evade signature recognition used by most antivirus vendors.

— Stop certain types of peer-to-peer (P2P) network file-sharing programs that can take up unauthorized bandwidth and transfer files into your environment of which you have no control.

— Stop instant messaging.

— Stop tunneling of protocols within other protocols, especially port HTTP.

— Enforce maximum number of connections allowed to a certain port to prevent CPU overload during peak usage or DoS attacks.

— Randomize TCP sequence numbers on a per-protocol basis to reduce the possibility of TCP hijacking.

— Apply quality of service to certain data flows or protocols.

Click the **Show Detail** option button at the bottom of the Security Policy panel to see which protocols are inspected by default. To see the details of each inspection, browse through the Edit panel's Traffic Classification, Traffic Match, and Rule Action tabs. In the Rule Action panel, click the **Configure** button to see a detailed inspection for each protocol.

NAT

Figure 4-15 shows the NAT panel, which has four main functions, as described in the list that follows. NAT is a feature that allows private addresses to be translated and routed to the Internet, as discussed in detail in Chapter 5. The options exist to add, delete, modify, or move any elements in any of the panels within the NAT panel. You can either right-click the panel and use the pop-up screen, use the icons across the top of the current panel, or use the pull-down menu labeled Rules.

Figure 4-15 *NAT Features Panel*

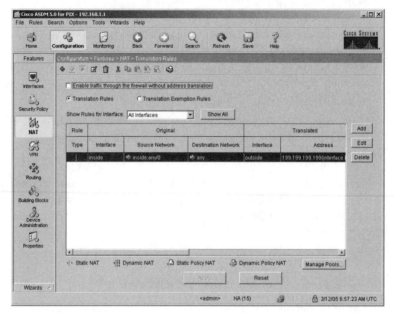

- **Enables Traffic to Traverse the Security Appliance Without Address Translation**—Checking this box will allow traffic to traverse back and forth through the security appliance without using address translation. The only time you should consider doing this is if all the addresses behind your security appliance are publicly routed Internet addresses.

- **Translation Rules**—This panel enables you to set up address translations that will allow you to use private Internet addresses on the inside of your security appliance while still accessing public Internet devices. The most common form of NAT used is port address translation, also called PAT. If you use PAT, the addresses from inside your security appliance assume the outside interfaces' IP addresses before they are routed to the Internet. Because all Internet devices know how to return traffic to your security appliance, the security appliance will know what to do when the traffic comes back to it. The security appliance will just check its NAT tables and be able to recognize the true source of the packet and send it back to the host on the inside of your network.

  For the purposes in this book, PAT is used for inside hosts, and static NAT is used for public servers. In Chapters 5 and 6, PAT and NAT are deployed to allow Internet access.

Note	NAT is a complex subject. For an in-depth discussion on implementing NAT, go the Cisco website and access the URL http://www.cisco.com/go/nat. Even though this link is for Cisco IOS, the concepts are the same for the ASA/PIX Security Appliance.

- **Translation Exemption Rules**—This panel enables you to exclude certain traffic from NAT translation, which is sometimes required in complex VPN deployments.
- **Manage Pools**—NAT pools are addresses allocated for use by NAT on a per-interface basis on the ASA/PIX Security Appliance.

VPN

The VPN panel is used to configure VPN tunnels that terminate on the ASA/PIX Security Appliance.

The VPN panel has four main functions:

- **General**—Allows basic high-level VPN configuration options
- **IKE**—Enables key setup and exchanges between the ASA/PIX Security Appliance and VPN clients
- **IPSec**—Allows the necessary configuration to encrypt traffic between the ASA/PIX Security Appliance and VPN clients
- **Address Management**—Enables the allocation of IP addresses to remote VPN clients

NOTE	IPSec VPN step-by-step configuration is addressed in detail in Chapter 11.

VPN General Features   The VPN General option has five different configuration panels:

- VPN System Options
- Client Update
- Tunnel Group
- Group Policy
- Default Tunnel Gateway

The following list describes each panel:

- **VPN System Options**—Enables you to configure high-level VPN commands that globally affect how the security appliance will use VPN. You have three options, as described in Table 4-3.

Table 4-3   *VPN System Options*

Option	Description
Enable IPSec Authenticated Connection Through the Security Appliance	If this option is selected, VPN tunnels that have been authenticated can pass any traffic through the security appliance, bypassing access lists. If this option is not selected, you must create access lists to allow traffic to the inside network after it is decrypted by the ASA/PIX Security Appliance.
Permit VPN Communication to Peers Connected to the Same Interface	This allows hub-and-spoke VPN. Traffic from the source peer is encrypted when it arrives on the security appliance. The ASA/PIX Security Appliance sees the destination is another VPN client and forwards it back out the same interface to another VPN client. This is useful for P2P communications such as VoIP and instant messaging.
Limit the Number of Active VPN Sessions	This limit affects the load-balancing calculation for VPN load balancing.

- **The Live Client Update**—From this panel, you can enable updates for VPN client software. You do so by first placing the client software on a web server and then setting the location with the edit key. When a client logs on to the server, it automatically starts the update process. By using the Live Client panel, you can optionally update all clients that are currently connected to the security appliance.

Figure 4-16   *VPN Live Client Update Panel*

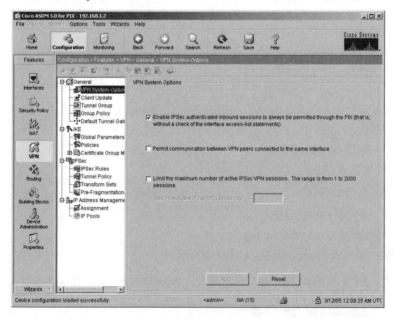

- **The Tunnel Group Configuration**—This panel enables you to set characteristics for IPSec VPN tunnels.

- **The Group Policy**—This panel enables you to configure policies for a group of VPN users. For example, you can set IPSec groups to perform the following:

  — Only access the ASA/PIX Security Appliance at certain times

  — Receive the same DNS and WINS server addresses

  — Enable Perfect Forward Secrecy to reduce the chance of key compromise

  — Enable compression to reduce the amount of traffic traversing the tunnel

  — Enable banners to be displayed by the client when connected

  — Enable IPSec over UDP to resolve some issues caused by NAT and VPN

  — Force a client security appliance to be active on the client before a connection can be established

  — Enable characteristics of a hardware VPN client connecting to the ASA/PIX Security Appliance

- **Default Tunnel Gateway**—This panel enables you to configure a static route to be applied to IPSec VPN tunnels.

IKE Features   The IKE (Internet Key Exchange) option has three different configuration panels, as follows:

- **Global Parameters**—These configuration options enable you to set parameters for all IKE sessions terminating on your security appliance. You can specify which interface the IKE sessions will terminate on, although it will almost always be on the outside interface. These parameters can be left as default unless, for some reason, a client is connecting that doesn't support the global options you have selected.

- **Policies**—This panel enables you to select values for the policies that are used for the key exchange process. The values in this screen must match the client IKE policies. If you are using the Cisco VPN client, you can use the defaults, which cause the policy to be downloaded to the client and a connection established.

- **Certificate Groups Management**—This panel has two subpanels; however, certificates are not yet widely used on the Internet, so they are not covered in this book. If you need information regarding certificate authentication, refer to Cisco.com.

IPSec Features   The IPSec option has four different configuration panels, as follows:

- **IPSec Rules**—This panel enables you to configure the entire set of IPSec policies. The policies allow the creation of the policies for encryption algorithms, the IPSec peers, and access lists that define traffic that will be protected by the IPSec tunnel.

- **Tunnel Policy**—This panel enables you to modify or create tunnel policy, which includes encryption algorithms, IPSec peers, and access lists that define traffic that will be protected by the IPSec tunnel.

- **Transform Sets**—Transform sets define how the IPSec data will be encrypted and authenticated. All of the commonly used transform sets have already been defined in ASDM. You use this configuration panel only if you need to add a new transform set or modify an existing transform set.

- **Pre-Fragmentation**—The enabling of prefragmentation is the default for the security appliance IPSec behavior. This means that if the ASA/PIX receives packets that exceed the maximum transmission unit of the VPN tunnel and must be fragmented, the packet will be encrypted, the don't fragment bit will be cleared, and the packet will be sent as an individual packet rather than as a set of fragmented packets.

IP Address Management Features   The purpose of IP address management is to allocate the IP addresses to clients that have successfully connected to the ASA/PIX Security Appliance using a VPN client.

The IP Address Management feature contains two panels:

- **Assignment**—This panel enables you to define the source that will be responsible for allocating addresses to VPN clients. The options are AAA server, DHCP, or internally defined address pools.

- **IP Pools**—The IP Pools panel enables you to manually configure the pool of IP addresses that will be allocated to remote VPN clients upon connection to the ASA/PIX Security Appliance.

Routing

The Routing panel shown in Figure 4-17 is used to configure routing protocols for the ASA/PIX Security Appliance. An exhaustive description of security appliance routing is beyond the scope of this book. This section highlights the available routing options with a brief description of their use.

Figure 4-17 *Routing Features Panel*

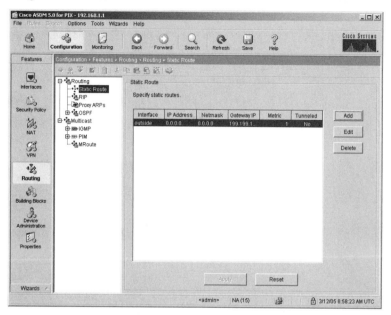

Table 4-4   *Routing Features*

Routing Element	Description
Static routing	Manually configured routing tables defining the next hop for a particular route.
RIP	A routing protocol that can learn routes based on the fewest number of hops.
Proxy ARPs	A configuration option that instructs the ASA/PIX to respond to ARP requests for hosts that it knows about or NAT addresses that it contains in its pools and addresses from the other end of VPN tunnels.
OSPF	A link-state protocol that determines the shortest path to a destination.
IGMP	Internet Group Management Protocol. Refer to http://www.cisco.com/go/multicast for complete information regarding multicast protocols.
PIM	Protocol Independent Multicast. Refer to http://www.cisco.com/go/multicast for complete information regarding multicast protocols.
mRoute	Refer to http://www.cisco.com/go/multicast for complete information regarding multicast protocols.

Building Blocks

The Building Blocks panel, shown in Figure 4-18, is used to build policies and network elements that can be easily used or shared by other features within ASDM.

Figure 4-18 *Building Blocks Features Panel*

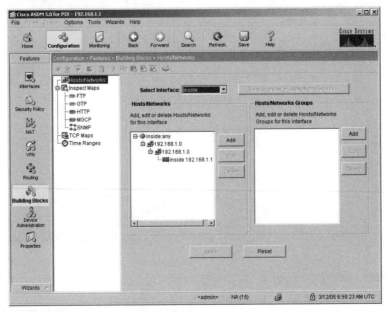

The Building Blocks feature contains four panels, as follows:

- **Hosts/Networks**—This panel enables you to create an entry for a network or host in ASDM that can then be used with building policies in other ASDM panels. This panel also gives the option of creating the hosts and networks in groups.

- **Inspect Maps**—This panel enables you to create custom inspect maps for specific protocols. After the map is created here, it can be accessed by other sections of ASDM that apply maps to rules. For example, if you decide that a hacker might be trying to compromise your web server by entering URLs that are more then 512 bytes, you can create an inspect map for HTTP defining the maximum URL size to be 511 and report this event to syslog. The inspect map can then drop the traffic.

- **Time Ranges**—You can use this panel to define time ranges that can then be applied to any policies created in the Security Policy feature. For example, by selecting Time Range, you can create a range that starts Saturday morning at 8 A.M. and ends Sunday nights at midnight. You can then name this time entry weekends. You can then apply the weekends time range to an access policy.

- **TCP Maps**—The TCP Maps panel provides you the option to configure inspection on your TCP traffic that goes through and terminates on the ASA/PIX Security Appliance.

Figure 4-19 *Device Administration Features Panel*

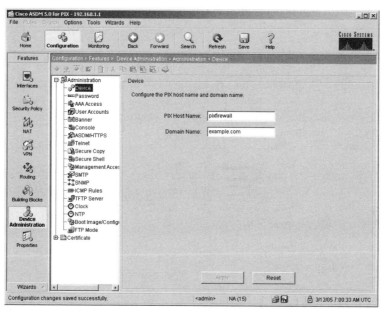

Device Administration

The Device Administration feature contains several panels, as shown in Figure 4-19. The functions in this list are all important in deploying a secure locked-down configuration on your security appliance. Pay special attention to warnings in this section that point out weaknesses in certain protocols:

- **Device**—The Device panel enables you to enter or modify the name of the ASA/PIX Security Appliance or the domain name associated with the security appliance.

- **Password**—This panel enables you to change the enable (privileged) password and the Telnet password on the security appliance.

Caution	Using Telnet is *highly discouraged* because during the logon sequence, the password is sent over the network in clear text. If an attacker is sniffing your network, this type of password will be easily stolen.

- **AAA Access**—Enable authentication, authorization, and accounting for device administration on the ASA/PIX Security Appliance.

Note	In this book, for simplicity, all authentication is performed from the local database.

- **User Accounts**—This panel enables you to enter users and passwords into your local ASA/PIX authentication database.

Caution	Use hard-to-guess passwords and usernames. Don't use words that are in the dictionary. Use at least eight characters, including uppercase, lowercase, numeric, and special characters. Attacks that use a dictionary to guess passwords are easy to run, and these guidelines provide fairly good mitigation against these types of attacks.

- **Banner**—You can define three banners that will then display when you log in to the ASA/PIX Security Appliance with a text tool such as SSH or through the console. The banners do not display when you connect to the security appliance using ASDM. The banners are as follows:
  - Session banner
  - Login banner
  - Message-of-the-day banner

  You can enter any text you like as banners. However, from a security perspective, in the Session and Login banners, you should say something such as, "You have logged on to a secure device. If you are not an authorized user, log out immediately or face the possibility of criminal consequences." Do not "welcome" users to your network devices, and do not say "please." There has been litigation in which this type of language was determined to be an open invitation to stay on a network device even if you were an intruder. RFC 2196 has guidelines on what information to put in your banner messages.

Caution	There have been cases where hackers have broken into a system and subsequently were caught. However, because the administrator didn't post a proper warning at login, the hackers were not prosecuted. So be sure to follow this best practice.

- **Console**—The Console panel enables you to configure the amount of idle time that lapses before the console session times out. A timeout will require the user to log back in if further access is required. The default is zero minutes, which means the console doesn't time out. However, from a security best practice point of view, you should set this option to 15 minutes or less. This ensures that if you do walk away, the console session will eventually time out. Therefore, the session cannot inadvertently be accessed by a random person who happens upon your PC or terminal with the connection still open.

- **ASDM/HTTPS**—The ASDM panel enables you to specify the IP address of a device or devices that can use ASDM to connect to the ASA/PIX Security Appliance.

- **Telnet**—The Telnet panel enables you to specify the IP address of a device or devices that can use Telnet to connect to the ASA/PIX Security Appliance.

Caution   Telnet passes the username and password in clear text on the network. These credentials can easily be stolen by anyone with a network sniffer. Telnet should not be used, if at all possible, because it can easily allow access to your security appliance.

- **Secure Copy**—This panel enables you to secure copy to transfer configuration files. There are some limitations with secure copy. To see these limitations, bring up the Secure Copy panel in ASDM and, from the Help menu, and choose the option **Help for Current Screen**.

- **Secure Shell**—The Secure Shell (SSH) panel enables you to specify the IP address of a device or devices that can use SSH to connect to the ASA/PIX Security Appliance. In addition to the IP address, you can specify the version of SSH supported by the security appliance. SSH version 1 and version 2 are supported in ASA/PIX version 7.

- **Management Access**—The Management Access panel enables you to specify an interface to be used strictly for management purposes.

- **SMTP**—This panel enables you to define a mail server to which alerts will be delivered if critical messages are sent to the syslog server. To configure the e-mail address where log messages are sent, go to the ASDM panel **Configuration > Features > Properties > Logging > E-mail Setup**.

- **SNMP**—This panel enables you to configure the ASA/PIX Security Appliance to send Simple Network Management Protocol information and traps to an SNMP server.

Caution   SNMP is not highly recommended by security experts because messages are sent in the clear and community strings; SNMP passwords can be captured off of the network.

- **ICMP Rules**—The ICMP Rules panel enables you to configure the ASA/PIX Security Appliance to allow certain types of pings to traverse the security appliance. In most cases, you would want to allow only ICMP reply, MTU discovery, and network unreachable messages to come in from the Internet. ICMP has a long and colorful history of being used as a protocol for DoS and even some unauthorized-access attacks.

- **TFTP Server**—TFTP is the most popular protocol for upgrading ASA/PIX images and ASDM images and for storing ASA/PIX configurations. This panel enables you to configure the default TFTP server to be used by your security appliance.

  TFTP is *not* secure! There is no password to authenticate the traffic, and the traffic passes the network in the clear. Therefore, you should take the following precautions:

  — The TFTP server must be located on the secure side (i.e., the inside) of your ASA/PIX Security Appliance.

  — The TFTP server should only be running when it is going to be used.

  — The TFTP server should be on an isolated management interface on this security appliance, if at all possible.

  — The TFTP server should be running both antivirus and host intrusion prevention software.

  — If you have switches on your network, your Layer 2 network should be locked down according to Cisco SAFE best practices. You can find more information on this on the Cisco SAFE home page at http://www.cisco.com/go/safe, "SAFE: L2 Application Note."

- **Clock**—If you don't have any time-sensitive applications that require all the devices on your network to have synchronized time, you can use this panel to set the time on the ASA/PIX Security Appliance. If you do have time-sensitive applications, you need to use NTP, which is described in the next paragraph.

- **NTP**—Network Time Protocol is used to synchronize clocks between network devices. There is an NTP server that runs the main system clock. All other devices communicate with that server to get the time to update their clocks on a periodic basis. From the NTP panel, you can enable the ASA/PIX Security Appliance as an NTP client. Optionally, you can specify authentication to NTP servers. Keeping your network device clocks in sync can make troubleshooting easier, because events from different devices can be correlated by time stamp. Using a common time source such as NTP makes this easier.

- **Boot Image Configuration**—This panel enables you to configure the default boot image for the ASA/PIX operating system. In addition to the default image, you can specify and list four boot images and specify a boot sequence for each image.

- **FTP Mode**—The FTP Mode panel enables you to configure the FTP mode as active or passive for uploading or downloading images. The client initiates the data and control sessions in passive mode.

- **Certificate**—Certificate administration is beyond the scope of this book. If you need information on certificate administration for the security appliance, refer to the Cisco website at http://www.cisco.com/go/pix and select technical documentation.

Properties Feature

The Properties panel, shown in Figure 4-20, is used to configure less-frequently used features and logging.

Figure 4-20 *Properties Features Panel*

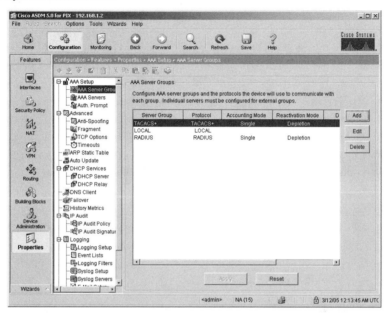

The Properties panel contains several subpanels. The features in this list represent global options such as DNS configurations, static ARP entries, management reporting, authentication parameters, intrusion prevention, and advanced security. Many of these features are discussed in more detail in Appendix B:

- **ARP Status Table**—This feature enables you to configure static ARP entries for certain IP addresses or to turn on proxy ARP on a per-interface and per-IP address basis.

- **DNS Client**—The DNS client enables you to configure as many as six DNS servers that can resolve IP addresses for the ASA/PIX Security Appliance.

- **DHCP Server**—This feature enables you to configure the ASA/PIX Security Appliance to be a DHCP server. As such, it automatically allocates IP addresses when requested by a network device. A detailed step-by-step procedure on how to do this is in Chapter 5.

- **DHCP Relay**—DHCP relay enables you to configure a server to which the ASA/PIX Security Appliance can forward requests if the DHCP server is not in the broadcast zone of the security appliance. The ASA/PIX will keep state when it sends the request so that it can forward the DHCP response to the originating network device.

- **Failover**—This feature enables you to configure failover between a primary and secondary security appliance. As stated before, failover is beyond the scope of this book. For more information, refer to the technical documentation on the Cisco website at http://www.cisco.com/go/pix.

- **Logging Setup**—This enables you to configure logging on the ASA/PIX Security Appliance. Many logging options are available, such as adding debug messages to syslog, changing the format of the syslog file, changing the ASDM and internal ASA/PIX buffer sizes, and configuring the logging to be sent to an FTP server or Flash before the syslog is written over. Syslog messages on the Home panel and the log viewer also rely on configurations applied using this panel.

- **Event Lists**—This feature enables you to create criteria for a syslog event as opposed to turning on logging by only syslog level. This enables you to reduce the number of syslogs, focusing on just the areas you're interested in.

- **Logging Filters**—Logging filters enable you to configure the ASA/PIX to send syslog events to the following different locations:
  - ASA/PIX console
  - ASA/PIX internal buffer
  - Telnet sessions
  - Syslog servers
  - SNMP traps
  - E-mail
  - ASDM event logger

- **Syslog Setup**—This feature enables you to determine which type of syslog messages will be sent to the syslog subsystem.

- **Syslog Servers**—This enables you to configure the IP addresses or syslog servers to which the ASA/PIX can send its syslog data. This panel also enables you to define the port to use for syslog, as well as define the format of the syslog file.

Caution   The syslog server should be on the inside of your security appliance and should have host intrusion prevention software installed and running. Attackers often look for hosts accepting syslog data for two reasons: 1) to find out information about your network, and 2) to edit the syslog data to cover their tracks after an attack.

- **E-Mail Setup**—This feature enables you to configure the IP address of the e-mail server to send critical events, the e-mail address to which to send the events, and a filter to define which events should be sent.

- **AAA Server Group**—This enables you to name an AAA group and assign either RADIUS, NT Domain, LDAP, SDI, Kerberos or TACACS+ as authentication protocols.

Caution	If you are running an authentication server, it is important that it is one of the most secure servers in your network. Think security best practices; the authentication server should be on the inside of your security appliance or on an isolated interface and should have intrusion prevention software running on it.

- **AAA Setup**—AAA Setup enables you to configure your AAA server IP address, the authentication protocol to be used, and the interface relative to your ASA/PIX Security Appliance. In addition, even though RFCs have defined the network port on which an authentication server listens, you can change this port in the Configuration panel. If you do this, you must also change the port on your authentication server. The only reason you might want to do this is to hide where authentication is happening. If a hacker runs a scan against your servers and sees TCP port 49 open, the hacker will know that it's a TACACS+ server. If you've changed the port to TCP 4646, when hackers see that on a scan, the information will be much harder for them to use for exploiting your system.

- **Auth Prompts**—This feature enables you to define three prompts that can be displayed to the user:

  - **Prompt**—Displayed upon Telnet, SSH, or console authentication
  - **User Accepted Message**—Displayed when a user passes authentication
  - **User Rejected Message**—Displayed when a user fails authentication

  Again, think security best practices. If you choose to create prompts, don't give anything away in your messages that might help a hacker. For example, don't give any hint of what type of device or operating system for which they are being presented a prompt. If authentication fails, the message should simply say, "Authentication failed." It is not possible on the ASA/PIX Security Appliance, but one of the mistakes early security programmers made was returning a prompt that said either invalid username or invalid password when a user failed authentication. Thus, a hacker easily knew that he had half of the credentials and he knew which half.

- **URL Filtering**—This feature enables you to configure third-party vendor software for URL filtering. As stated earlier in this chapter, URL filtering enables you to control which websites your users can access from the inside of your network. The software packages are easy to use; often with a single click, you can filter out all known porn sites, hacker sites, sport sites, or file-sharing sites. URL filtering can also catch URL attacks such as a Unicode attack. This panel is more specific than the previous panel discussed because it enables you to define which third-party server you are using as a filtering server.

- **Auto Update**—This feature enables you to configure the ASA/PIX Security Appliance to connect to a VMS AutoUpdate server and automatically have its operating system updated. Either HTTP or HTTPS can be used to accomplish this task. You can specify that certificate authentication and username password authentication must take place before the auto-update can occur. You must specify the location on the auto-update server where the new ASA/PIX operating system is located.

- **IP Audit Policy**—The IP Audit Policy enables you to define intrusion detection and prevention policies. The default policies are set up for intrusion detection, as opposed to intrusion prevention. This means that the policies don't prevent attacks from happening. Instead, they send an alarm to the syslog server if a signature is triggered. You can use this panel to define a custom policy to drop packets and then apply that policy to an interface.

- **IP Audit Signatures**—This panel enables you to view and enable or disable the 51 default intrusion detection prevention signatures. These signatures are common attacks and don't normally generate false positive alarms. Therefore, a drop action with these signatures is not an overly dangerous policy to enforce. It might be wise to configure your e-mail syslog events to send you an e-mail if an intrusion detection signature is triggered; this will give you the opportunity to research the alarm and determine whether it poses a serious problem to a device on your network.

- **Anti-Spoofing**—This feature enables you to configure your security appliance to not pass spoofed source addresses to the Internet. A spoofed address is a source address that has been changed from its real source and then sent on to the network. Normally, if you are seeing spoofed addresses from the inside of your network, it means that a device is trying to do some sort of malicious activity. Anti-Spoofing on the ASA/PIX uses a technology called Unicast Reverse Path Forwarding (uRPF) to determine whether an address is spoofed. When you turn on the Anti-Spoofing feature, packets containing spoofed addresses are dropped by the ASA/PIX Security Appliance. You can enable this option per interface on the security appliance.

| Note | If you want more information about uRPF, refer to RFC 2267 at http://www.ietf.org. You can find all RFCs online at http://www.ietf.org/rfc/rfc*xxx*.txt, where *xxxx* is the number of the RFC. If you do not know the number of the RFC, you can try searching by topic at http://www.rfc-editor.org/cgi-bin/rfcsearch.pl. |

- **Fragments**—This feature enables you to configure protection from fragment attacks (frag attacks) by configuring how long fragments can be queued until the fragment cache is flushed, the size of fragmented packets, and the number of fragments in a chain. The ASA/PIX Security Appliance uses this configuration information to determine whether fragmented packets are valid or whether they need to be dropped.

- **TCP Options**—This feature enables you to configure the following:
  - The TCP packet sizes for proxy connections, which can help cause less TCP fragmentation if a proxy is used to handle web requests and responses.
  - The forcing of a TCP connection to linger in a wait state for 15 seconds, which can help TCP connects to gracefully close down during some unexpected timing conditions.
  - The resetting of inbound TCP connections sends a reset to the source address if a connection is blocked by an access list. If this is not set (or reset), the request is silently discarded.
  - The resetting of outbound TCP connections sends a reset to the source address if a connection is blocked by an access list. If this is not set, the request is silently discarded.

- **Timeouts**—This feature enables you to configure the ASA/PIX Security Appliance to clean up sessions and connections that have been opened but rendered inactive after a certain amount of time. This condition could represent a hacker probing the security appliance for open ports, DoS attacks, or just connects where one end or the other has gone silent. Timeouts are set for each common web protocol, as well as for address translations and authentication events. The pull-down Help menu for this panel provides an in-depth discussion for each of the 14 timeout values.

  The default values are usually adequate for most companies deploying the ASA/PIX Security Appliance. If you know you are being hit with a DoS attack targeting a specific port or protocol, you might want to decrease the timeout period so that the security appliance cleans up the dead connections more frequently. If you are using authentication, the default to re-authenticate you is 5 minutes. If you want a longer or shorter timeout period, you must modify the authorization absolute parameter.

  You can also apply timeouts using the Service Policy Rules panel. The rules set up in these panels take priority over the default rules described.

- **SUNRPC Server**—This enables you to determine which Remote Procedure Calls (RPCs) you want to allow through your security appliance. This is not an issue for most users. However, for some, their applications need RPC functionality to traverse their security appliance. This panel enables these users to define which RPC calls will be allowed.

- **History Metrics**—This panel enables you to configure the security appliance so that it can store ASDM data that can be viewed for time intervals up to 5 days.

Monitor Navigation Icon

The Monitor feature menu contains functions needed to monitor traffic and services on the ASA/PIX Security Appliance.

Seven features are listed under the Monitor navigation icon. (See Figure 4-21.)

Figure 4-21 *Monitor Navigation Icon*

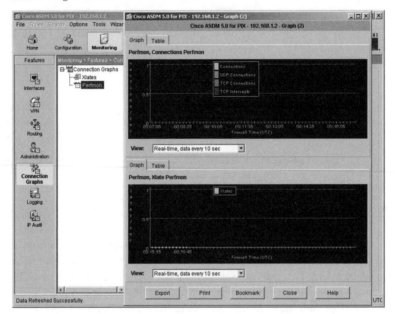

The following features are available under the Monitor navigation icon:

- Interfaces
- VPN
- Routing
- Administration
- Connection graphs
- Logging
- IP audits

This list of features represents a comprehensive set of ASDM options to monitor many keys features of the ASA/PIX Security Appliance.

Interface Monitor Features

Table 4-5 provides a summary of all the panels available in the Interface Monitor navigation screen, along with the data that is reported for each element of the Interface Monitor feature.

Table 4-5   *Interface Monitor Features*

Interface Monitor Feature	Data Displayed
ARP Table	Interface, IP address, MAC address
DHCP Server Tables	IP address, MAC address, lease expiration
DHCP Client Leases	DHCP lease information pertinent if one of the ASA/PIX interfaces is set up as a DHCP client
DHCP Statistics	Counters for all DHCP message types
Dynamic ACLs	Hit counters for access control lists
Interface Graphs (inside and outside)	Dynamic graphing for all packet and error information for each ASA/PIX interface.

Routing Monitor Features

Table 4-6 provides a summary of all the panels available in the Routing Monitor features screen, along with the data that is reported for each element of the Routing Monitor feature.

Table 4-6   *Routing Monitor Features*

Routing Monitor Feature	Data Displayed
Routes	Protocol, type, destination, gateway, metric/administrative distance
OSPF LSAs	For LSA types 1,2,3,4,5,7 area, router ID, advertiser, age, sequence number, checksum, link count
OSPF Neighbors	Neighbor, priority, state, dead time, address, interface

VPN Monitor Features

Table 4-7 provides a summary of all the panels available in the VPN Monitor features screen, along with the data that is reported for each element of the VPN Monitor feature.

Table 4-7   *VPN Monitor Features*

VPN Monitor Feature	Data Displayed
Sessions	Session counts, username, encryption type, login time, client type, bytes in and out
Encryption Statistics	Sessions and percentage per algorithm
Protocol Statistics	Sessions and percentage per protocol
Global IKE/IPSec Statistics	Various IPSec and IKE statistics and hit counts
Crypto Statistics	Various statistics and hit counts for IPSec, IKE, and SSL
IPSec Tunnel Graphs	Graph IPSec and IKE active tunnels

Administration Monitor Features

Table 4-8 provides a summary of all the panels available in the Administration Monitor features screen, along with the data that is reported for each element of the Administration Monitor feature.

Table 4-8   *Administration Monitor Features*

Administration Monitor Feature	Data Displayed
ASDM/HTTPS Sessions	Sessions ID, IP address
Telnet Sessions	Sessions ID, IP address
Secure Shell Session Statistics	Client, user, state, version, and encryption statistics
AAA Locked Out Users	Locked time, failed attempts, users
Authenticated Users	User, IP address, dynamic ACL, and timeout statistics
AAA Servers	Server group, IP address, protocol, and request statistics
CRL	CRL info per trust point
DNS Cache	Host, IP address, permanent, idle time, active
Block Graphs	Graph blocks used, blocks free
CPU Graphs	Graph CPU utilization
Memory Graphs	Graph memory used, memory free
Failover Status	Output of **show failover** command
Failover Graphs	Graph various failover statistics

Connection Graphs Monitor Features

Table 4-9 provides a summary of all the panels available in the Connection Graphs Monitor features screen, along with the data that is reported for each element of the Connection Graphs monitor feature.

Table 4-9   *Connection Graphs Monitor Features*

Connection Graphs Monitor Feature	Data Displayed
Graph Xlates	Graph xlate utilization
Graph Perfmon	Graph performance for AAA, inspects, web, connections, xlates

Logging Monitor Features

Table 4-10 provides a summary of all the panels available in the Logging Monitor features screen, along with the data that is reported for each element of the Logging Monitor feature.

Table 4-10   *Logging Monitor Features*

Logging Monitor Feature	Data Displayed
Live Log	Displays real-time syslog messages
Buffer Log	Displays buffered syslog messages

IP Audit Monitor Features

Table 4-11 provides a summary of all the panels available in the IP Audit Monitor features screen, along with the data that is reported for each element of the IP Audit monitor feature.

Table 4-11   *IP Audit Monitor Features*

IP Audit Monitor Feature	Data Displayed
IP Audits	Displays graph information for 16 attack signatures

Back Arrow Navigation Icon

The Back arrow navigation button is analogous to the back arrow on a web browser. It takes you back to the previously viewed screen.

Forward Arrow Navigation Icon

The Forward arrow navigation button is analogous to the forward arrow on a web browser. If you have backed up while navigating, it will take you forward to the previously viewed screen. If you haven't navigated backward, the button remains inactive.

Search Navigation Icon

The Search button on the navigation bar is one of the handiest tools available to help you navigate through ASDM; its purpose is to assist you in finding any panel in the ASDM application. When you click the **Search** button, you are prompted with a search panel, as shown in Figure 4-22.

Enter a keyword into the Feature Keyword text box, click the **Search** button, and the feature search will display all the paths that contain the keyword in your search. The results include a link that you can click to take you straight to the desired feature panel. Figure 4–30 shows the results from the keyword "access," where three navigation paths were displayed:

- AAA Access
- Access Group
- Access Rules

Figure 4-22 *Search Navigation Tool*

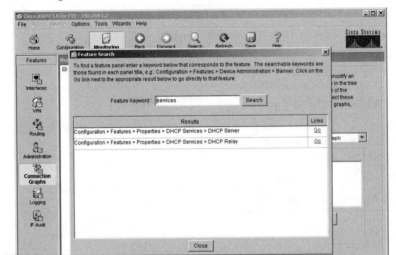

From the result list, clicking the **Go** link at the end of the navigation path will take you directly to that panel.

Refresh Navigation Icon

The Refresh navigation icon enables you to refresh ASDM with the current configuration on the ASA/PIX Security Appliance. Use this button when you have made changes to a panel that you haven't saved and you want the panel to revert to its previous state. If you want to see the changes in *your* ASDM session when a change was made to the security appliance via either another ASDM connection or a console connection, you should use this button.

CAUTION   A warning prompt displays before ASDM is refreshed with the running configuration if you have unsaved changes.

Save Navigation Icon

The Save navigation icon enables you to write the current ASDM configuration to Flash on the ASA/PIX Security Appliance. This action is equivalent to the **write memory** command in the security appliance CLI. Changes take effect immediately when they are applied using ASDM, but they do not become permanent until you perform a save.

Help Navigation Icon

The Help navigation icon brings up the Adaptive Security Device Manager Online Help screen. This screen enables you to access context-sensitive help, which includes the following:

- Help contents
- Help screen
- Help search
- Help glossary
- Help index
- About ASDM
- Using Help

Summary

This chapter explored each component of ASDM:

- The pull-down menus
- The navigation bar icons
- Features available in each navigation icon

The following tables summarize all components of ASDM.

Table 4-12 *Pull-Down Menu Command Summary*

Pull-Down Menu Tab	Summary
File	Contains commands to save configuration files to the Flash in the ASA/PIX Security Appliance and various other locations.
Rules	Used to insert items into a rules list. This pull-down is only active when the Configuration icon is selected in the navigation bar.
Search	Used to search items that exist in a rules list. This pull-down is only active when the Configuration icon is selected in the navigation bar.
Options	Sets cookies in your browser to control how ASDM will behave in certain circumstances such as logout and command displays.
Tools	Contains tools for common command-line tasks for the security appliance. This includes Flash, file management, image and ASDM upgrades, ASA/PIX command execution, and system reloads.
Wizards	This pull-down starts the two wizards that are available with ASDM: the VPN Wizard and the Startup Wizard.
Help	This pull-down contains context-sensitive help for ASDM. You can also access the ASA/PIX Security Appliance User Guide from the Cisco website if you have Internet connectivity.

An overview of each item on the navigation bar was discussed in this chapter. These items are contained in Table 4-13.

Table 4-13 *Navigation Bar Overview*

Navigation Icon	Summary
Home	This is the default screen seen when ASDM launches. It primarily contains status and device information of the ASA/PIX and ASDM.
Configuration	This is the main portion of ASDM. It contains all the configuration options for the ASA/PIX Security Appliance.
Monitoring	The Monitoring icon offers options to monitor all the security appliance features and functions. This includes graphing and table views.
Back Arrow	This allows backward navigation through previously viewed ASDM screens.
Forward Arrow	This allows forward navigation through previously viewed ASDM screens.
Search	This icon finds the ASDM screen that matches user-entered search criteria.
Refresh	The Refresh icon reloads the current ASA/PIX configuration to the ASDM application.
Save	This icon saves any changes made through ASDM to the ASA/PIX Security Appliance's running configuration.
Help	This contains context-sensitive help.

Features available for each item on the navigation bar that were discussed in this chapter are contained in Table 4-14.

Table 4-14 *Navigation Bar Overview*

Navigation Icon	Features
Home	Information panels displaying:
	Host name
	ADSM user
	ASDM version
	Browser running ASDM
	Operating system running ASDM
	ASA/PIX device type
	ASA/PIX operating system version
	User privilege level
	Java version installed
	Interface status
	VPN status
	System resource status
	Interface status

Table 4-14   *Navigation Bar Overview (Continued)*

Navigation Icon	Features
Configuration	Interfaces
	Security policies
	NAT
	VPN
	Routing
	Building blocks
	Device administration
	Properties
Monitoring	Interfaces
	Routing
	VPN
	Administration
	Connection graphs
	Logging
	IP audits
Back Arrow	Used to move back to the previously accessed ASDM screen
Forward Arrow	Used to move forward to the previously accessed ASDM screen
Search	Finds the ASDM screen that matches user-entered search criteria
Refresh	Reloads the current ASA/PIX Security Appliance configuration to the ASDM application
Save	Saves any changes made through ASDM to the ASA/PIX Security Appliance's running configuration
Help	Context-sensitive help

Securing Network Infrastructures with ASDM

This chapter provides you with the necessary information to use the ASDM Startup Wizard to perform the initial configuration of your network. There are three major sections in this chapter.

This chapter addresses the following topics:

- **Introduction to the ASDM Startup Wizard**—This first section provides a brief overview of the ASDM Startup Wizard and its capabilities.

- **Understanding the Basic Network Topology**—The second section is a discussion of your basic network topology, explaining some high-level concepts of IP addressing and how it's used in configuring your network. The intent is to give you the basic concepts to enable you to easily move ahead with your firewall and Internet deployment.

- **Using the ASDM Startup Wizard to Configure Your Network**—The third section is the bulk of the chapter and is a step-by-step tutorial on how to use the wizard to configure your firewall.

CHAPTER 5

Deploying Secure Internet Connectivity

This chapter is a step-by-step procedure explaining how to use the ASDM Startup Wizard to set up the initial configuration for your ASA/PIX Security Appliance.

These steps are intended to show you how to achieve secure connectivity to the Internet. After completing these steps, you will have access to the Internet. In addition, you will be protected from both Internet-sourced attacks against the hosts on the inside of your network and denial-of-service (DoS) attacks against your firewall.

Chapter 6, "Deploying Web and Mail Services," covers how to configure ASDM to advertise and secure public services such as web servers and e-mail.

Introducing the ASDM Startup Wizard

The ASDM Startup Wizard is an easy-to-use tool that steps you through the procedures necessary to get your firewall functional. It provides the configurations necessary for both Internet connectivity and protection for your network resources. The wizard queries you for all items pertinent to the configuration of your firewall, including the following:

- Inside IP addresses
- Outside IP addresses
- Default gateway
- Domain name
- Public services
- Network address translations
- Firewall name
- Access passwords
- Interface options
- Inside addressing options (DHCP)

Before you begin, take a look at Table 5-1, which defines the network terms used in the preceding list.

Table 5-1   *Networking Terminology*

Terminology	Definition
Inside IP address	The IP address of the inside interface of your firewall, which connects to your internal network.
Outside IP address	The IP address of the outside interface of your firewall, which connects to your service provider for Internet connectivity. This address is provided by your service provider.
Default gateway	The next-hop IP address of your firewall outside interface. This is provided by your service provider.
Domain name	This is optional. If you are providing public services, you need to identify a domain name for those services. Either your ISP or a web registration service provides your domain name.
Public services	These are services that you are providing to other people over the Internet. Common public services are web servers, mail servers, or DNS servers. You can elect not to manage your own services and have your ISP manage the services for you.
Network address translation	This feature enables you to use private addresses inside your network and still obtain Internet access.
Access passwords	This password allows you privileged access to your firewall.
Inside addressing options (DHCP, static)	These are IP addresses that you assign to devices on the inside of your firewall. You have two options for configuring your inside hosts with IP addresses: You can manually set up each address on each PC, or you can use DHCP on the ASA/PIX Security Appliance to assign addresses for you.

Basic Network Topology

This chapter provides a common and basic network topology as an example for the ASDM Startup Wizard procedure. The topology is such a standard template that, unless you have a unusual circumstance, you can follow these steps verbatim and have secure Internet connectivity upon completion.

Figure 5-1 shows the topology you will use for your ASDM Startup Wizard procedure.

It's important to understand the basic elements and terminology used in this topology:

- Internet
- Service provider
- Default gateway
- IP address and subnet masks
- Inside address

- Inside network
- Internet server addresses

Figure 5-1   *Basic Network to Internet Topology*

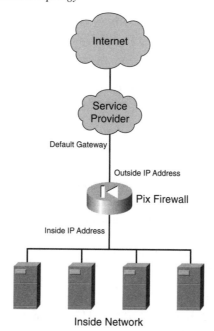

Understanding the Elements of Your Network

Before you begin, let's review some basic Internet terminology to ensure that we are all on the same page.

The Internet

The *Internet*, which of course everyone is familiar with, is millions of networks and hosts that reach all over the globe. Most companies want to be connected to the Internet to either tap into this vast array of information, communicate with others who have Internet access, or provide services or advertisement to other Internet users.

The Internet Service Provider

The *Internet service provider* (ISP) is your entry point into the Internet. There are many different providers throughout the world. Your first step to connect to the Internet is to select a local ISP. Your local ISP might be a local telephone company or a small company that focuses on providing Internet coverage in small target areas. It is beyond the scope of this book to recommend ISPs. It is recommended, however, that you talk to other companies or use the web to find out who provides the best service in your area.

The ISP provides you with a physical point of entry into its network. This is usually a networking device such as a DSL/cable modem or a router. The outside of your ASA/PIX Security Appliance plugs into this device.

Default Gateway

Your ISP will provide an IP address called a *default gateway address*. This is the address of a router that the ISP owns that will be the next hop toward the Internet from your ASA/PIX Security Appliance.

Internet IP Address and Subnet Mask

Along with a default gateway, the ISP will provide you with an *IP address* and a *subnet mask*. The IP address and subnet mask are applied to the outside of your firewall. The IP address always has four octets and might look something like 199.200.2.4. The address and mask work together to form a network number and a host number. You don't have to worry about this for now; suffice it to say that if you correctly enter your IP address and mask, you will be properly connected to the Internet.

NOTE   A new addressing scheme called *IPv6* will be used in the Internet a few years from now. The format of the v6 address will be different. However, the IPv6-style addresses will be designed so that they work seamlessly with IPv4 addresses. Therefore, no changes will need to be made to your configuration when IPv6 comes of age. It is also important to note that the ASA/PIX Security Appliance supports IPv6 in the version 7 release.

Inside Addresses

The concept of *inside addresses* could get complex if you let it. Don't let it! It can also be simple. Addresses on the inside of your network are usually defined as private or reserved addresses.

Don't be intimidated if you don't understand IP addressing. If you enter the addresses correctly from your ISP and follow the procedures in this book, the details of IP addressing are insignificant. The most commonly used private addresses are the following:

- **Class A**: 10.0.0.0 through 10.255.255.255 (subnet mask: 255.0.0.0)
- **Class B**: 172.16.0.0 through 172.31.255.255 (subnet mask: 255.255.0.0)
- **Class C**: 192.168.0.0 through 192.168.255.255 (subnet mask: 255.255.255.0)

It doesn't matter which of these addresses you elect to use because they all function in exactly the same manner. In this book, you use 192.168.1.x and a subnet mask of 255.255.255.0 as your private inside network addresses.

Network Address Translation

One thing you must understand about private inside addresses is that they are not routable on the Internet. This means that if you were to send traffic out from a host that has a private address to http://www.cisco.com, the packet would make it out to the Internet. However, because it's a private nonroutable Internet address, it cannot be returned to the host that originated the request. Therefore, your web request would never be returned and your connection would time out.

The ASA/PIX Security Appliance handles this situation by using a concept called *network address translation* (NAT). When NAT is applied on the firewall, it uses the following process to ensure that the traffic is both delivered to the destination address and then returned back to the host that has the private address:

1 Looks at the address of the host requesting Internet access

2 Stores the original private address in its NAT lookup table

3 Replaces the private address with either the outside interface IP address of your ASA/PIX Security Appliance or another address provided by your service provider

4 Accepts the return packet, looks up the host that made the original request in its NAT table, and replaces the private address

5 Routes the return packet back to the correct host

Inside Network

The *inside network* refers to the hosts that will be behind your firewall. Normally, these hosts are connected to a switch or a series of switches and routers, depending on the complexity of your network. Because this book is a beginner's guide, you are going to use the topology shown in Figure 5-1, which is a flat network, which means that the inside of your firewall and all of your hosts will be connected to a single switch comprising your inside network.

Your inside network addresses *must* be in the same subnet as the inside interface of your ASA/PIX Security Appliance. You could manually configure the IP addresses of each of your inside hosts so that they are in the same subnet. However, the security appliance can also do this for you. You will use a function of the ASA/PIX Security Appliance called *Dynamic Host Configuration Protocol* (DHCP) to automatically assign IP addresses to your inside host. This protocol will save you many hours of initial labor and ongoing maintenance.

Public Servers: Mail DNS, Web Servers

Public servers provide services that you plan to allow Internet users to access. The most common of these are web servers, mail servers, and DNS servers. If you plan to offer public services, you must request an IP address for each of the servers from your ISP. Also, remember from earlier reading, that if you are going to offer public services, you need to have a firewall (such as a PIX 515E) that has more than two interfaces. This way, you can put your servers on an interface separate from your inside users. This setup ensures that if hackers do compromise one of your public servers, your inside network is still isolated from the hackers. Chapter 6 covers the deployment of these servers.

Using the ASDM Startup Wizard

It's time to start with ASDM. At the end of this section, you will have a secure connection established to the Internet.

You complete the following tasks in this section:

- Connect to the ASA/PIX Security Appliance with ASDM.
- Configure the ASA/PIX Security Appliance host name and domain name and enable password.
- Configure the outside interface information.
- Configure other interface characteristics.
- Configure NAT.

Connecting to the ASA/PIX Security Appliance with ASDM

If you haven't completed the steps from Chapter 3, "Getting Started with the ASA/PIX Security Appliance," to install ASA/PIX version 7 and ASDM, you cannot proceed. You must complete the configuration portion of that chapter before you can do any of the step-by step portions of this section.

You need to complete three steps before you can connect to the ASA/PIX Security Appliance using ASDM:

Step 1   Configure an interface port.

Step 2   Allow ASDM access to the box.

Step 3   Ensure you have the appropriate Java Runtime Environment on your host that will be running ASDM.

Configure an Interface Port

These steps assume that there is currently no configuration on your ASA/PIX Security Appliance. If it is the first time you boot your ASA/PIX Security Appliance, it will prompt you with a question asking whether you want to configure the device. Enter **No**. All of your configuration steps are outlined in the following steps.

If you already configured your security appliance as described in Chapter 3, you can skip to the section titled "Configure Your PC to Access the ASA/PIX Security Appliance."

Step 1   Plug your PC serial port into the console of the ASA/PIX Security Appliance using the serial cable. Using HyperTerminal or any terminal emulator application, set your parameters to match those in Figure 5-2. These setting show speed at 9600 bps, 8 data bits, no parity checking, and 1 stop bit.

Figure 5-2 *HyperTerminal Parameter Setup*

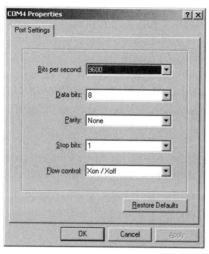

Step 2 Power on the ASA/PIX Security Appliance. The Security Appliance will go through its boot sequence and you will be presented with a pixfirewall> prompt.

Step 3 You must now configure the inside interface of the ASA/PIX Security Appliance with a valid inside address so that you can access it using ASDM. At the prompt, enter the commands in the following example that are in bold text. Comment lines have been added to indicate what each command does. Comment lines are preceded with an exclamation point (!):

```
pixfirewall> enable
! en - puts you in Enable (Privileged) mode.
Password:<CR>
! <CR> - is the default password for the PIX.
pixfirewall# configure terminal
! conf t - specifies that the following commands will be configuration
    commands.
pixfirewall(Config)# interface ethernet
! int e1 - specifies that the commands following will be applied to the
    Ethernet 1 interface.
pixfirewall(Config-if)# nameif inside
! nameif inside - defines Ethernet 1 as the inside or protected
    interface.
INFO: Security level for "inside" set to 100 by default.
pixfirewall(Config-if)# ip address 192.168.1.1 255.255.255.0
```

```
! ip add 192.168.1.1 255.255.255.0 - sets the IP address and subnet mask
    for the inside interface.
pixfirewall(Config-if)# no shut
! no shut - enables the interface for operating.
pixfirewall(Config-if)#
```

In this book, this is the only time you use the native ASA/PIX Security Appliance
command-line interface (CLI) to enable the security appliance to accept ASDM
connections.

Configure Your PC to Access the ASA/PIX Security Appliance

Because you will be accessing ASDM with your PC on the inside interface of the ASA/PIX
Security Appliance, you must configure your PC with an inside IP address. You will use
192.168.1.2 with a subnet mask of 255.255.255.0 (same as the security appliance subnet
mask). The gateway is the next-hop address; so in this case, it is the address you gave to the
inside of the security appliance: 192.168.1.1.

Figure 5-3 illustrates how your Network Control Panel should look when configured if you
are using Windows 2000.

Figure 5-3   *PC Network Configuration*

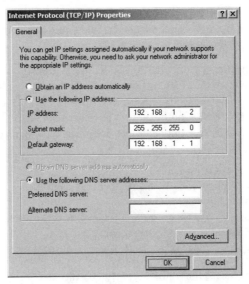

You can connect the PC to the ASA/PIX Security Appliance in one of two ways. You can
directly connect to the interface labeled Ethernet 1 using a crossover cable, or you can plug
the PC and Security Appliance Ethernet 1 into a switch using straight-through Ethernet
cables. You should now be able to ping the firewall from your PC using the command **ping
192.168.1.1**. If your pings are not successful, recheck your addressing and cabling. Make

sure that the PC Ethernet card and Ethernet 1 on the security appliance are enabled. You should see link lights on the security appliance interface and the network card of your PC when properly configured.

Allow ASDM Access to the ASA/PIX Security Appliance

You must now tell the ASA/PIX Security Appliance that you are enabling it to run ASDM. You are also defining what IP address can access the security appliance with the ASDM application.

Follow these steps:

Step 1   The first thing you need to do is tell the PIX the name of the ASDM file. Enter the following command on the PIX: **asdm image flash:/asdm.bin**.

Step 2   Now, you must enable the ASA/PIX Security Appliance to start its secure web server. Enter the command **http server enable**.

Step 3   After the ASA/PIX Security Appliance web server is enabled, you must tell the security appliance who can access ASDM and where they are located. To accomplish this, enter the address of your PC and tell the security appliance you are located on the inside interface. Enter the command **http 192.168.1.2 255.255.255.255 inside**.

Caution   You can enable ASDM on the outside interface of the ASA/PIX Security Appliance, but it is not recommended. If you do, you open yourself to the possibility that someone can guess your username and password and gain full access to your firewall.

Step 4   Enter the command **show running http** on the ASA/PIX Security Appliance and ensure that the output matches the following output:

```
pixfirewall(Config)# show running http
http server enabled
http 192.168.1.2 255.255.255.255 inside
pixfirewall(Config)#
```

At this point, you should have full connectivity to your ASA/PIX Security Appliance via ASDM.

Launching ASDM

The instructions in this section show you how to launch ASDM. Just follow these steps:

Step 1   Open the browser on your PC and enter **https://192.168.1.1/admin**.

This action downloads the ASDM applet to your PC. The first time you do this, it might take a minute to load. However, in subsequent connections, ASDM will start in just a few seconds.

ASDM will also present you with an option to download a utility called the *ASDM Launcher*. This launcher is an application that functions exactly the same as the Java applet. Using this application will eliminate the need to launch a browser to access the ASA/PIX Security Appliance.

The browser-based ASDM applet requires Java 1.4.2 or 1.5.0. If you don't have one of these Java versions installed on your PC, you will get the following message and you must download the required software: "Your browser does not have the required Java Plug-in. ASDM requires Java Plug-in version 1.4.2 or higher." We will point you to a web page from which you can download the correct Java version to your PC.

Because ASDM is using a connection secured by SSL, you will see the various security warnings as described in the following steps.

Step 2   The first pop-up (Figure 5-4) is a message that lets you know that the secure connection has a valid certificate, but that the certificate is from an untrusted source. This certificate is a self-generated certificate by the ASA/PIX Security Appliance. You must click **Yes** to continue.

Figure 5-4   *Valid Certificate Alert*

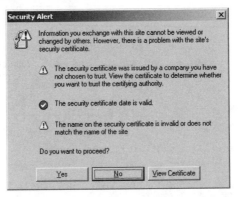

Step 3   When you get the prompt for the ASA/PIX Security Appliance username and password (Figure 5-5), leave the fields empty and click **OK**. You haven't set a password yet, so no input is required.

Step 4   Figure 5-6 informs you that the certificate is going to be used as a key to encrypt data but that the issuer isn't trusted. You must click **Yes** to continue. Don't be concerned when you see these messages that say that certificates are not trusted. Trust is a technical concept in public certificate authentication related to the prior knowledge of a certificate.

Figure 5-5   *ASA/PIX Security Appliance Username and Password Prompt*

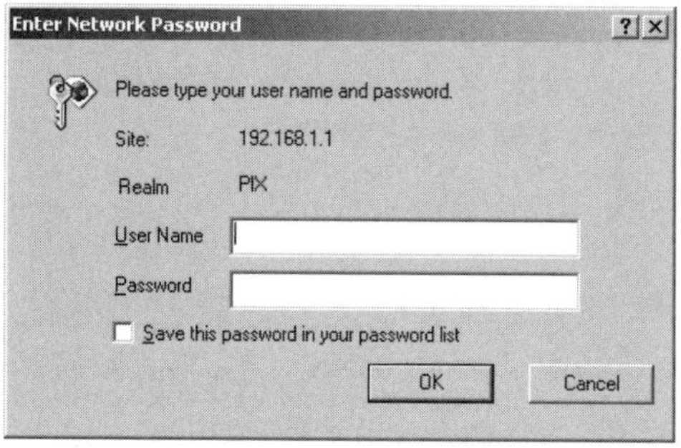

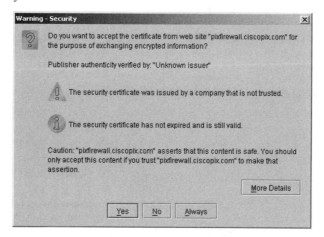

Figure 5-6   *Valid Certificate Alert*

Step 5   Figure 5-7 prompts you again for username and password because the Java applet is now running. Again, because you haven't set passwords at this point, you should click **Yes**. If you are using the ASDM Launcher application rather than the web browser, you won't get this prompt.

Figure 5-7   *Network Password Access*

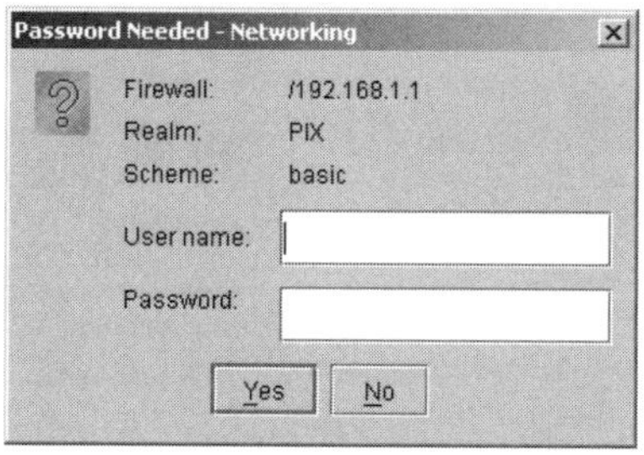

Step 6   Figure 5-8 is a certificate that needs to be approved to download the ASDM applet to your PC. Click **Yes** to continue.

Figure 5-8   *Certificate to Download ASDM*

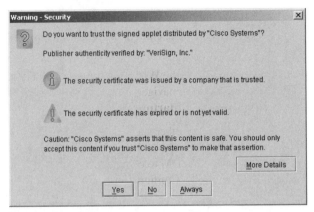

You are now presented with Figure 5-9, which is the ASDM Welcome screen.

Figure 5-9   *ASDM Welcome Screen*

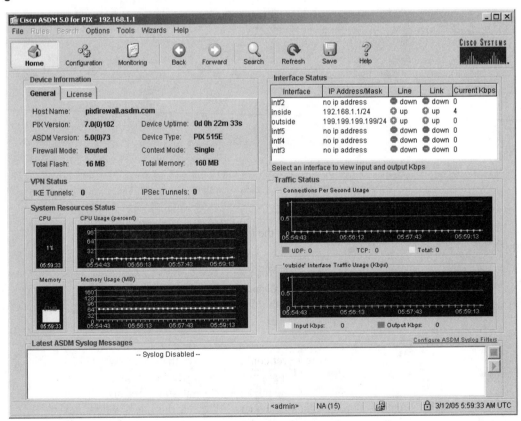

You are now logged on to your ASA/PIX Security Appliance using ASDM.

Using the ASDM Startup Wizard to Configure the ASA/PIX Security Appliance

Now, you are ready to begin entering configuration information into ASDM. Just follow these steps:

Step 1   To start the wizard, click the **Wizard** pull-down menu item or the click the **Wizard** option on the navigation panel to the far left of the ASDM home screen and choose **Startup Wizard**.

Step 2   You will first be asked whether you want to use the existing configuration. The only existing configuration should be your IP address and the command that allows ASDM to communicate with your browser. Click **Continue with Existing Configuration**, and then click **Next**. (See Figure 5-10.)

Figure 5-10   *ASDM Starting Configuration*

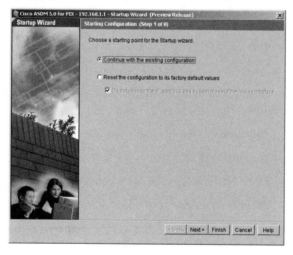

Step 3   You are than prompted for the basic configuration (see Figure 5-11).

Enter the name you want to call your ASA/PIX Security Appliance. Enter the domain, if you have one. You can enter anything you want in these fields; Figure 5-11 shows pixfirewall and example.com entered in these fields. The default domain name is default.domain.invalid until you enter your own domain name into this field.

Step 4   You need to enter an enable password (privileged) for the firewall. Because no password is yet configured, leave the old password blank. According to security best practices, you should enter a password at least eight characters long, using numerals, special characters, and containing uppercase and lowercase characters. Following this rule will significantly reduce the chances of an attacker being able to run a brute-force or guessing attack against your firewall to get the password and gain full access. Click **Next**.

Figure 5-11 *ASDM Basic Configuration*

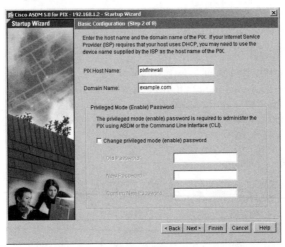

Step 5   The next step is to configure the connectivity to the Internet. This consists of the following:

— The name of your firewall's outside interface

— The outside IP address of your firewall provided to you by your ISP

— The subnet mask provided by your ISP

— The default gateway provided by your ISP

In Figure 5-12, you can see that outside is entered as the name the interface, 199.199.199.199 as the IP address, 255.255.255.0 as the subnet mask, and 199.199.199.254 as the default gateway. A default security level will be set to 0 on your outside interface. These addresses were randomly chosen for the step-by-step procedures in this book. The address you actually enter will be provided by your ISP. Although not addressed in this book, your ISP might ask you to accept a DHCP address on the outside interface. To do this, you just click the **Use DHCP** option button.

Security level is important. In the ASA/PIX Security Appliance, traffic will flow unimpeded from a high-security level to a low-security level. Conversely, traffic from a low-security level to a higher-security level will be blocked by default. Later when you configure access lists, you will allow traffic from low to high.

Figure 5-12 *Outside Interface Configuration*

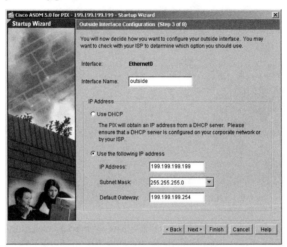

By default on the ASA/PIX Security Appliance, because the inside interface has a security level of 100 and the outside has a default of 0, traffic originating from the inside is allowed to pass to the outside interface. Because the ASA/PIX Security Appliance is a stateful device, this means that all traffic going through the firewall will also be allowed to return. The default security appliance behavior blocks traffic sourced from the Internet, effectively mitigating against thousands of possible attacks that can be launched against your network from the Internet.

The IP addresses for the outside interface listed are only an example and will not work for your network deployment. You must use the values provided by your ISP.

Your service provider might not give you an IP address for the outside interface of your security appliance; they might require you to run DHCP and automatically configure your outside address using its DHCP server.

The next screen is titled Other Interface Configuration. (See Figure 5-13.) In this chapter, you do not make any changes to other interfaces. In Chapter 6, you add another interface if you plan to host a web or mail server.

Step 6 You shouldn't need to make any changes to this screen. Click **Next** to proceed.

Figure 5-13 *Other Interface Configuration*

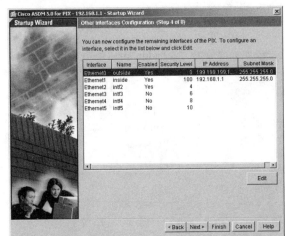

Step 7 The next screen, DHCP Server, allows you to automatically configure the IP addresses of your inside hosts. (See Figure 5-14.) As mentioned earlier in this chapter, the most expeditious way to deliver addresses to the inside is to use DHCP. If you use DHCP, the ASA/PIX Security Appliance assigns an address to each host on your inside network when the host boots up.

To activate DHCP, click the box next to **Enable the DHCP Server on the Inside Interface**.

Figure 5-14 *DHCP Server Configuration*

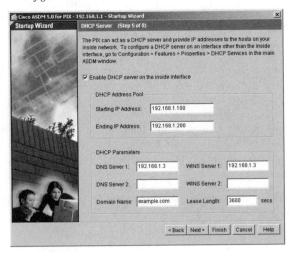

Step 8 Enter a range of IP addresses that will be allocated by DHCP for your hosts. Make sure you allow enough IP addresses for all of your hosts. Use a starting address of **192.168.1.100** and an ending address of **192.168.1.200**. You need to make sure that the range you use does not overlap with any other IP addresses, such as the inside interface of your security appliance (192.168.1.1) or the static address of your PC (192.168.1.2).

Step 9 You now need to enter the DNS and WINS address that you want automatically configured on your inside hosts. If you don't have your own DNS server, the address will be given to you by your ISP. A WINS server is required if you plan to use Microsoft File or Print Sharing on your network. You need to consult with Microsoft on how to enable this on your system. You can leave this field blank. In the example, the same address as my DNS and WINS server is used.

Step 10 To enable your PCs to accept DHCP addresses from your ASA/PIX Security Appliance, you need to go to the Network Control Panel, choose **Properties**, highlight **Internet Protocol**, choose **Properties**, check **Obtain an IP Address Dynamically**, check **Obtain a DNS Server Address Dynamically**, and then click **OK**.

After the wizard has completed and the PCs have been configured, addresses are automatically allocated when a PC is started and connected to the inside network.

Step 11 If you have a domain name given to you by your ISP, enter it into the Domain Name field. This is an optional field.

Step 12 After you have filled in the values, click **Next** to proceed.

Step 13 The next screen is the Address Translation screen. (See Figure 5-15.) As mentioned previously in this chapter, private inside addresses are not routable on the Internet. Therefore, you must use NAT to translate the private addresses and allow them access to and from the Internet. In your case, you are going to use something called *port address translation* (PAT), which uses a combination of something called a port and the outside address of the ASA/PIX Security Appliance. Using PAT simplifies the configuration steps for address translation; in addition, because you are using an existing address, you don't need to purchase additional addresses from you ISP.

Click the **Use Port Address Translation** option button, click the **Use Port on the Outside Interface** option button, and then click **Next** to continue.

Figure 5-15 *Address Translation*

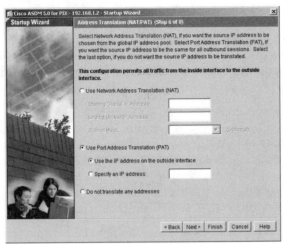

Step 14 Now, you must select which IP addresses are allowed to have administrative access to your ASA/PIX Security Appliance. This specification should already be set or you wouldn't have access to ASDM. If you need to add additional authorized IP addresses, choose an interface and click **Add**. Then, enter the data for the PC for which you need to allow access. Click **Next**. This value should already be set from when you used the CLI to configure the security appliance to allow access from 192.168.1.2. (See Figure 5-16.)

Figure 5-16 *ASDM Configuration Panel*

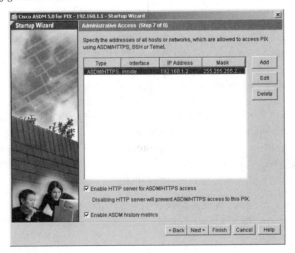

Step 15 Click **Finish**.

The ASA/PIX Security Appliance then automatically generates and sends commands to the security appliance according to the selections that you made during the wizard configuration process.

Congratulations! You now have a secure, working connection to the Internet.

When the Startup Wizard has completed, the resulting addresses of your network display, as shown in Figure 5-17.

Figure 5-17 *Server Topology*

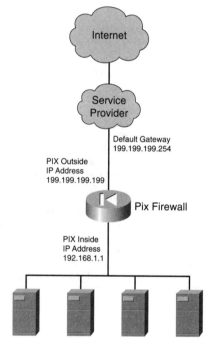

Inside Network 192.168.1.100 – 192.168.1.200

You are now protected from several hundred attacks that can originate from the Internet because traffic is allowed only from the inside out. In addition, by default, many processes are running on your firewall to help protect it from DoS attacks. You are still susceptible to many other attacks, such as mail- and web-based viruses, but in subsequent chapters, you are instructed on how to mitigate these threats.

Summary

In this chapter, you used ASDM to configure the ASA/PIX Security Appliance to enable the users inside your business or enterprise to securely access the World Wide Web.

In this chapter, you did the following:

- Gained an understanding of basic networking terminology
- Defined a network topology
- Assigned IP addresses to the network devices
- Configured connectivity between the ASA/PIX Security Appliance and the PC running ASDM
- Used the ASDM Startup Wizard to configure your network

Table 5-2 provides a summary of the network terminology defined in this chapter.

Table 5-2 *Network Terminology Summary*

Terminology	Definition
Inside IP address	The IP address of the inside interface of your firewall.
Outside IP address	The IP address of the outside interface of your firewall. This is provided by your service provider.
Default gateway	The next-hop IP address of your firewall outside interface. This is provided by your service provider.
Domain name	This is optional. If you are providing public services, you need to identify a domain name for those services. Either your ISP or a web registration service provides the domain name.
Public services	The public services include mail, web, or DNS servers. The intent of a public server is to share or exchange data with other Internet users. You may elect not to manage your own services and have your ISP manage the services for you.
Network address translation	This protocol enables you to use private addresses inside your network and still obtain Internet access.
Access passwords	These passwords allow privileged access to your firewall.
Inside addressing options (DHCP)	These are IP addresses that need to be assigned to devices on the inside of your firewall.
Internet	Several thousands of networks and hosts interconnected that reach all over the globe.
Service provider	The Internet service provider is a company that provides you with your access point into the Internet.

You then defined a topology that described your Internet connection in relation to your firewall and your protected users. The firewall outside interface, Ethernet 0, was plugged into a network connection provided by your ISP. Your inside users were connected to the inside of your firewall on the interface Ethernet 1.

IP addresses were then defined for both the outside and the inside interfaces of the ASA/PIX Security Appliance.

You were then stepped through the following three-step process to connect your PC to your ASA/PIX Security Appliance using ASDM:

1   You used the ASA/PIX Security Appliance console and a series of native commands to configure a security appliance interface port.

2   You used the security appliance console and a series of native commands that allowed your PC to have ASDM access to the ASA/PIX Security Appliance.

3   You upgraded the Java Runtime Environment on your PC so that it could run ASDM.

After connectivity was established between the ASA/PIX Security Appliance and your PC, you used the ASDM Startup Wizard to configure the ASA/PIX Security Appliance. The following parameters were configured during these steps:

- **ASA/PIX Security Appliance host name**—Device identification
- **Domain name**—Unique Internet suffix associated with all of your hosts
- **Enable password**—Allows privileged access to the ASA/PIX Security Appliance
- **Outside interface**—IP address, gateway address, and security level
- **Inside interface addressing**—DHCP addresses to be automatically given to hosts as they access the inside network
- **Network address translation**—Translates private inside addresses so that they can use the Internet
- **Access filter for DNS**—Allows DNS to go through the ASA/PIX Security Appliance so that inside users can resolve URLs

Now that you have finished this chapter, you have secure connectivity to the Internet. Traffic can be sourced only from the inside and sent to the Internet. Any traffic sourced from the Internet will be blocked by the firewall.

This chapter represents only step one in securing your network. The following chapters provide you with step-by-step instructions on how to fully integrate security into your network. If you have no plans to host public mail or web servers, you can skip Chapter 6 and proceed to Chapter 7.

- Chapter 6, "Deploying Web and Mail Services"
- Chapter 7, "Deploying Authentication"
- Chapter 8, "Deploying Perimeter Protection"
- Chapter 9, "Deploying Network Intrusion Prevention"
- Chapter 10, "Deploying Host Intrusion Prevention"
- Chapter 11, "Deploying VPNs"

This chapter provides you with all the necessary information to successfully use the ASDM Startup Wizard for adding both a web server and a mail server to your Internet deployment.

This chapter addresses the following topics:

- **Reviewing Your Current Network Topology**—This section is a review of the network topology deployed in Chapter 5, "Deploying Secure Internet Connectivity."

- **Updating Your Network Topology to Include Web and Mail Services**—This section discusses the addition of a web server and a mail server to your network topology. You use basic concepts to make it as easy and secure as possible, enabling you to move forward with your security appliance and Internet deployment.

- **Using the ASDM Startup Wizard to Add Web and Mail Internet Services to Your ASA/PIX Security Appliance**—This section provides step-by-step instructions on how to use ASDM to add both a web server and a mail server to your network.

Deploying Web and Mail Services

If your business has no intention of hosting a web server or mail server on the inside of your network, you can skip this chapter—unless, of course, you want to know how to do it just out of curiosity. Whether you plan to deploy a web or mail server, read Chapters 7 through 11 and continue your deployment of defense in depth to ensure that your network is as secure as possible.

This chapter is a step-by-step procedure explaining how to use the ASDM Startup Wizard to securely add a web server and a mail server to your network topology.

Upon completion of the steps outlined in this chapter, you will have achieved the following:

- Secure access to the Internet
- Protection from Internet-sourced attacks against the hosts on the inside of your network
- Secure deployment of a web server and a mail server that can be accessed by other Internet users
- Protection of your security appliance and servers from denial-of-service and other Internet-based attacks

Chapters 7 through 11 cover how to use ASDM (and host intrusion prevention software) to deploy defense in depth and additional security best practices within your network:

- Chapter 7, "Deploying Authentication"
- Chapter 8, "Deploying Perimeter Protection"
- Chapter 9, "Deploying Network Intrusion Prevention"
- Chapter 10, "Deploying Host Intrusion Prevention"
- Chapter 11, "Deploying VPNs"

Review of Your Current Network Topology

In Chapter 5, you used the ASDM Startup Wizard to securely connect a private network to the Internet. This topology allowed users to browse the Internet. As well, it did not allow any connectivity sourced from the Internet to the inside of the private network.

In this chapter, you build on that topology by adding a web or mail server to that private network.

First, take a look at Figure 6-1 for a quick review of the network you created in Chapter 5.

Figure 6-1 *Basic Network-to-Internet Topology*

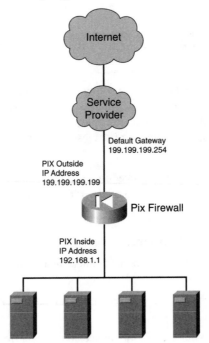

Inside Network 192.168.1.100 – 192.168.1.200

This figure shows the ASA/PIX Security Appliance relative to both the Internet and the private inside network of your topology. It includes current IP addressing. Table 6-1 shows the full addressing scheme and network elements configured in Chapter 5.

Table 6-1 *Networking Terminology*

Network Entity	Value	Subnet Mask
Inside IP address	192.168.1.1	255.255.255.0
Outside IP address	199.199.199.199	255.255.255.0
Default gateway	199.199.199.254	255.255.255.0
Domain name	example.com	n/a
NAT address pool	199.199.199.199 (Outside Interface)	n/a
Inside addressing (DHCP)	192.168.1.100 through 192.168.1.200	255.255.255.0

Designing the Network Topology to Include Web and Mail Services

Before you use ASDM to add a web and mail server to your topology, you need to make the following decisions regarding the architecture:

- Where to logically place the servers relative to the ASA/PIX Security Appliance
- What IP addresses to give the servers on the inside network
- What IP addresses to give the servers on the outside network
- What services are going to be offered on these servers

Logical Placement of the Servers

Logical placement of the servers in your network is a critical decision. It is important to remember that the servers will be hosting data and will be reachable by anyone with Internet connectivity—both legitimate users and hackers alike.

You have four options for placement of your new public web servers:

- Connected on the inside network, with the rest of your users
- Connected on the outside network interface of your ASA/PIX Security Appliance
- At the location of your ISP, which would entail paying them to co-locate and secure the servers
- On a dedicated isolated interface of your ASA/PIX Security Appliance (often called a *demilitarized zone*, DMZ)

You have only two options to seriously consider when deciding where to locate Internet-facing servers. To keep them secure, you should either put them on a separate interface of your ASA/PIX Security Appliance or co-locate them at your Internet service provider (ISP).

If you put the server on the inside interface with the rest of your users, you will have created a substantial security risk and will not have fully deployed defense in depth. Remember that these servers have addresses that can be accessed from the Internet, and any Internet-facing address is a target for outside attacks. If a hacker successfully penetrates the server, the hacker will already be on the inside of your network (which presents an excellent opportunity to attack other hosts also located on the inside of your network).

CAUTION   Even though it's recommended that intrusion prevention software be run on your servers, you still don't want to put your public servers on the inside of your network. It is extremely important to remember that defense in depth, or layered security, is the key to deploying a secure network. Why take the chance of putting a device that can be compromised in a location where it can immediately compromise other devices? Such a setup just makes it easier for hackers to get to all of your network assets and data.

Putting the server on the outside of your ASA/PIX Security Appliance is also asking for trouble, because there would be no perimeter protection between the server and the Internet. This scenario would successfully isolate a hacker from the rest of the network if he did happen to compromise the server. However, the server would still be compromised, and the hacker would have access to all data on the server.

If your web server is just an advertising tool and doesn't contain critical data to your business, this might not be such a big deal. However, even in this scenario, the risk does exist that the hacker can cripple the server and make it unavailable to other Internet users.

For an e-mail server, on the other hand, this could be potentially disastrous. Because most companies use e-mail for confidential data, all this information would be available to a hacker to use as desired.

Letting your ISP host your servers is a viable option. However, there are both pros and cons to this scenario. The downsides are as follows:

- The cost may be high.
- The servers will not be physically at your location, which limits your troubleshooting capabilities.
- You will manage the servers remotely, which can sometimes be slow depending on available network bandwidth.
- You will not have control over the security of the server's perimeter.
- Managing servers sometimes requires the uploading and downloading of large amounts of data. This can be slow depending on the bandwidth you have to manage the remote servers.

Your ISP might be able to minimize these factors for you. They could provide very high-speed connections for you to manage your data, they could guarantee that someone will be available to do physical troubleshooting, and so on. If you don't have resources to manage your own machines, using an ISP to host and maintain your servers might be the best option.

The last option discussed is the placement of the servers on a separate interface of your ASA/PIX Security Appliance, allowing you to manage your own machines. This allows you to do the following:

- Eliminate the cost charged by ISPs.
- Have physical control over your servers.
- Mange the servers locally.
- Control the security posture of your network and server environment.
- Easily move large files to or from your servers during upgrades and maintenance.
- Control access to your servers using the ASA/PIX Security Appliance.

- Physically separate your servers and your users by having users on one security appliance interface and servers on another interface. This essentially isolates your servers, ensuring that if a hacker does compromise it, he will still need to get through the security appliance to get to your remaining network assets.

If you have decided that having an ISP is the best way for you to deploy Internet servers, there is no need to read the rest of this chapter. However, because you still need to deploy defenses to ensure the security of your network, you should skip to Chapters 7 through 11 and continue using ASDM, ASA/PIX Security Appliance, and host intrusion prevention to complete the secure lockdown of your network.

Defining Inside and Outside Server Addresses

Now that you have decided that the most secure way to proceed is to place the servers on an isolated interface on the ASA/PIX Security Appliance, you need to decide on an addressing scheme. This should not be too difficult; you can follow the precedence set in Chapter 5 and use private addresses.

NOTE   An isolated security appliance interface is often called a DMZ interface. This will be the terminology used throughout this book.

You need to define the following addresses before you configure the ASA/PIX Security Appliance:

- A private inside "network" address of the ASA/PIX Security Appliance DMZ interface where you will place the web and mail servers
- A private inside IP address for the ASA/PIX Security Appliance DMZ interface where you are going to place the servers
- A private inside IP address for each of the new servers
- A public address that Internet users can enter when they access the new servers

Defining a Private "Network" Address on the DMZ

First, you need to define a network address for the DMZ interface. You elected to use the private address of 192.168.1.0, with a subnet mask of 255.255.255.0, for the inside addresses. When you define network addresses, it is important to ensure that different interfaces have completely different addresses than other interfaces; for example, select another private address that isn't the same as any of the inside addresses.

For example purposes, use 192.168.2.0 with a subnet mask of 255.255.255.0.

Defining a Private Address for the Servers

You need to define an address for both the web server and the mail server. The only restrictions are that the address needs to be part of the network address range that you used for the DMZ and that you cannot reuse an existing address. You used 192.168.2.1 for the ASA/PIX interface; therefore, you can use any address in the range between 192.168.2.3 through 192.168.2.254. Keep it simple and use 192.168.2.3 for the web server and 192.168.2.4 for the mail server. The subnet masks need to be the same as the DMZ interface, so use 255.255.255.0. The gateway for these machines will be the DMZ interface of the ASA/PIX Security Appliance, which again is 192.168.2.1. You complete the address configurations later in this chapter.

Defining a Public Address for the Servers

You do not need to make any decisions about defining public Internet addresses. Public addresses are allocated by your ISP. You must contact them and let them know that you will need two public Internet addresses—one for your web server and one for your mail server. They allocate addresses that are in the same subnet as your outside ASA/PIX Security Appliance address. In this example, the outside address is 199.199.199.199. (Your outside address will be different, because every publicly addressable device on the Internet needs to have a unique address.)

For the configuration outlined in this book, use 199.199.199.203 for the web server address and 199.199.199.204 for the mail server address.

Defining Services

The next items to decide upon are the services you plan to make available on these two servers. For this example, keep it relatively simple. Use HTTP for the web server and SMTP for the mail server. These are the most common services used for these two types of servers.

HTTP, which stands for Hypertext Transfer Protocol, is the Internet standard that allows users to browse a web server and access web pages.

SMTP, which stands for Simple Mail Transport Protocol, is the Internet standard for exchanging mail messages.

New Topology

Your design is now complete. Table 6-2 provides a summary of the addresses you will be entering in ASDM to configure our new network topology.

Table 6-2   *Server IP Addressing*

Network Device	Address	Subnet Mask
PIX DMZ network address	192.168.2.0	255.255.255.0
PIX DMZ interface address	192.168.2.1	255.255.255.0
Private web server address	192.168.2.3	255.255.255.0
Private mail server address	192.168.2..4	255.255.255.0
Web server gateway	192.168.2.1	255.255.255.0
Mail server gateway	192.168.2.1	255.255.255.0
Public web server address	199.199.199.203	255.255.255.0
Public mail server address	199.199.199.204	255.255.255.0

Figure 6-2 shows the topology after adding the web and mail servers.

Figure 6-2   *New Network Topology*

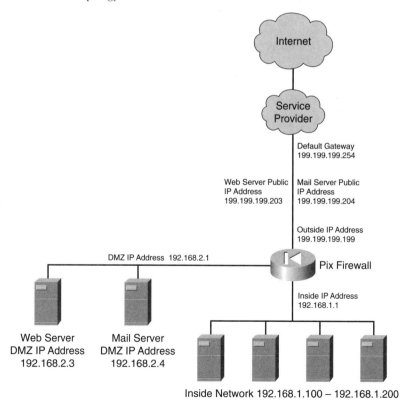

Inside Network 192.168.1.100 – 192.168.1.200

Use the ASDM Startup Wizard to Deploy Web and Mail Services

Congratulations! Now that you have successfully defined all of the network entities and designed a new network topology, you are ready to deploy mail and web services using the ASDM Startup Wizard. To fully deploy your new servers, you must do the following:

- Configure and connect your web and mail servers to the DMZ of the ASA/PIX Security Appliance.

- Use ASDM to configure the security appliance to allow Internet users access to your new servers.

Connect the New Servers to the ASA/PIX Security Appliance

Before you can run ASDM and configure the ASA/PIX Security Appliance, you must first connect the new servers to the security appliance (a straightforward task).

You need to do the following:

- Configure your mail and web servers with the new IP addresses, subnets, and gateways.

- Obtain a Layer 2 network switch and connect it to both the DMZ interface of the ASA/PIX Security Appliance and the network interface cards on your servers.

- Verify Layer 2 connectivity to the ASA/PIX Security Appliance using the **ping** command.

Here are the steps:

Step 1 **IP address setup on the servers** — Use the Network Control Panel on the mail and web servers to configure the inside IP addresses, the subnets, and the gateway.

The web server address will be 192.168.2.3, the gateway address will be 192.168.2.1, and the subnet mask will be 255.255.255.0.

The mail server address will be 192.168.2.4, the gateway address will be 192.168.2.1, and the subnet mask will be 255.255.255.0.

Step 2 **Connect the servers to the ASA/PIX Security Appliance** — Now that the servers have been configured with the correct IP addresses, you need to physically connect them to the DMZ interface of the ASA/PIX Security Appliance. Use the port labeled Ethernet 2 on the security appliance.

Obtain a network switch. Plug a straight-through Ethernet cable from the switch to Ethernet 2 on the security appliance. Plug a straight-through cable from the switch to the Ethernet interface of each of the servers. The

LEDs on the switch should show a link indication a few seconds after they are connected.

Step 3   **Verify that you have connectivity** — You cannot connect to the ASA/PIX Security Appliance yet because it isn't configured. However, you should be able to ping between the two servers, 192.168.2.3 and 192.168.2.4. The inability to successfully ping points to a Layer 2 problem. If this happens, check your IP address configuration, check your cables, and, ultimately, contact your switch vendor if you are still having problems.

Configure Your ASA/PIX Security Using ASDM

Now that the new servers have been successfully configured and physically connected to the ASA/PIX Security Appliance, you are ready to run ASDM. Using ASDM, you configure the ASA/PIX Security Appliance to secure your servers and allow Internet users access to your servers.

NOTE   Although it is beyond of the scope of this book, it has been assumed that your ISP is managing DNS for you. Before you can allow users to access your servers using a name such as http://www.mywebserver.com, you need to make sure that your ISP has entered the DNS names for both your web and mail servers:

Step 1   Use the same PC that was configured and connected in Chapter 5 and launch ASDM using your browser by entering **https://192.168.1.1**. An ASA user will use a slightly different URL, https://192.168.1.1./admin.

Step 2   Enter the appropriate responses to certificate pop-ups and usernames and passwords. Upon completion, the ASDM home page displays. (See Figure 6-3.)

Step 3   Choose the pull-down menu wizard and choose **Startup Wizard**.

Step 4   When the Startup Wizard launches, the first screen asks whether you want to continue with the existing configuration. Because you are adding to your configuration and not changing anything you have already configured, click this option and then click **Next**.

Step 5   Continue clicking **Next** until you see the Other Interface Configuration screen. (See Figure 6-4.)

Step 6   Highlight **Ethernet 2** and click the **Edit** button.

Figure 6-3 *ASDM Home*

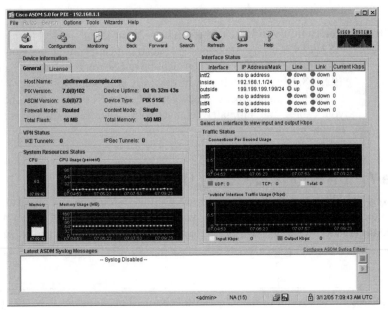

Figure 6-4 *ASDM Interface Configuration*

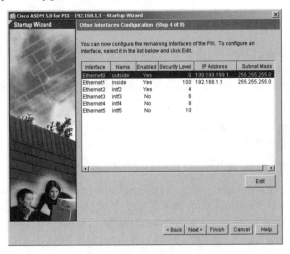

Step 7 In the display panel, enter the configuration information for the DMZ interface as indicated in Figure 6-5. (Don't forget to check **Enable**). Then click **OK**. You will get a warning about a security level change, to which you should click **OK**.

Figure 6-5   *DMZ Configuration Panel*

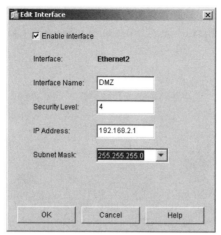

Traffic between ASA/PIX Security Appliance interfaces is determined by security level. By default, traffic can flow unimpeded from an interface with a higher security level to an interface with a lower security level. Traffic in the reverse direction is blocked unless an access rule is in place to allow traffic. The outside interface has a security level of zero, and all other security appliance interfaces are greater than zero. This means that traffic originating inside the ASA/PIX Security Appliance can flow in and out, but if traffic is originated outside the security appliance, you need to write an access rule to allow traffic flow.

Step 8   Click **Next** until the wizard is done, and then click **Finish**.

You have now finished configuring the security appliance interface. It is now time to create an address translation and access lists, which together will allow Internet users to access your servers:

Step 1   Navigate to **Configuration > Features > NAT Translation Rules** in ASDM. The NAT Configuration Panel will display. Click **Add**.

Step 2   Choose **DMZ** as the interface.

Step 3   Enter the IP address **192.168.2.3** for the web server.

Step 4   Enter the mask as **255.255.255.255**.

Caution   This entry is not really a subnet mask. The ASA/PIX Security Appliance is expecting a selection of 255.255.255.255 to let it know you are adding a host, rather than a network, to the NAT table.

Step 5 Click the **Static** radio button and enter **199.199.199.203** in the IP Address field.

Step 6 Click the **Static** button and enter the public IP address **199.199.199.203**. (See Figure 6-6.)

Figure 6-6 *Add Translation for HTTP Server*

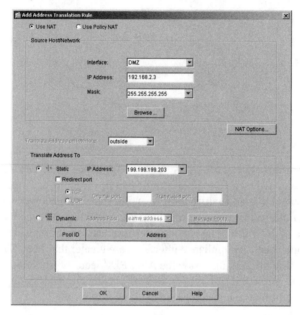

Step 7 Click **OK**.

Step 8 Click **Apply** when you are back to the main panel to save the changes.

Now, you need to add a translation for the mail server:

Step 1 Select configuration "NAT feature" in ASDM to display the NAT configuration panel. Click **Add**.

Step 2 Choose **DMZ** as the interface.

Step 3 Enter the IP address **192.168.2.4** for the mail server.

Step 4 Enter the mask as **255.255.255.255**.

Caution This entry is not really a subnet mask. The ASA/PIX Security Appliance is expecting a selection of 255.255.255.255 to let it know you are adding a host, rather than a network, to the NAT table.

Step 5   Click the **Static** radio button and enter **199.199.199.204** in the IP Address field.

Step 6   Click **OK**.

Step 7   Click **Apply** when you are back to the Mail NAT panel to save changes.

Figure 6-7   *Add Translation for Mail Server*

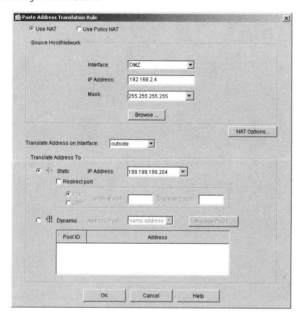

You need to complete one last sequence of steps before Internet users will have access to your new servers. You need to create an access policy that allows Internet users access to the web and mail services on the IP addresses you just defined.

First, set up an access list for the web server:

Step 1   Navigate to the ASDM panel **Configuration > Features > Security Policy > Access Rules**. The default panel will be Access Rules. Click **Add** and fill in the panel as shown in Figure 6-8.

Step 2   Click the **Interface** pull-down in the Source Host/Network section and choose **Outside**. As indicated by an IP address of 0.0.0.0 and a mask of 0.0.0.0, the default is to allow access for all Internet users.

Step 3   Click the **Interface** pull-down in the Destination Host/Network section and choose **DMZ**. Enter the IP address **192.168.2.3**. You can do so either manually or by using the pop-up button to the right of the text box. Make sure that the mask is set to 255.255.255.255.

Figure 6-8 *Access Policy Panel—HTTP*

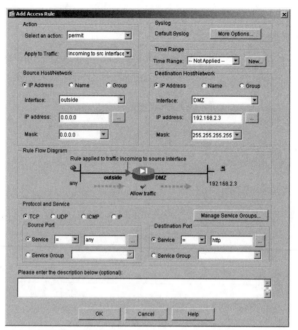

Caution   This entry is not really a subnet mask. The ASA/PIX Security
Appliance is expecting a selection of 255.255.255.255 to let it
know you are adding a host, rather than a network, to the
access rule.

Step 4   Choose the **TCP** option in the Protocol and Service section.

Step 5   Click the pop-up button next to the text box in the Destination Port
Service section. Choose **HTTP**.

Step 6   Click OK.

Step 7   When you are redirected back to the Main Access Rules panel, click
Apply to download the new configuration to the ASA/PIX Security
Appliance.

Now, you need to do the same steps for the mail server.

NOTE	Most mail servers will work with this configuration, but some servers will need additional ports opened on the security appliance. If mail doesn't work after the completion of these steps, check with your mail vendor to identify the additional ports that you need to open. Then, follow this guide to open the ports they are expecting.

Step 1   Click the **Configuration Navigation** button, and then choose the **Security Policy** feature. The default panel is Access Rules. Click **Add**. Fill in the panel as shown in Figure 6-9.

Figure 6-9   *Access Policy Panel—SMTP*

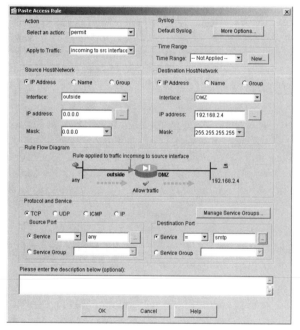

Step 2   Click the **Interface** pull-down in the Source Host/Network section and choose **Outside**.

Step 3   Click the **Interface** pull-down in the Destination Host/Network section and choose **DMZ**. Enter the IP address **192.168.2.4**. You can do so either manually or by using the pop-up button to the right of the text box. Make sure that the mask is set to 255.255.255.255.

Caution	This entry is not really a subnet mask. The ASA/PIX Security Appliance is expecting a selection of 255.255.255.255 to let it know you are adding a host, rather than a network, to the access rule.

Step 4   Choose the **TCP** option in the Protocol and Service section.

Step 5   Click the pop-up button next to the text box in the Destination Port Service section. Choose **SMTP**.

Step 6   Click **OK**.

Step 7   When you are redirected back to the Main Access Rules panel, click **Apply** to download the new configuration to the ASA/PIX Security Appliance.

Congratulations! Successful completion of these steps has given you a network where your inside users can browse the Internet. You have also deployed a web server and mail server that Internet users can access.

Many people stop their Internet deployment networks at this point. They have connectivity and are relatively secure. Why shouldn't they stop? As discussed several times previously, the only way to achieve full security is with several layers of defense. You still need to lock down the perimeter of you system, perhaps deploy VPN, and definitely deploy host intrusion prevention.

With your current network security posture, you are still susceptible to the most costly attacks—day-zero attacks. You may feel secure, but the first Blaster, Slammer, Sasser, Code Red, Nimda, or major mail virus that hits will potentially affect your servers and the hosts on the inside of your network. This can potentially cost you several thousands of dollars to clean up. Following through with defense in depth is an incidental expense in comparison.

Summary

In this chapter, you leveraged the work you did in Chapter 5 and added a web and mail server to your secure network topology.

You started by reviewing the work done in Chapter 5, gaining a good understanding of the existing IP addressing and interface configuration on the ASA/PIX Security Appliance.

Then, you went through a process of deciding how and where to deploy the web and mail servers. It was an easy decision based on security best practices to deploy the servers on an isolated (or DMZ) interface on the ASA/PIX Security Appliance. This architecture ensured that if by chance the servers were compromised, the attackers would not be able to also compromise hosts on the inside of your network unless they were able to get through the security appliance. But because of the restrictive nature of the ASA/PIX Security Appliance, where traffic is not allowed to be sourced from the DMZ to the inside network, this would be very unlikely.

After deciding on the topology, you defined IP addresses for the ASA/PIX Security Appliance DMZ interface, the servers in the DMZ, and the public addresses that Internet users would use.

You then physically connected the servers to the DMZ interface of the security appliance and verified connectivity between the servers.

After making the topologies and address choices, you launched ASDM and entered commands to set up the DMZ and allow access for the new web servers. The following steps enabled you to complete this deployment:

- You used the Startup Wizard to define address information and to enable the DMZ interface on the ASA/PIX Security Appliance.

- You used the Configuration NAT panel and defined the public addresses for the web and mail servers and translated them to their private DMZ addresses.

- You used the Configuration Access Rules panel to allow HTTP and SMTP traffic from the outside interface of the ASA/PIX Security Appliance to the DMZ where the servers are located.

In this chapter, you learn how to deploy authentication, the first layer of defense in depth, as described in Chapter 2, "Principles of Network Defense."

This chapter addresses the following topics:

- **Defining Authentication**—This section provides a brief description of authentication.
- **Purpose of Authentication**—This section explains why you need authentication in your network.
- **Deploying Authentication**—This section explains how you can use ASDM to deploy authentication at different levels in your network.

CHAPTER 7

Deploying Authentication

Now that you have completed the initial configuration of the ASA/PIX, you must start securing the security appliance so that an attacker cannot compromise the device. You can do this with the first layer of defense in depth, described in Chapter 2, called *authentication*. This chapter explains authentication and provides a step-by-step procedure on how to secure your security appliance from unauthorized access from both inside and outside of your network.

As well as covering how to authenticate users to access the ASA/PIX Security Appliance, this chapter explains how to use the security appliance to authenticate inside users and Internet users requesting certain access, such as web services.

Defining Authentication

Authentication is a means to enforce a policy of who can access your network devices and who can access certain network services that traverse your security appliance, such as web, Telnet, and FTP. You can enforce authentication on both inbound and outbound users. When a user is authenticated, it means that the user has passed proper credentials, such as a username and password. Therefore, the user should be granted access to the service or device requested.

In today's Internet environment, you see authentication frequently. Two common examples of authentication are when users access their e-mail account and when users attempt to access a website for financial transactions. In both cases, users are prompted for both a username and a password. Whenever critical data is to be accessed, it's considered a best practice to authenticate users before granting them access. Similarly, whenever a critical device is to be accessed, it's considered a best practice to authenticate users before granting them access. The ASA/PIX Security Appliance is one such crucial device that, if compromised by an attacker, can be used to weaken the security of your entire network.

There is also another part of authentication possible with the ASA/PIX Security Appliance called *authorization*, which is a feature that defines what users can do after they have successfully authenticated on to a system. For example, if you have someone in your organization to whom you want to give access to the security appliance, but you want him to be able to only monitor syslog usage, you can configure the ASA/PIX Security Appliance to achieve this requirement.

The ASA/PIX Security Appliance also supports AAA *accounting*, which logs user activity on the security appliance, including device logon information, authentication stop and start events, elapsed time on the device, and commands that were entered after someone authenticated on to the device. AAA accounting is supported with both the TACAS+ and RADIUS protocol.

In this book, you learn to store all usernames and passwords locally on the ASA/PIX Security Appliance. You can, however, use the Cisco Access Control Server (Cisco ACS) instead of the local ASA/PIX data. The Cisco ACS allows you the flexibility to authenticate on to the following:

- A one-time password authentication server
- A Microsoft domain controller
- An LDAP server
- A TACACS+ database
- A RADIUS database

The Purpose of Authentication

You need authentication so that you can lock down devices, hosts, and services in your network and make them accessible only via authentication credentials such as username and password or one-time passwords.

Your network devices, such as security appliances and routers, are prime targets for hackers. If hackers can gain access to a network device, they can change configurations to a point where they can hijack data, sniff data on your network, open back doors for future access, and change tables to weaken the security posture of your system. Therefore, you should consider authentication a primary feature to deploy in your network.

Implementing Authentication

In this book, you use ASDM to implement authentication on the ASA/PIX Security Appliance. The following list of authentication tasks are performed:

- Secure Telnet security appliance access
- Secure SSH security appliance access
- Secure ASDM/HTTPS security appliance access
- Secure inbound and outbound web users (optional)
- Authorize security appliance users

Securing Access to the Security Appliance

Now that you have a basic understanding of both authentication and its importance, you can start ASDM and follow these procedures to deploy authentication.

This step-by-step procedure leverages off of the configuration work that you have already done on your ASA/PIX Security Appliance in Chapter 5, "Deploying Secure Internet Connectivity," and Chapter 6, "Deploying Web and Mail Services."

Start ASDM

To connect to the ASA/PIX Security Appliance using ASDM and then to authenticate access to your security appliance, follow these steps:

Step 1 Use the same PC that you configured and connected in Chapter 5 and launch ASDM by entering **https://192.168.1.1./admin**.

Step 2 Enter the appropriate responses to certificate authentications and usernames and passwords. After you do so, the ASDM home page displays. (See Figure 7-1.)

Figure 7-1 *ASDM Home*

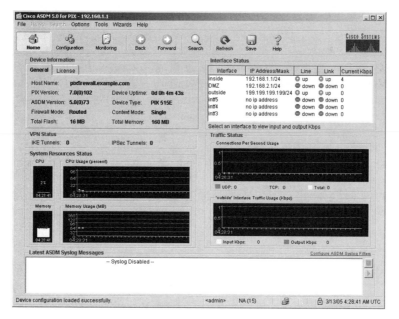

> **Step 3**   Because you are using the LOCAL security appliance database, you must set that parameter before you configure users or services. Access the following Authentication panel, as follows:
>
> **Configuration > Features > Device Administration > Administration > AAA Access > Authentication**
>
> **Step 4**   On the Administration screen, click **Enable**.
>
> **Step 5**   Select **LOCAL** from the Server Group.
>
> **Step 6**   Click **Apply** to save the changes.

Securing Telnet Access

Do *not* use Telnet to administer your security appliance. As stated several times in this book, Telnet is a clear text protocol. Therefore, it sends usernames and passwords on the network in clear text. The same occurs if you use Telnet for Line mode configuration of your security appliance, in that the configuration of the security appliance would be passed on the network in clear text. In such a case, hackers can easily intercept the information and thereby gain unlimited access to your security appliance.

CAUTION   From a security best practices perspective, do not use Telnet to administer your security appliance. You cannot secure the Telnet protocol unless it is used in conjunction with virtual private networks (VPNs), which is beyond the scope of this book. The "SAFE Blueprint" white paper at http://www.cisco.com/go/safe has some recommendations for using VPN as a means to protect clear text management protocols.

Securing SSH Access

Secure Shell (SSH) is a utility that you can safely use to manage your security appliance. It is a Line mode tool; therefore, it is important to be familiar with the native ASA/PIX version 7 command set if you elect to use SSH. If you aren't familiar with the command set, ASDM is the option you would want to use.

To set up SSH, just in case you have this requirement in your network deployment, follow these steps:

> **Step 1**   Before you can authenticate an SSH user, you must generate an RSA key pair on the ASA/PIX. Navigate to **Configuration > Features > Device Administration > Certificate > Key Pair**.
>
> **Step 2**   Click **Add** to generate a key. In the Add Key panel, click **Generate Now**.

Step 3   You now need to create a user to log in to the ASA/PIX. Navigate to **Configure > Features > Device Administration > Administration > User Accounts**.

Step 4   Click **Add** and create a username and password. Remember to use security best practices and create a difficult-to-guess username and password. Include uppercase, lowercase, numeric, and special characters. Make sure that both the username and password are at least eight characters in length. If you are configuring a user for security appliance management access (ASDM), you need to select a privilege level of 15.

Step 5   Navigate to the **Configuration > Device Administration > Administration > Secure Shell** panel.

The default parameters on this page are SSH version 1 and a timeout of 5 minutes. Most implementations would keep this as default. However, if you know that you are using a certain version of SSH, you can set the version value appropriately. You can always change the timeout to a value that suits you. Don't set the timeout value too low, however. If you leave your SSH session for a long period of time, you don't want the session to stay active for long because someone could sit down at your station and have access to your ASA/PIX.

Step 6   Click **Add** to configure the IP address of a PC that can use SSH to connect to your ASA/PIX.

For this example, the added device has the address 192.168.1.2 on the inside interface of the ASA/PIX. (See Figure 7-2.)

Figure 7-2   *SSH Add Panel*

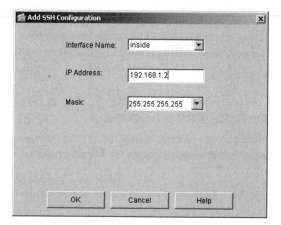

Step 7 Click **OK**. When you return to the main panel, click **Apply** to enable the changes.

You should now be able to access the ASA/PIX Security Appliance, using SSH, from 192.168.1.2 with the username and password you created.

Securing ASDM/HTTPS Access

The preferred method of access for the ASA/PIX Security Appliance running version 7 is ASDM. It is both secure and easy to use. In this section, you configure the security appliance to add ASDM users. You have already configured the security appliance to use ASDM, but the steps are repeated here again briefly for emphasis:

Step 1 You need to create a user to log in to the ASA/PIX. Navigate to **Configure > Features > Device Administration > Administration > User Account**. Click **Add** and create a username and password. Again, use a difficult-to-guess username and password that includes uppercase, lowercase, numeric, and special characters. Make sure that both the username and password are at least eight characters in length. Also, because this user is an ASDM user, you must select privilege level 15.

Step 2 Now, you need to add IP addresses of the PCs you are allowing to access your ASA/PIX using ASDM. Navigate to **Configuration > Device Administration > Administration > ASDM > HTTPS**.

Step 3 Click **Add** and enter the interface, IP address, and mask of the device you are allowing to use ASDM. Click **OK**, and then click **Apply** to save the changes.

Step 4 To verify that the changes worked, go to the device you just configured to use ASDM. Access ASDM through the browser as normal. This time, however, when you are prompted for the username and password, enter the username and password you created in the preceding steps. Respond appropriately to the certificate warnings. If done correctly, you should have access to the ASA/PIX through ASDM from this device.

Monitoring Security Appliance Access

Monitoring system access is a critical task for any network administrator. The ASA/PIX Security Appliance offers several options for keeping track of who is logged on to your system.

If you navigate to **Monitoring > Features > Administration**, you will see a list of all the ASA/PIX access methods, including the following:

- ASDM/HTTPS
- Telnet

- Secure Shell
- Authenticated users
- AAA servers

By just clicking any of these categories, you can immediately see who is connected to your system and the method by which they established their connection.

Syslog can also be an excellent tool to see who has connected to your system. However, you would need to write a script or utility to search the syslog file for keywords that indicate that someone has connected or disconnected from your system.

AAA Authentication Access

By using the AAA features of the ASA/PIX Security Appliance, you can limit the hours that users can log on to your ASA/PIX. AAA also has utilities that enable an administrator to see what time a user logged on or off and, in some cases, what the user did while on the system. Adding an AAA server is an additional expense, but considering the additional features and reporting, many customers have little problem justifying the purchase. You can find out more about AAA on the Cisco website at http://www.cisco.com/go/acs.

Authentication for Inbound and Outbound Services

Another compelling feature of the ASA/PIX Security Appliance is the ability to authenticate users before you allow them to access certain inbound and outbound services. For example, if you have a website on your demilitarized zone (DMZ) that is to be accessed only by a few choice users, the ASA/PIX Security Appliance can prompt anyone trying to access that site for a username and password before allowing access.

The following are the services that can be authenticated:

- **HTTP**—Web traffic
- **HTTPS**—Encrypted web traffic
- **Telnet**—Text-based terminal traffic
- **FTP**—File Transfer Protocol

To deploy this authentication, you must complete the following steps. In this example, HTTPS is used and users are authenticated before they can access your web server at 199.199.199.202:

Step 1   Navigate to **Configure > Features > Device Administration > Administration > User Accounts** to create a username and password.

Step 2 Click **Add** and create a username and password. Remember to use security best practices and create a difficult-to-guess username and password. Include uppercase, lowercase, numeric, and special characters. Make sure that both the username and password are at least eight characters in length.

Step 3 To enable authentication, navigate to **Configure > Features > Security Policy** and click the **AAA Rules** button. Click **Add** to add a rule. The panel shown in Figure 7-3 displays.

Figure 7-3 *AAA Access Panel*

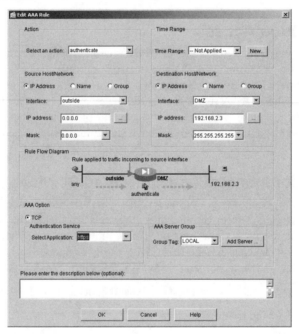

Step 4 Choose **Outside** as the source network.

Step 5 Choose **DMZ** as the destination network.

Step 6 Click the pop-up next to the Address text box and choose **192.168.2.3**, which is your web server.

Step 7 Click the Application pull-down and choose **HTTPS**.

Step 8 Choose **LOCAL** from the Group pull-down.

Step 9 Click **OK**, and then click **Apply** to save the changes.

Step 10 To test this feature, go to a machine on the outside of your network. Enter the address **https://199.199.199.203** in your browser. You should be prompted with a standard username and password prompt. Enter the user credentials from your local database, and you should be authenticated.

You can authenticate outbound users in the same manner, except, when you create the AAA rule, choose **Inside** as the source and **Outside** as the destination.

Outbound URL Filtering for Public Services

As discussed in Chapter 4, "Exploring the Adaptive Security Device Manager," in the ASDM overview, outbound URL authentication can be a powerful security and network bandwidth-management tool. You can block access to certain websites or classes of websites and thereby limit access to certain sites such as porn, free download, and file-sharing sites, which in turn will help reduce the following threats to your hosts:

- The spread of spyware
- Pop-up advertisements
- Trojan downloads
- Web viruses
- Downloading of dangerous software

The ASA/PIX version 7 operating system supports URL filtering from several different vendors. This feature enables you to stop access to several different classes of websites that might be responsible for the spread of spyware, Trojans, web viruses, and data-mining cookies. Examples of classes of websites that might be blocked by this software include the following:

- Hacker sites
- Music download sites
- Pornography sites
- Sports sites

NOTE	The classes of sites listed here are not considered bad sites, per se. But they represent some of the classes of sites that could be blocked using URL filtering. Unfortunately, many web servers that fit in these classes have chosen to do things such as download spyware, data miners, and Trojans. The result of this activity has led to client computers experiencing excessive pop-up ads, significantly slower CPUs, and usage of unnecessary network bandwidth.

URL blocking servers enable you to block classes of URLs that you deem dangerous or inappropriate. If you elect to block a class called "hacker sites," the software automatically blocks several hundred URLs that are known hacker sites. You can also use URL blocking to improve bandwidth usages in some businesses (especially if users previously had been downloading large files such as MP3s, WAVs, MPEGs, or streaming audio). You can deploy URL blocking to reduce these traffic classes.

CAUTION   A few states in the United States consider URL blocking illegal. Check with a legal representative before deploying this feature.

Step 1   You can deploy URL blocking by navigating to the **Configuration > Features > Properties > URL Filtering** panel. You can select the vendor on that panel and then click **Add**. On the Add subpanel, you can choose the IP address of the server running the URL-filtering software and the protocol supported by that server. (See Figure 7-4.)

Figure 7-4   *URL Filtering Panel*

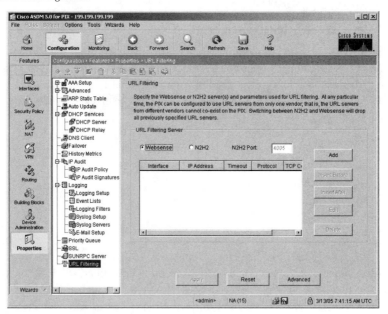

Step 2   Click **OK** and **Apply** to save your changes to the ASA/PIX Security
Appliance.

Step 3   After defining the URL server, you need to define a filter to tell the
security appliance which traffic to block and what to do if the URL server
goes down. Navigate to **Policy > Filter Rules**.

Step 4   Set the Select Action to **HTTP**.

Step 5   Set the Host/Source Network to **Inside**.

Step 6   Set the Host/Destination Network to **Outside**.

Step 7   If you want to allow traffic flow if the URL server is down, check
the box Allow Outbound Traffic If the URL Server Is Not Available.
(See Figure 7-5.)

Figure 7-5   *Add Filter Rule*

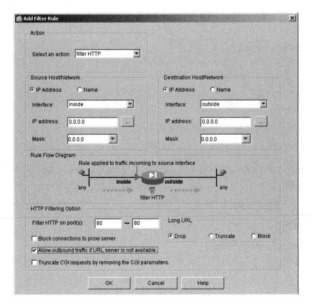

VPN Authentication

VPN authentication is discussed in Chapter 11, "Deploying VPNs."

Summary

Authentication represents one of the basic foundations of defense in depth and should be deployed in every network infrastructure. You should follow a few basic best practices to keep your network secure, including the following:

- Don't allow privileged access to the outside of your security appliance.
- Use hard-to-guess usernames and passwords.
- Do not use clear text protocols such as HTTP and Telnet for device management.
- Use ASDM or SSH for ASA/PIX Security Appliance management. Both use full encryption for data, as well as authentication credentials.
- Check your logs frequently to make sure that there is no unauthorized access occurring.
- Consider AAA to add value in logging and authentication flexibility.

In addition to device management authentication, you can deploy authentication for the following web services:

- HTTP
- HTTPS
- FTP
- Telnet

Authenticating services enables you to grant only certain users access to the services listed here. You can also use outbound authentication for the same services.

Besides merely blocking access to certain websites or classes of websites, URL blocking can prove effective to stop malware from installing itself on the PCs behind your security appliance. It can mitigate the following web- and browser-based problems:

- Spyware
- Pop-up advertisements
- Trojan downloads
- Web viruses
- Downloading of dangerous software

You have now deployed authentication, the first layer of defense in-depth. Chapter 8, "Deploying Perimeter Protection," covers locking down the perimeter of your network, adding protection assistance against denial-of-service attacks, and filtering your traffic.

The remaining steps to fully deploy defense in depth in your network are covered in the following chapters:

- Chapter 8, "Deploying Perimeter Protection"
- Chapter 9, "Deploying Network Intrusion Prevention"
- Chapter 10, "Deploying Host Intrusion Prevention"
- Chapter 11, "Deploying VPNs"

This chapter explains how to deploy perimeter protection for your network using the ASA/PIX Security Appliance. This chapter addresses the following topics:

- **The Importance of Perimeter Protection**—This section is a brief description of why perimeter protection is important and how it can add additional security to your network.

- **Deploying Perimeter Protection**—This section explains how you can use ASDM to deploy perimeter protection in your network.

CHAPTER 8

Deploying Perimeter Protection

By this point in the book, you have completed the steps to connect your network to the Internet, deploy public services, and lock down authentication on your network devices and services. The next step, which is addressed in this chapter, is to lock down the perimeter of your network.

The following are the four steps you need to accomplish to lock down your network perimeter using the ASA/PIX Security Appliance:

- Ensure that traffic traversing your security appliance matches protocol specifications.
- Customize protocol application inspection.
- Ensure that appropriate filters are in place, allowing only desired traffic through your security appliance.
- Deploy ASA/PIX Security Appliance denial-of-service protection.

Because the ASA/PIX is shipped pre-optimized for perimeter protection, you might be surprised at how little you need to do to deploy additional perimeter security.

Perimeter Protocol Enforcement

The ASA/PIX Security Appliance comes with a standard set of protocol application inspections. *Inspections* are functions within the ASA/PIX to ensure that data isn't passing through the ASA/PIX, inside of a packet, that could cause damage to a server or network to which the packet is destined.

NOTE Some application inspections have non-security-related features. For example, NetBIOS inspections look into the data portion of the packet at source IP addresses and make sure that those addresses are properly represented in the packet header. All security appliances need this functionality to ensure that network address translation (NAT) functions correctly.

The ASA/PIX performs application inspection for the protocols listed in Table 8-1. This is a list of the most commonly used protocols; for a more in-depth list, refer to the Cisco ASA/PIX web page at http://www.cisco.com/go/pix/.

Table 8-1   *Inspected Protocols*

Protocol	Protocol Definition
DNS	Domain Name Services—used to translate names to IP addresses
FTP	File Transfer Utility—Internet standard for moving files
HTTP	Hypertext Transfer Protocol—the Internet standard for browsing Internet websites
H323 H225	A standard to support visual telephony services
H323 RAS	A standard to support telephony gatekeeper services
ILS	Provides name/address resolution for IP video conferencing
RSH	Remote Shell Protocol—allows users to execute commands on a remote system without logging in to the remote system
RTSP	Real Time Streaming Protocol—the Internet standard for delivering real-time video and audio streaming
ESMTP	Extended Simple Mail Transfer Protocol—SMTP with enhanced extensions
SQLNET	The Internet standard for allowing the delivery of queries to SQL-compliant databases over the network
SKINNY	Skinny Client Control Protocol (SCCP)—enables IP telephony communication between voice clients
XDMCP	X Display Manager Control Protocol—used to communicate between devices running X Windows sessions
SIP	Session Initiation Protocol—used to establish sessions for IP telephony
NETBIOS	Microsoft Windows Network Protocol—used to connect devices running Windows operating systems
CTIQBE	Computer Telephony Interface Quick Buffer Encoding—IP telephony encoding standard
TFTP	Trivial File Transfer Protocol—used to update many device images and configurations
ICMP	Internet Control Message Protocol—a standard used to communicate status and error messages between network devices using the TCP/IP protocol
SNMP	Simple Network Management Protocol—a standard used to manage network devices

You can browse these protocol application inspections at the following ASDM location:

Step 1   Navigate to **Configuration > Features > Security Policy** and click the **Service Policy Rules** option button.

Step 2   Choose the line that says inspection default and click **Edit**. The panel shown in Figure 8-1 will display.

Figure 8-1   *Add Service Policy*

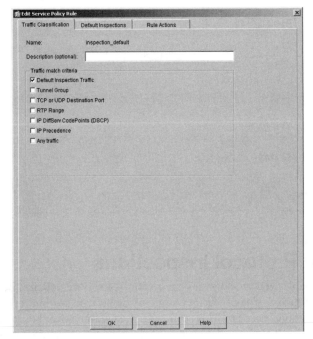

Step 3   From here, you can open the panel Traffic Classification, which lists the protocol port numbers.

Step 4   To see the default protocols that are inspected, click the tab **Rule Actions**. (See Figure 8-2.)

The details of the default actions of an application inspection are Cisco proprietary. Generally speaking, however, default inspections look into a packet and ensure that a protocol command is valid. As well, they confirm that certain lengths of protocols packets haven't been exceeded. Finally, they ensure that a source address embedded in Layer 7 payload is written to the header of the packet to fix potential problems with NAT. For an in-depth discussion on ASA/PIX application inspection, go to the technical documentation link at http://www.cisco.com/go/pix.

Figure 8-2 *Default Inspections*

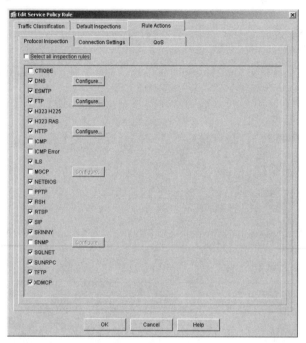

Customizing Protocol Inspections

ASDM enables you to add your own customized service policies. Because the ASA/PIX ships with such a strong security posture by default, no customizations are "required" to ensure additional security. This section does, however, cover how to create a customized service policy should you decide that it's important for your deployment.

The example used is the creation of a service policy that checks the length of a URL and drops the packet if the length is too long. This policy could be effective for preventing hackers from both attempting to guess a URL that could cause buffer overflows or passing URLs that contain SQL commands in an attempt to gain access to a back-end SQL database.

This policy is only one example of what you can do with custom service policies. You will notice when you browse these panels that ASDM gives you a wide range of options to drop or log suspect traffic traversing your security appliance.

You can customize protocol checking using the Service Policy panel as follows:

Step 1   Navigate to the **Configuration > Features > Security Policy** panel.

Step 2   Click the **Service Policy Rules** option button.

Step 3   Click **Add** to launch a wizard to step you through the process. (See Figure 8-3.)

Figure 8-3   *Service Policy Wizard*

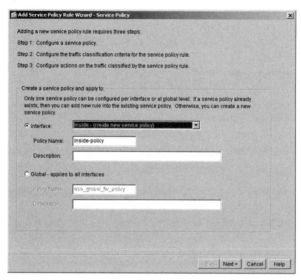

Step 4   On the first panel, click the **Interface** option button. Then, choose the **Inside** interface from the pull-down list to create a policy for traffic going to the inside interface. Click **Next** to continue.

Step 5   On the next panel (Figure 8-4), check the box next to **TCP or UDP Destination Port**.

Figure 8-4   *Traffic Classification*

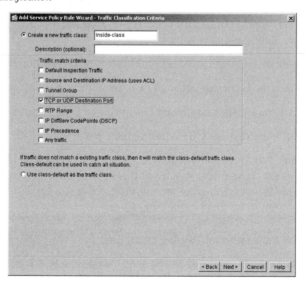

Step 6 On the next panel (Figure 8-5), enter **80** in the Port Number box and ensure that **TCP** is enabled. The TCP option button applies this policy to your web traffic only.

Figure 8-5 *Destination Port*

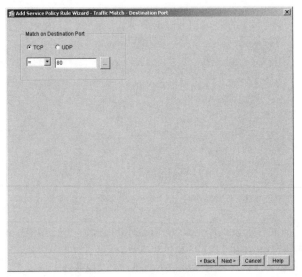

Step 7 On the next panel, Protocol Inspection, click **HTTP** and then click the **Configure** button to the right of the HTTP selection. Doing so displays a dialog box to select an HTTP map. Click the **New** button to display the Add HTTP Map dialog box. (See Figure 8-6.)

Step 8 Enter the text **URLength** in the HTTP Map Name box. This field cannot contain spaces in the name.

Step 9 In the RFC Compliance section, ensure that **Reset Connection** is chosen.

Step 10 Check the **Generate Syslog** box to the right of the action box.

Step 11 Click the **Entity Length** tab. The panel shown in Figure 8-7 will display.

Step 12 Check the **Inspect URI Length** check box.

Enter **128** for maximum number of bytes. The value of 128 is just an example. If you were deploying this in production, you would find out the longest URL in your web server and use that value.

Step 13 Choose the action **Reset Connection**.

Step 14 Check the **Generate Syslog** check box.

Step 15 Click **OK**. A panel will display with the existing HTTP maps. Choose the map you just created and click **OK**.

Figure 8-6   *Add HTTP Map*

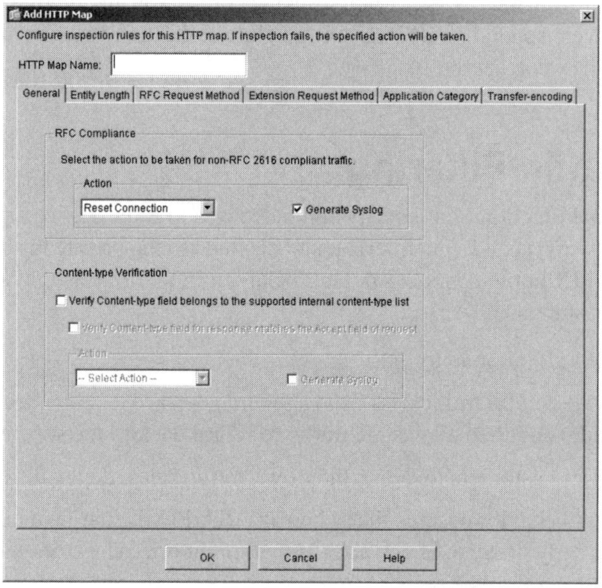

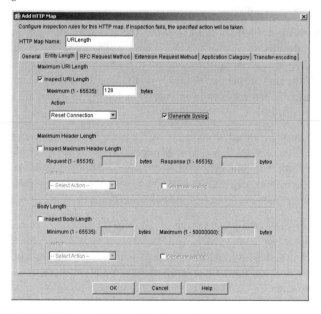

Figure 8-7   *Entity Length*

Step 16 Click **Finish** in the last wizard panel.

Step 17 Click **Apply** to write this configuration to the ASA/PIX Security Appliance.

You have now created a rule that will inspect HTTP traffic. If a packet is found with a URL greater than 128, the ASA/PIX will reset the connection and report the policy violation to a syslog server. Appendix A, "Deploying Effective Security Management," explains how to configure a syslog server.

Perimeter Traffic Filtering

The original function of a security appliance was to filter traffic originating from a less-secure network, such as the Internet, and destined to the private inside network of a device. The ASA/PIX implements this default behavior in the following way, presenting a strong security posture:

- Blocks all inbound traffic
- Lets all stateful traffic pass from a secure interface to a less-secure interface (inside to outside) and then allows the traffic to return back to the secure interface
- Enables customers to create their own traffic rules, depending on their requirements

This default behavior ensures that when an ASA/PIX is first installed, the private secure network is fully protected from attacks that might originate from the Internet (outside network).

One of the only possible attacks that could be launched from the Internet against an inside host is a TCP hijack attack.

However, this is unlikely because it would mean that an attacker randomly found a TCP stream and decided to pose as the target device. The most damage that a hacker could probably do in this scenario is to send a Trojan back to a host as a web response (which is essentially the same thing that websites do to inject spyware and adware). The defense for this isn't actually in the security appliance; the defense is in host intrusion prevention (CSA) and antivirus software.

Because of the work already completed in Chapter 5, "Deploying Secure Internet Connectivity," Chapter 6, "Deploying Web and Mail Services," and Chapter 7, "Deploying Authentication," there is very little if anything you need to do as far as setting up additional filters on your security appliance. To gain an understanding of how to set up access rules, in this chapter, you will go into the appropriate panels but not make any additional changes to access rules.

You will now step through an exercise on how to create a new access rule on your ASA/PIX Security Appliance using ASDM. Just to be clear, access rules are known by several different names, depending on the vendors with whom you are working or the books and articles that you read. Don't be confused, because all of these terms are used interchangeably:

- Access control lists
- Filters
- Security appliance filters

- Access rules
- Policy rules
- Policy filters

All these terms mean essentially the same thing. The term most commonly used in the past has been *access lists*, but the terminology used in ASA/PIX version 7 with ASDM is *access rules*.

This step-by-step procedure instructs you on how to open a port to allow Secure Sockets Layer (SSL) traffic from the Internet to the web server on your security appliance's demilitarized zone (DMZ) interface.

CAUTION   As a matter of security best practice, if you are not using HTTPS on your web server, delete this rule when you have completed the exercise or take care that you don't click Apply when you have finished the steps.

Step 1   Click the **Configuration Navigation** button.

Step 2   Choose the security policy feature. The default panel will be Access Rules. Click **Add**. Complete the following steps to fill in the panel as illustrated in Figure 8-8.

Figure 8-8   *Add Access Policy—HTTPS*

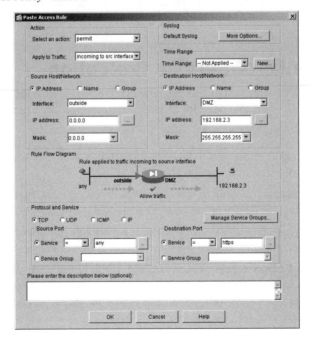

Step 3   Click the **Interface** pull-down in the Host/Source Network section and choose **Outside**.

Step 4   Click the **Interface** pull-down in the host/Source Network section and choose **DMZ**. Enter the IP address **192.168.2.2**. You can do this either manually or by using the pop-up button to the right of the text box. Make sure the mask is set to **255.255.255.255**.

Step 5   Check the **TCP** option in the Protocol and Service section.

Step 6   Click the pop-up button next to the text box in the Destination Port Service section. Choose **HTTPS**.

Step 7   Click **OK**.

When you are redirected back to the main access rules panel, and if you are planning to allow HTTPS, click **Apply** to save and initiate the rule. It is not good practice to add a rule that you don't need. Doing so just gives hackers a small opening where they might be able to exploit your web server. If you are not planning to run HTTPS on your web server, do not click Apply to enable this rule.

The procedures that you have just stepped through are the same for adding or deleting any access rules on your ASA/PIX Security Appliance. Be very careful to make sure that you have chosen the proper interfaces and IP addresses for the source and destination of the access rules. The best-case scenario is if a rule is misconfigured, no traffic will pass through the security appliance. The worst case, however, is that you will have opened a security hole that can be exploited and your inside hosts or services might be compromised.

Perimeter Denial-of-Service Protection

The ASA/PIX Security Appliance has default protection built in for denial-of-service (DoS) attacks. However, it also provides an interface to change the parameters, if required.

DoS attacks come in different flavors:

* An attack that attempts to take up so much bandwidth on your network that the network becomes unusable

* An attack that takes up so much of a system resource or CPU on a network device that it renders the device or the network unusable

* A single-packet attack design so that a network device doesn't know what to do with the packet and the device stops forwarding traffic or crashes

Unfortunately, DoS attacks are easy to launch and not so easy to protect against. The ASA/PIX Security Appliance, however, does have some built-in functionality to reduce the impact of the attacks. As well, you should follow some best practices to mitigate the effect of these attacks.

The ASA/PIX Security Appliance mitigates against various types of DoS attacks by deploying different technologies to protect the perimeter of your network. The specific features that the ASA/PIX uses include the following:

- **DNSGuard**—Protects against DoS attacks aimed at DNS servers. DNSGuard allows only a single response to multiple outgoing DNS queries, thereby preventing DNS storms.

- **FloodGuard**—Prevents DoS attacks caused by multiple AAA authentication attempts.

- **FragGuard**—Prevents a class of DoS attacks based on sending fragmented packets to the ASA/PIX Security Appliance.

- **IPVerify**—Most DoS attacks use invalid or spoofed addresses so that the attack cannot be traced back to the attacker. IPVerify ensures that the source traffic is valid before the security appliance will respond to the request, effectively mitigating spoofing DoS attacks.

- **TCP Intercept**—Protects against the most popular DoS attack, a TCP SYN flood. In this attack, a hacker sends thousands of requests to open a connection through the security appliance. TCP Intercept recognizes these packets as being an attack and cleans up the resources, allowing only valid traffic to go through the security appliance.

Mitigating Network Bandwidth DoS Attacks

If an attacker has taken it upon himself to try to consume all the bandwidth on the outside of your security appliance, you will need to get your Internet security provider (ISP) involved. It would not be that difficult, depending on how much bandwidth you have available between you and your ISP, for an attacker to use several zombie machines. With these machines, attackers can start streaming data destined for your web server or your mail server until those services are no longer usable.

Your ISP will have several options to help out. Most of the time, they are willing to help, because the attacks destined for you also take up bandwidth and slow down their network and the networks of their customers. Following is just a partial list of simple steps the ISP can do to help protect you under these circumstances. Most ISPs have several other options besides these that they can deploy to help stop DoS attacks:

- Most DoS attackers use spoofed source addresses such as private and bogon addresses because attackers don't want the attack to be traced back to them. Therefore, ISPs can filter these invalid source addresses to protect your network.

- ISPs can implement a technology called *rate limiting*. Rate limiting slows down the traffic and thereby returns some bandwidth.

- ISPs now have technology available to them that enables them to differentiate invalid DoS traffic from valid traffic, filter the bad traffic out, and send you only valid traffic destined for your network.

You should always contact your ISP if you believe that you are the victim of a DoS attack so that it can deploy these methods to get you back on line as soon as possible.

On your ASA/PIX Security Appliance, the default configuration called Anti-Spoofing can help during these attack conditions.

Anti-Spoofing will ensure that DoS attacks are not launched from inside your own network.

You should follow this procedure to enable Anti-Spoofing on your inside interface to ensure that DoS attacks are not inadvertently being launched from the inside of your security appliance:

Step 1   Navigate to **Configurations > Features > Properties > Advanced** to see the default setting for Anti-Spoofing. Highlight the **Inside** interface.

Step 2   Click **Enable**. The interface status will change to Enabled.

Step 3   Click **Apply** to effect the change.

Figure 8-9 shows the Anti-Spoofing panel with the inside interface enabled.

Figure 8-9   *Anti-Spoofing Panel*

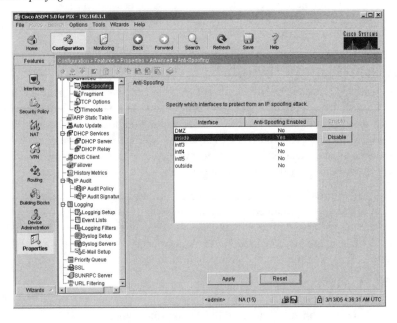

Mitigating Resource-Intensive DoS Attacks

DoS attacks designed to take up system resources can, but don't *usually*, have the same volume of traffic as an all-out bandwidth attack described previously. These attacks are more "finesse" oriented. They are crafted attacks that try to use the features of network protocols against the devices that they are attacking.

An example of this is a TCP SYN attack. In this type of attack, malicious software sends millions of requests to open network sockets on a security appliance. When a security appliance gets a SYN packet (for example, a request to open a connection), it might do the following:

- Use the CPU to allocate a certain amount of memory to establish this connection, taking up both CPU and memory.

- Send a SYN request to the device it is destined for and wait until the device on the inside responds, maintaining the memory resource.

- Use the CPU to check for a response for the destination device.

- Receive the response and send an acknowledgment that the connection is open. This connection remains open until the security appliance or the device sends a request to tear down the connection.

If a security appliance is capable of handling only one million connections and the software running the SYN attack sends five million connections, the security appliance could conceivably crash or, at the very least, be rendered useless.

To mitigate these types of attacks, the ASA/PIX Security Appliance has a mechanism built in to it that enables it to delete connections that don't have data following the acknowledgment packet after a certain amount of time.

Navigate to the following ASDM panel to see the default timeouts set for the ASA/PIX Security Appliance: **Configurations > Features > Properties > Advanced > Timeouts**. You will see the panel shown in Figure 8-10.

Figure 8-10 *ASA/PIX Default Timeouts*

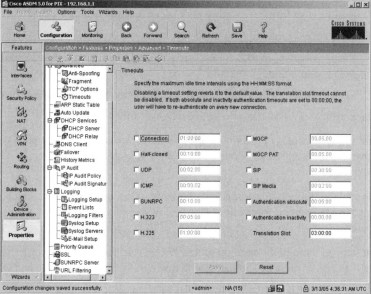

The default settings on the ASA/PIX are generally good enough to mitigate the attacks described in the previous paragraphs. However, if you find that you have an attack that isn't effectively being mitigated, you should first classify the type of traffic present in the attack and then either lower your timeouts or contact your ISP (or the Cisco Technical Assistance Center at http://www.cisco.com) for help.

Summary

So far in Part II, "Securing Network Infrastructures with ASDM" (the deployment section of this book), the following has been completed:

- **Chapter 5, "Deploying Secure Internet Connectivity"**—The initial configuration of your security appliance and connection of the security appliance to the Internet

- **Chapter 6, "Deploying Web and Mail Services"**—The addition of a web and a mail server

- **Chapter 7, "Deploying Authentication"**—The deployment of authentication to the device and the instruction of how to deploy authentication to web services

In this chapter, perimeter protection on your ASA/PIX security appliance has been deployed.

Perimeter protection has mitigated several different forms of attacks. Most of these attacks have been DoS attacks. However, by also using restrictive access rules, you have blocked unknown other types of attacks.

Specifically, within this chapter, you

- Ensured that traffic traversing your security appliance matches protocol specifications

- Customized protocol inspection

- Ensured that appropriate filters are in place, allowing only desired traffic through your security appliance

- Gained an understanding of ASA/PIX Security Appliance DoS protection

Attack mitigation was achieved with each one of these items listed.

Enforcing protocol specification stops an attacker from exploiting a protocol to attack your network. This is effectively done with the default inspection parameters set by default in the ASA/PIX.

You stepped through an exercise customizing protocol inspections, which enabled you to dynamically create a new filter that discovers and classifies new attacks against your system.

You stepped through the creation of new access rules, and you enforced restrictive inbound filtering on your security appliance, which will mitigate more attacks than you can calculate.

You then went through an exercise of examining and understanding the importance of ASA/PIX timeouts. The timeout defaults are effective in both reducing the amount of overhead caused by DoS attacks and returning CPU and memory back to the device so that it can better handle the traffic that you want to allow through your security appliance. The remaining steps to fully deploy defense in depth in your network are covered in the following chapters:

- Chapter 9, "Deploying Network Intrusion Prevention"
- Chapter 10, "Deploying Host Intrusion Prevention"
- Chapter 11, "Deploying VPNs"

This chapter covers steps to deploy the third layer of defense in depth. This layer is called *intrusion prevention*.

This chapter addresses the following topics:

- **The Importance of Intrusion Prevention**—This section describes why intrusion prevention is important and how it can add additional security to your network.
- **Deploying Intrusion Prevention**—This section addresses how you can use ASDM to deploy intrusion prevention in your network.

CHAPTER 9

Deploying Network Intrusion Prevention

As outlined in Chapter 2, "Principles of Network Defense," intrusion prevention is a key component in the defense-in-depth strategy for protecting your network from Internet-based network attacks.

Chapter 7, "Deploying Authentication," and Chapter 8, "Deploying Perimeter Protection," addressed deploying authentication and perimeter security on your security appliance. Authentication enforces who can get into your network, whereas perimeter security enforces what traffic can get into your network. The problem that now exists is that, even though the inbound traffic has been restricted and filtered, this filtering isn't enough to stop all attacks. Hackers have tools to detect the traffic you are letting into your network, and it's *that* traffic they will try to exploit to compromise your systems. You don't need to look further than the major attacks of the past few years to verify this: Code Red, Nimda, Sasser, Slammer, and Blaster all exploited valid traffic.

This chapter explains the features that the PIX security appliance and ASA 5500 series security appliance have in place to stop known attacks from getting into your network. You learn how to deploy intrusion prevention with a step-by-step procedure similar to previous chapters.

This chapter includes information about the new ASA 5500 series of security appliances with the Security Services Module (SSM). The SSM is a card that you can insert inside the ASA 5500 series to provide additional Internet service provider (ISP) features. Because this appliance is so new, there are no step-by-step implementation guidelines as of the original publishing of this book. After public introduction of this product, there will be a section on the Cisco website dedicated to information regarding this device. If you have any additional questions about the features or deployment of the ASA/SSM, you should be able to find the answers on this website.

This chapter references two distinctly different intrusion prevention technologies: IPS and IP Audit. Don't get confused by this; it's pretty straightforward, as follows:

- **IP Audit**—IP Audit is the default intrusion protection built in to both the PIX and the ASA security appliance. This prevention mechanism drops traffic but is limited to 51 commonly seen Internet attacks.

- **IPS**—IPS stands for Intrusion Prevention System. IPS is available only with the ASA 5500 series security appliance with an SSM installed. It includes more than 1500 signatures and, as described in this chapter, has much more advanced features than what is available on the PIX security appliance.

You can configure the features of the SSM modules the same way as you configure the security appliance, by using ASDM and browsing to the device. If you have the SSM installed, you will see an additional icon in the Features panel labeled IPS.

What Is Intrusion Prevention?

All ASA/PIX Security Appliances include intrusion protection features, specifically IP Audit, which contains 51 signatures of well-known Internet attacks, and IPS. IPS and IP Audit are capable of looking into packets that come into the ASA/PIX Security Appliance, matching the contents of the packets to an attack signature, and then either reporting or stopping the attack. In addition to signature-based IP Audit protection, the ASA/PIX Security Appliance supports HTTP application inspection, user-definable protocol configurations, instant messaging and peer-to-peer protection, and customized application inspection.

Table 9-1 describes the features supported by the ASA/SSM solution.

Table 9-1   *ASA/SSM IPS Features*

ASA/SSM IPS Feature	Feature Description
Multiple packet-drop actions	The ASA SSM is capable of dropping a single packet, an entire TCP flow, or all traffic from a possible attacking source.
SNMP support	ASA SSM users can define alarms or events to be sent as traps to SNMP management servers. The SSM module also supports an SNMP MIB and will respond to SNMP polling, which allows the sensor to respond to and participate with SNMP-compliant network management products.
Traffic normalization	*Traffic normalization* is a new term for Inline mode, where the SSM enforces order upon the packets traversing the network. It removes ambiguous packets from the network. For example, if two packets are seen on the network with the same headers but different data (shouldn't happen), only one of these packets is allowed through to the end host. The other is dropped. This action prevents a hacker from injecting two packets into a stream trying to confuse an IPS device as to which packet the end host actually accepts.
VoIP Inspection Engine	Added signatures for the evaluation of H.323 and H.225 VoIP traffic.
Meta Event Generator	An on-box correlation technology that enables the user to define multiple alarms as one event, which helps to simplify alarms.
Risk rating	A set of parameters that customers can configure to define the criticality of an event as well as what actions the sensor will take based upon the event.

Why Use IPS and IP Audit?

Up to this point, you have applied all the security preprocessing you can on your traffic by deploying authentication and perimeter security. You are now seeing only valid traffic traversing your security appliance. With the security deployed at this point, your ASA/PIX Security Appliance is looking only into the first few headers of a packet. IPS and IP Audit look further into the data portion of a packet to determine whether an attack is in process.

What Are the ASA/PIX IPS and IP Audit Signatures?

The ASA/PIX has 51 signatures of well-known, easily identifiable network and host attacks; the ASA/SSM combination has more than 1500 signatures that provide a comprehensive suite of IPS protection. The IP Audit signatures built in to the ASA/PIX are the following:

- 1000 IP options-Bad Option List
- 1001 IP options-Record Packet Route
- 1002 IP options-Timestamp
- 1003 IP options-Provide s, c, h, tcc
- 1004 IP options-Loose Source Route
- 1005 IP options-SATNET ID
- 1006 IP options-Strict Source Route
- 1100 IP Fragment Attack
- 1102 Impossible IP Packet
- 1103 Teardrop
- 2000 ICMP Echo Reply
- 2001 ICMP Host Unreachable
- 2002 ICMP Source Quench
- 2003 ICMP Redirect
- 2004 ICMP Echo Request
- 2005 ICMP Time Exceeded for a Datagram
- 2006 ICMP Parameter Problem on Datagram
- 2007 ICMP Timestamp Request
- 2008 ICMP Timestamp Reply
- 2009 ICMP Information Request
- 2010 ICMP Information Reply
- 2011 ICMP Address Mask Request

- 2012 ICMP Address Mask Reply
- 2150 Fragmented ICMP Traffic
- 2151 Large ICMP Traffic
- 2154 Ping of Death Attack
- 3040 TCP - No Bits Set in Flags
- 3041 TCP - SYN and FIN Bits Set
- 3042 TCP - FIN Bit with No ACK Bit in Flags
- 3153 FTP Improper Address Specified
- 3154 FTP Improper Port Specified
- 4050 UDP Bomb
- 4051 Snork
- 4052 Chargen
- 6050 DNS Host Info
- 6051 DNS Zone Transfer
- 6052 DNS Zone Transfer High Port
- 6053 DNS All Records
- 6100 RPC Port Registration
- 6101 RPC Port Unregistration
- 6102 RPC Dump
- 6103 Proxied RPC Request
- 6150 ypserv Portmap Request
- 6151 ypbind Portmap Request
- 6152 yppasswdd Portmap Request
- 6153 ypupdated Portmap Request
- 6154 ypxfrd Portmap Request
- 6155 mountd Portmap Request
- 6175 rexd Portmap Request
- 6180 rexd Attempt
- 6190 statd Buffer Overflow

NOTE   For a more in-depth description of these signatures, refer to http://www.cisco.com/go/pix and browse to Software Center and Documentation.

The important message that should be received from looking at this list of signatures is that the ASA/PIX is capable of stopping several of the popular attacks that plague the Internet today. If you add the ASA/SSM into the mix of protection, you increase the number of signatures to more than 1500, and you add a high level of confidence that false positives will not affect your production network. Any attacks that cannot be stopped with IPS or IP Audit on the security appliance will be stopped on the desktop with host intrusion prevention software (Cisco Security Agent).

Deploying Intrusion Prevention on the ASA/PIX

Using ASDM, you can perform three operations on the ASA/PIX Security Appliance associated with IP Audit:

- View a list of the signatures and choose which signature will be triggered by the ASA/PIX.

- Apply an IP Audit policy and action to an interface.

- Monitor which signatures have been triggered.

When you use ASDM in conjunction with ASA and SSM, you have the following key IPS GUI features available:

- **Signature Configuration**—This GUI option enables you to perform the following tasks:
  - Enable/disable signatures.
  - Set actions such as packet drops.
  - Alert using SNMP traps.
  - Packet captures on alarm traffic.
  - Customize existing signatures.
  - Create new custom signatures.
  - View details of existing signatures.
  - Browse to signature definitions.
  - Set custom severity per signature.
  - Custom configuration definitions.
  - Configure blocking devices.
  - Configure IP management accounts.
  - Enable signature update management.
- **Meta Event Definitions**—A *meta event* is when you take several events and consolidate them into a single event. For example, when the Nimda attack hit the web, it fired several signatures. If a meta event had been in place when this attack hit, you could have defined your IPS in such a way that only the single meta event would have triggered. The ASA/SSM solution provides a number of meta events and enables you to generate your own events based on your requirements. By default, meta events correlating to high-profile worm attacks are provided with the ASA/SSM solution.

- **Target Value Asset Configuration**—You can apply a variable to the devices in your network. If the device is important, you would set a high rating to indicate that you want to know about any alarms that are triggered with this device as the destination.

- **Event Action Override**—You can consolidate several network assets and perform a single event based on the risk rating of the alarm with a single operation. This setup gives you the option, for instance, to apply a drop action if any alarm triggers that could be considered serious. Serious alarms "generally" have a risk rating between 85 and 100.

- **Event Action Filter**—You can override alarms generated by certain IP addresses. For example, you might have devices in your network, such as vulnerability scanners or load balancers, that normally generate hundreds of alarms. Using the Event Action Filter option, you could tell the ASA/SSM device not to generate an alarm from these devices.

Note   Load balancer uses pings as a means to validate that devices are available. This ping sequence can look like a ping sweep to IPS devices.

- **Event Viewing**—The ASDM GUI enables you to look at events generated by the ASA/SSM module. These events could include a summary of why an alarm was triggered, a packet dump of an attack, or attack flows. The information in the event viewer includes signature ID and actions that the security appliance took against these packets.

- **Signature Updates**—The ASA with the SSM card is capable of running all of the Cisco IPS signatures, which will also include some network virus signatures. These signatures are different from the ASA/PIX signatures, which tend to remain static. This feature of the GUI enables you to install new signature definitions for the SSM. Signatures come out at least once every two weeks. If a critical new attack is found, signature updates come out sooner, which gives you the flexibility to quickly download signatures and keep your network protected.

Viewing and Changing ASA/PIX IP Audit Signatures

IP Audit signatures do represent overhead on the CPU of the security appliance; therefore, it is recommended, to preserve CPU, that you disable signatures that you might not need. For example, if you are not going to allow pings (ICMP) or FTP through your security appliance, you can use the following general steps to disable all the signatures related to those two protocols.

The modification of which signatures the ASA/PIX uses to protect your network is a simple operation, as follows:

Step 1   To view and modify the default signatures in the ASA/PIX, use ASDM to navigate to the **Configuration > Features > Properties > IP Audit > IP Signature** panel. (See Figure 9-1.)

Figure 9-1   *IP Audit Signatures*

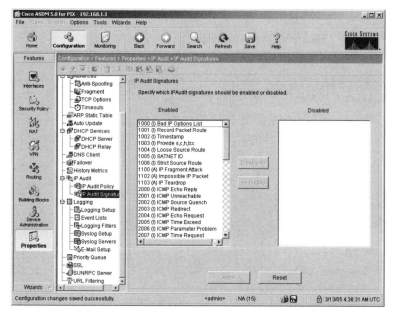

You can use the scroll bar on the right to view the signatures.

Step 2   Highlight the signature on the left that you want to disable.

Step 3   Click the **Disable** button to move the signature into the Disabled window.

Step 4   Click the **Apply** button to save the configuration to the ASA/PIX Security Appliance.

When you finish this procedure, you will have defined which signatures will be activated when you apply IP Audit to an ASA/PIX interface.

Enabling IP Audit Policy on an Interface

By default, the ASA/PIX ships with IP Audit turned off. You must follow the steps in this section to turn on IP Audit for a specific interface.

Before reviewing the steps to activate IP Audit, it is important that you understand the types of signatures and the actions you can select for each signature type.

The ASA/PIX Security Appliance has two different classes of IP Audit signatures, attack and informational:

- **Attack signatures**—These indicate that an attack is in progress.

- **Information signatures**—These indicate suspicious traffic.

You can take three actions whenever a signature is matched, as follows:

- **Alarm**—Sends a message to syslog
- **Drop**—Silently discards the packet
- **Reset**—Resets the TCP connection that sent this packet

The ASA with the SSM card allows for significantly more control when an IPS alarm is generated. It can perform any combination of the following actions:

- **Deny attacker inline**—Does not forward the packet that triggered this alert or other packets from this source address
- **Deny connection inline**—Does not forward the current packet and all following packets in this TCP connection
- **Deny packet inline**—Does not forward the packet that triggered this alert (IPS mode only)
- **Log attacker packets**—Logs all packets coming from the source IP address that triggered this alert
- **Log pair packets**—Logs all packets that have the same source and destination IP address that triggered this alert
- **Log victim packets**—Logs all packets that have the same destination address of the packet that triggered this alert
- **Produce alert**—Logs this event to the event store as an alert
- **Produce verbose alert**—Logs the content of the packet that triggered this alert
- **Request block connection**—Sends a request to block this connection
- **Request block host**—Sends a request to block this attacker host
- **Request SNMP trap**—Sends a request to forward a trap to your SNMP to log the triggering of this alert
- **Reset TCP connection**—Sends TCP resets to stop the current TCP flow

In the example in this chapter, you turn on all alarm policies and tell the ASA/PIX to drop the traffic. Subsequently, you turn on all the informational policies and ask the ASA/PIX to report to syslog when a policy triggers.

The following steps walk you through how to enable alarms on the ASA/PIX. One thing to keep in mind when enabling alarms is that you don't want to try to do too much and waste CPU cycles. For this example, you create a policy to drop and report packets that have triggered alarms and then report informational packets, which is where the ASA with the SSM card can really help. It is optimized for inline network intrusion prevention. It stops attacks without a high impact on the ASA/PIX Security Appliance CPU.

To deploy IP Audit on your ASA/PIX, follow these steps:

Step 1   Set up the alarm policy. Navigate to **Configuration > Features > Properties > IP Audit > IP Policy** panel.

Step 2   Click **Add**.

Step 3   Name the policy **AttackPolicy**.

Step 4   Click the **Attack** option button in the Policy Type section.

Step 5   Click the **Alarm** and **Drop** option buttons in the Action section. Your screen should look like Figure 9-2.

Figure 9-2   *IP Audit Attack Policy Setup*

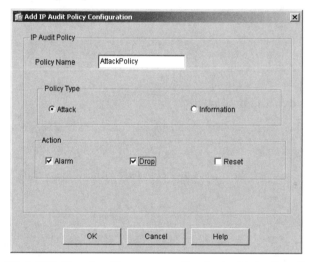

Step 6   Click **OK**. You should see your policy in the IP Audit policy list.

Step 7   Set up the informational policy. Navigate to **Configuration > Features > Properties > IP Audit > IP Policy** panel. Click **Add**.

Step 8   Name the policy **InfoPolicy**.

Step 9   Click the **Information** option button in the Policy Type section.

Step 10 Click the **Alarm** option button in the Action section. Your screen should look like Figure 9-3.

Step 11 Click **OK**. You should see your policy in the IP Audit policy list.

You now need to take the following steps to apply the policies to the outside interface:

Step 1   Next to the Outside Interface tag, click the **Attack Policy** pull-down menu and select **AttackPolicy**.

Figure 9-3 *IP Audit Info Policy Setup*

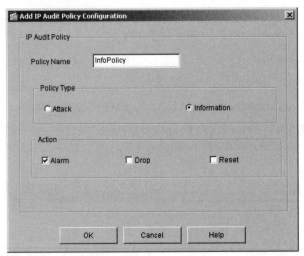

Step 2 Next to the Outside Interface tag, click the **Info Policy** pull-down menu and choose **InfoPolicy**.

Step 3 Click **Apply** to save the changes to the ASA/PIX Security Appliance.

You have now successfully deployed IP Audit on your ASA/PIX Security Appliance.

When you complete the preceding steps, the IP Audit Policy Panel should look like Figure 9-4.

Figure 9-4 *Completed IP Policy Panel*

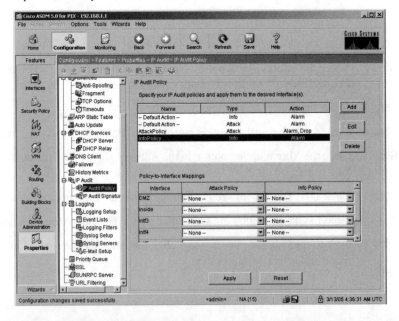

Monitoring the Triggering of IP Audit Policies

While using IP Audit, it is important to track any alarms that might be triggered. An alarm doesn't mean that an attack was successful, but it does warrant follow-up on your part just in case. The chances are quite high that you didn't experience any problems as a result, because the alarms are set to drop the packet.

A best practice to follow to ensure that attacks were not successful on your network is to do the following:

- View and store your alarms in case a forensic investigation is required in the future.

- Look at the dates and times of all IP Audit alarms. Many times, if you are under attack, you will see repetitive time occurrences.

- Compare security appliance alarms to alarms that might have been generated by your host intrusion prevention software (CSA) to ensure that CSA caught any attacks that weren't dropped.

The best way to view ASA/PIX IP Audit alarms is to do so through syslog. Syslog best practices are discussed in Appendix A, "Deploying Effective Security Management."

Syslog works best if you send the data to a remote computer. From there, you can save it as a text file and run search utilities on it to find certain data strings.

The following procedure shows you how to enable syslog and how to look at IP Audit syslog messages:

Step 1 Using ASDM, navigate to the following panel: **Configurations > Features > Properties > Logging > Logging Setup**. Click the check box **Enable Logging**, and then click **Apply** to activate the logging of syslog data.

Step 2 Navigate to **Configuration > Features > Properties > Logging > Logging Filters** and enable the ASA/PIX device to report IP Audit or IPS events.

Step 3 Using ASDM, navigate to the following panel: **Monitoring > Features > Logging > Live Buffer**.

Step 4 Choose **Informational** for the logging level.

Step 5 Click **View**.

Step 6 To trigger some events, ping to the outside IP address of your web server 199.199.199.203. Your ping will fail. It fails because you don't allow pings through your security appliance. However, the pings still trigger an alarm.

Step 7 In the text search box at the top of the panel, enter **IDS** and click **Find Next**. You will see an error message similar to this:

400014: IDS:2004 ICMP echo request from 199.199.199.200 to 199.199.199.203 on interface outside

Step 8 If you are running the ASA with the SSM card, you can navigate to the **Monitor > View** panel to see the alarms that were generated.

To view syslog messages, you can create a script that runs on your syslog server to search for the string IDS: This will give you a good idea of whether anyone is trying to get into your system and triggering any of the signatures deployed in the ASA/PIX.

As another alternative, ASDM has a feature called Live Log that enables you to view desired syslog messages in real time. To use Live Log, follow these steps:

Step 1   Navigate to the following ASDM panel: **Monitoring > Features > Logging > Live Log**.

Step 2   Click the **View** button.

Step 3   When the Syslog screen displays, choose **Filter by Text** in the Incoming Messages section.

Step 4   Enter **IDS** next to the Filter button. Now only IDS messages will display.

As an alternative to syslog, you can set alarms in real time by completing the following procedure:

Step 5   Navigate to **Monitoring > Features > IP Audit > Miscellaneous Graphs > IP Audit**.

Here, you can select a grouping of signatures to graph and watch what's happening on your system in real time. Set up the ping scenario again, but view it by graph this time.

Step 6   Choose **ICMP Requests** and click **Add**.

Step 7   Click **Show Graphs**.

Step 8   Trigger the same event. Ping to the outside IP address of your web server 199.199.199.203.

Step 9   View the graph in real time as data traverses the security appliance.

Summary

So far in Part II, "Securing Network Infrastructures with ASDM" (the deployment section of this book), the following has been covered:

- **Chapter 5, "Deploying Secure Internet Connectivity"**—The initial configuration of your security appliance and connection of the security appliance to the Internet

- **Chapter 6, "Deploying Web and Mail Services"**—The addition of a web and a mail server

- **Chapter 7, "Deploying Authentication"**—The deployment of authentication to the device and the how to deploy authentication to web services

- **Chapter 8, "Deploying Perimeter Protection"**—The deployment of perimeter prevention

In this chapter, you deployed intrusion prevention (IPS and IP Audit) on your ASA/PIX Security Appliance, and you examined the advanced features made available to you with the ASA Security Appliance in conjunction with the SSM module.

IPS and IP Audit mitigate several attacks that are sourced from the Internet, including some, but not all, worms, viruses, and directed attacks. IP Audit on the ASA/PIX Security Appliance is signature-based. The ASA/PIX Security Appliance has 51 signatures in its default audit profile, and ASA/SSM has more than 1500 signatures. Both the ASA/PIX Security Appliance and the ASA 5500 series also provide RFC compliance checks and port-misuse checks.

The signatures deployed in the ASA/PIX stop many attacks; however, if attackers are determined enough, they might eventually circumvent signature prevention either by finding an attack not included in the signature database or by changing a string in their attack so it no longer triggers the signature. For this reason, host intrusion prevention, described in Chapter 10, "Deploying Host Intrusion Prevention," is important.

The following has been covered in this chapter:

- **Intrusion detection versus intrusion prevention**—Intrusion prevention drops and reports packets that are identified as attack packets. Intrusion detection lets the packets pass but logs the alarm to a syslog server.

- **The importance of IPS and IP Audit**—In the first few deployment chapters, you authenticated your data, filtered it, and then ran protocol checks on it. As a final step, IPS looks into the packet to ensure that the data in the packet doesn't match that of an attack string. If it does match, IPS drops the packet, thus protecting the resource for which the packet was destined.

- **ASA/PIX IP Audit and IPS signatures**—A list of all ASA/PIX default signatures has been provided. For an explanation of these signatures, check the Cisco website at http://www.cisco.com/go/pix. IPS signatures have been referenced in this chapter only as a quantity of more than 1500; listing all signatures in this book would not add any value. For a complete description of the IPS signatures, navigate to the ASDM panel **Configuration > IPS > Signature Configuration**. From that panel, highlight a signature and click the **NSDB** button. That button takes you to a web location that has a detailed description of the signature.

  You then deployed intrusion prevention on the ASA/PIX. In doing so, you learned how to use ASDM to do the following:

  — View and modify the IP Audit signatures.

  — Build an IP Audit policy.

  — Enable IP Audit policy on an interface.

  — Monitor the triggering of IP Audit policies.

The remaining steps to fully deploy defense in depth in your network are covered in the following chapters:

- Chapter 10, "Deploying Host Intrusion Prevention"

- Chapter 11, "Deploying VPNs"

This chapter addresses the following topics regarding host intrusion prevention software:

- **The Importance of Host Intrusion Prevention Software**—This section describes the layers of defense that we have already deployed and underscores the importance of installing host intrusion prevention software to ensure that your network is fully secured. The model used for this book is the Cisco host intrusion prevention software called the *Cisco Security Agent*.

- **CSA Internals**—This section will help you understand how CSA works, what components in your host or server are affected, and how CSA goes about recognizing and stopping a computer attack.

- **CSA Deployment**—This portion provides you with a high-level step-by-step process that explains how to roll out CSA into your business or enterprise.

- **Antivirus Deployment**—This section helps you to understand what antivirus software will and will not do for you. The importance of using antivirus software in conjunction with CSA is also discussed. It is important to use both technologies for a complete solution.

CHAPTER 10

Deploying Host Intrusion Prevention

This chapter provides you with information regarding a new security technology called *host intrusion prevention software*. The Cisco implementation of intrusion prevention software is called *Cisco Security Agent* (CSA).

CSA is security software that runs on servers or desktops and recognizes behavior indicative of a present attack on these devices. When CSA sees this behavior, it either stops the behavior or stops the process or application that is performing the malicious activity.

Why Use Host Intrusion Prevention

The primary purpose of this book is to show you how to use PIX version 7 and ASDM to deploy defense in depth in your network. As explained in Chapter 2, "Principles of Network Defense," the ASA/PIX Security Appliance does an excellent job of providing security services at the network level and some services at the application level. By following the steps in the previous chapters, you have already mitigated numerous potential attacks, providing examples on how to implement the following:

- Device authentication
- Traffic authentication
- Public server isolation (DMZ)
- Network device hardening
- Traffic filtering
- DoS protection
- Protocol violation protection
- Intrusion prevention and detection

In the Internet of yesterday, one could feel safe with the security deployed so far in this book. However, in this modern day, new vulnerabilities are constantly discovered and exploits (malicious code) are being written that take advantage of these vulnerabilities.

Most of these new attacks (called *day-zero attacks*) use valid traffic, follow valid protocol rules, and are still capable of exploiting a vulnerability and compromising your systems. Because a valid protocol was followed and valid traffic was used, firewalls (or any signature-based or most protocol behavior-based systems) cannot recognize these attacks. For this reason, it is important to deploy intrusion prevention software on hosts and servers as the final layer of defense for attack mitigation.

NOTE   Do not make the mistake of thinking that intrusion prevention needs to be deployed only on servers; many virus or worm outbreaks are targeted at hosts. After a host is infected, it will, in turn, infect the remaining hosts or servers in your network that are not adequately protected. Not all attacks focus on taking your systems down. Some are focused on gathering information or using your system as a zombie to launch other attacks.

Day-zero attacks are the most costly to you and your organization. They are designed to take advantage of the time lapse between when the attack is let loose in the wild and when a signature is created to stop them. The bad news is that, in most cases, a tangible cost is already incurred before a signature is created. Slammer was a worm that hit the Internet in 2002. It infected 1.4 million hosts in less than 48 hours. Blaster infected approximately 400,000 hosts in the same amount of time. The list goes on with Nimda, Sasser, Code Red, and many others. The cost of cleaning up after these incidents is staggering. Companies needed to perform some or all of the following to recover from these attacks:

- Install hot fixes
- Update security signatures
- Reinstall operating systems
- Reinstall old security patches
- Reinstall applications
- Reinstall application patches
- Recover data from backup to the best of theory ability
- Recover data manually where backups were not current

It would be impossible to know exactly how much these attacks cost consumers, but a simple web search investigating costs of viruses reveals that even LoveBug, which had relatively low interest as far as viruses or worms are concerned, costs consumers between $8 billion to $10 billion dollars to mitigate, isolate, and clean up. The same investigation for the Slammer and Blaster worm indicates that each of these attacks cost companies in excess of $3 billion dollars.

Customers that had deployed CSA fortunately did not incur any tangible costs as a result of these costly security incidents. In all cases, CSA (with its default rules) recognized that malware was trying to run on host machines and stopped the attempt. The net cost for these customers was zero dollars.

Anatomy of a Host or Server Attack

One of the reasons that host intrusion prevention software can be so effective in stopping day-zero or unknown attacks is because the same attack paradigm has been used since the first recorded attack, the Morris worm, on November 2, 1988.

This attack paradigm is divided into five phases, as shown in Figure 10-1.

NOTE   Later, this chapter explains how CSA mitigates attacks in each of the attack phases.

Figure 10-1   *Worm/Virus Attack Model*

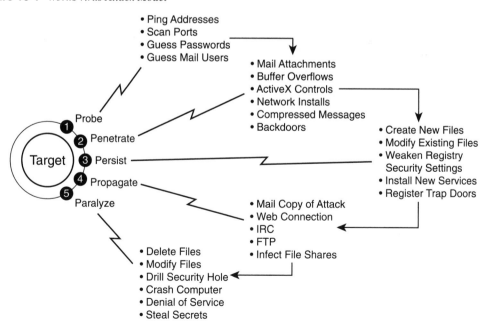

Probe Phase

In the probe phase, attackers attempt to learn as much as they can about the hosts or servers that they plan on attacking. They do this usually by using off-the-shelf freeware tools such as NMAP or Nessus. These tools probe systems and then return the following:

- Open network ports
- Operating systems and versions
- Applications and version that are listening on the open port

After hackers obtain this information, they can easily access databases on the Internet that tell them how to exploit the specific operating systems and applications. In the case of Nessus, it is easier for hackers; this freeware tool creates a report that also lists the vulnerabilities. Several tools perform this function; these just happen to be two popular and free ones.

NOTE	Don't be too quick to pass judgment on these tools and their authors. Many businesses and enterprises use these same tools to do security assessments on their systems to ensure that they know and have addressed all of their systems' own vulnerabilities. In most cases, these tools were not meant for malicious purposes.

Penetrate

The penetrate phase is where the hacker actually runs the exploit and injects his attack code onto a host or server. In many cases, this is done via a buffer overflow, but it can also be accomplished by other means such as malware running as follows:

- E-mail attachments
- ActiveX controls
- Network installations
- Compressed messages
- Back doors

If the penetrate phase is successful, the malware has either already run on your machine or will run when the e-mail attachment or the ActiveX code is executed.

Persist

The persistence phase is the hacker's attempt to maintain a presence on the host or server he has penetrated the device. This phase involves one or more malicious actions by the attacking software:

- Create new files
- Modify existing files

- Write to the registry
- Weaken the security posture of the device
- Install new services
- Register trap doors
- Install fake system files (Trojans)

If the persistence phase is completed, the hacker has compromised your host or server to a point where not only can he access it any time he wants, but he also probably has administrative or root access and can easily gain access to other machines inside your network.

Propagate

During the propagation phase, hackers try to spread the attack to other devices within your network. They might even go outside your firewall to infect machines on the Internet that belong to other companies and individuals. It was during the propagation phase that attacks such as Slammer and Blaster infected millions of devices in a short period of time.

Many small businesses believe that they won't be compromised because they have nothing that anyone else wants. Unfortunately, this isn't correct. Many times, an attack just needs your CPU cycles and a network connection. For example, in a distributed denial-of-service (DDos) attack, a hacker needs several machines to participate in the attack. In this case, the malicious software installs itself on any machine it can compromise. These machines are called *zombies*; they are usually devices that have limited security, such as those in the following locations:

- Doctor offices
- Retail stores
- Universities
- Home DSL or cable (always-on networks)
- Small businesses

At a predefined time, the software on these machines will all start simultaneously and attack a specific target. Whitehouse.gov was a victim of such an attack.

Another reason an attacker might want to gain access to your PC is to use "your" machine for an attack against someone else. In this case, if law enforcement gets involved, the attacker's tracks are covered and it looks like you launched the attack.

CAUTION   Propagation attacks could also be used against critical-infrastructure websites. Therefore, it is important to be a good web citizen and take steps to protect your systems even if you think that no one *wants* the data on your machines.

The propagation phase can be done using several different methods:

- Mail a copy of the attack
- Web connections
- IRC
- FTP file transfers
- Infected file shares

Paralyze

If you are a small business or an enterprise, the paralyze phase of an attack could be the most devastating. The paralyze phase usually consists of one or more of the following malicious activities:

- File deletion
- File modification
- Opening of security holes
- Broadcasting to hacker communities that you have been compromised to further expose you to attacks
- Crashing of servers and hosts
- Denial of service
- Stealing secrets
- Stealing customer lists
- Stealing customer financial data, such as credit cards and account numbers

This phase of the attack can be costly. Both intangible and tangible costs can be quite high; intangible costs can be a high factor if the attack stole business secrets and customer data; tangible costs of recovery can be quite high. Recently, attackers have favored stealing information and then extorting money from these companies to keep the attack or information secret.

To take a deeper look at the paralyze phase of an attack, consider the damage Slammer, which infected 1.4 millions hosts, could have done. The widespread effects could have been devastating to many corporations. An attacker had full administrative or root access to every machine it compromised; the attacker could have decided to do some or all of the following operations on those servers:

- Delete security hot fixes from operating system vendors or application vendors. Such deletions are bad because they weaken the security posture of your system and make it vulnerable to future attacks.

- Delete or modify system files, which would intermittently crash your systems.

- Scan your disk drives for numbers that match the format of a credit card number.

- Copy your password file to a hacker server for analysis of usernames and passwords.

Depending on how a hacker wrote her malware, you might be in a position where you need to do a full recovery on all infected devices on your networks. This recover could include the following:

- Reinstallation of the operating systems

- Reinstallation of all operating system patches

- Reinstallation of all applications

- Reinstallation of all application patches

- Restoring of data from backup

- Manually updating any data between the last backup and the attack

- Evaluating and installing a host intrusion prevention system to prevent a recurrence

It is precisely because of these reasons that host intrusion prevention is included as a layer of defense in depth. A firewall can protect and mitigate against many attacks, but your systems are not completely secure until you have deployed host intrusion prevention software on your systems.

CSA Internals

CSA is unique in the way it stops attacks against hosts and servers. Many prevention technologies use anomaly-type detection or attack signatures, both of which can be subverted by a knowledgeable attacker. Anomaly detection can be circumvented by launching an attack that uses only normal valid data packets. Signatures can be circumvented by using a variation of known attacks. A simplistic example that does not represent a real-world way to circumvent Nimda is where a signature for Nimda might be looking for a string that has the string "NIMDA" in the payload. An attacker can easily change that string to add null characters between the text letters, with the result "N00I00M00D00A00". The attack packet no longer has the string "NIMDA" and could now possibly be a successful attack.

CSA doesn't look for signatures and it doesn't do anomaly detection. CSA looks for behavior on a device that indicates that it could be under attack. For example, code injected onto a buffer after a buffer overflow and then executed is always going to be bad behavior. CSA will stop this behavior or kill the process before it can execute the code.

CSA in Action

The CSA has three engines that work together to protect a device against a malicious attack. These engines all use default or custom rules to stop bad behavior on a processor. These rules are flexible and easy to change with a Java-based GUI management console.

The three parts of CSA are as follows:

- Behavior engine
- Application engine
- Firewall engine

These engines are implemented in two software modules that run on a protected device. One module runs on top of the operating system kernel; the other runs on the network stack.

The module that runs on top of the kernel can recognize actions important to the behavior engine and the application engine. The module that runs on the network stack recognizes actions that are important to the firewall engine.

Behavior Engine

The behavior-based engine looks for generalized bad behavior on the processor from applications that might exhibit the following:

- Buffer overflows
- Code executions off of the stack
- System directory writes
- Registry writes

Any of these actions *could* indicate an attack in process on a device; however, it is important to note that just because an application might be performing one of these actions, it doesn't mean an attack is definitely happening. CSA "talks" to the other engines and correlates their events to determine whether an attack is actually in process.

Application Engine

The application engine recognizes bad behavior of a certain application and stops that application if it violates its behavioral rules.

For example, it is known that a web browser should have the following behaviors:

- Browsing the web
- Storing cookies
- Writing history files
- Running ActiveX or Java applets within a defined context
- Requesting GETs and POSTs to websites, as defined by the HTTP protocol

We know that a web browser should not have the following behaviors:

- Copying cmd.exe into a scripts directory
- Executing cmd.exe or any executables
- Writing to the system registry
- Modifying system files
- Randomly opening outbound network ports
- Listening for incoming traffic on random ports
- Randomly sending data to websites without the user initiating the transfer

If CSA detects an application performing an action that violates its application rules, it correlates with the other three engines and determines whether an attack is in process. If CSA decides that an attack is in fact occurring, it stops the behavior or the process, effectively mitigating the attack.

Firewall Engine

The firewall engine is similar to many personal firewalls in the sense that it filters only wanted traffic. However, it also has the advantage of being able to share information with the behavior and application engines to determine whether an attack is really in progress.

NOTE Correlation has been brought up many times in this chapter. Correlation is one of the many strengths of CSA and a key to a successful host intrusion prevention solution. With endpoint prevention, you need to ensure that you stop a process only if an attack is definitely occurring. Effective correlation is the key to making sure that processes are not being stopped unnecessarily.

The firewall engine watches the behavior of both inbound and outbound network traffic and takes appropriate action if bad behavior is detected. On the inbound side, it blocks or rate limits unwanted traffic. On the outbound side, it stops traffic or kills a process that starts to send unsolicited or invalid network traffic.

One of the features of the firewall engine is a function called *Net Shield*. Net Shield can mitigate the probe portion of an attack. As mentioned previously in this chapter, the first part of an attack on a host or server is a probe to determine the operating system, open ports, and applications running on a network device. Net Shield can fool probing applications into thinking they are communicating with a Linux box when the target of the probe might actually be a machine running the Windows operating system. Like almost all functions in CSA, this feature is implemented as a rule and can be turned on or off by the system administrator.

CSA Architecture

The CSA architecture consists of two separate parts:

- **The host or server agent**—Consists of software modules that are installed on a host or a server, as mentioned earlier in the chapter. These modules recognize and stop bad behavior. The agent reports every event (including pings and probes) to a centralized management server. The agent polls the CSA management server every few minutes to see whether any rules have been changed that need to be updated on the hosts.

- **CSA Management Console**—Rules are stored and modified via the Management Console. If a rule is changed, it is downloaded the next time an agent polls the server. The server is also the repository for event logging and notification. It can be programmed to send critical security alarms to an administrator's pager or e-mail.

Another valuable part of the CSA Management Console is that it looks at data that has been collected and can create rules on-the-fly that might help stop attacks. For example, each agent reports to the Management Console if he has been pinged or probed. If the Management Console determines that a ping has come from the same machines several times, it can put that device into a quarantine list and disallow all traffic from that device until there has been a chance to determine whether the traffic is valid. With this, as well as all rules within CSA, the rules can be modified or turned off. For example, if you have a management workstation or a load balancer that needs to do ping sweeps as part of its job, you can let CSA know and it will not take action against those hosts.

NOTE If the CSA agent is not connected to the Management Console, as the situation would be if a user took his laptop home, CSA would still protect the laptop using the last downloaded policy.

CSA Attack Mitigation

The number of attacks that CSA can mitigate with the three behavior-based rule engines and the Management Console are endless. When you look closely at the attack paradigm examined earlier in the chapter, you will see that all phases of an attack are mitigated by at least one of the CSA behavior-based rules engines.

Note that because of the way CSA works, if an attack did indeed circumvent part of the CSA defense, the attack would be stopped in the next phase of the attack. For example, CSA stopped a worm called Korgo when it tried to execute code off of an overflowed buffer. If CSA didn't stop Korgo at that point, Table 9-2 lists how many ways it would have been stopped by the CSA. This list is derived in the lab by the following procedure:

1 Run Korgo, documenting where CSA stopped the attack.

2 Disable the rule that stopped the attack.

3 Run Korgo again, documenting where CSA stopped the attack.

4 Loop through this process, recognizing all of the rules that Korgo would have triggered.

Table 10-1   *Korgo Rule Triggering*

Rule	Behavior Mitigated
Desktop module	This Trojan-detection rule prevents the shell code from executing ftpupd.exe.
Common security module	This rule prevents ftpupd.exe from opening itself.
Common security module	This rule prevents ftpupd.exe from creating a randomly named copy of itself.
Common security module	This rule prevents the randomly named copy of the worm from deleting ftpupd.exe.
Desktop module	The worm triggers this rule when it (as downloaded content) tries to connect to IRC servers.

Table 10-3 takes a practical look at how CSA stops attacks. Using the attack paradigm discussed previously in this chapter, this table maps the CSA engine (or rule type) that stops the malicious behavior. With this breadth and flexibility of mitigating attacks based on behavior, a combination of CSA and antivirus software has been reported to have stopped all known zero-day attacks from infecting PCs.

NOTE   Some of these attack actions have "not applicable" (n/a) under the mitigation engine. This designation appears because that the action cannot be stopped because the action being done is a user trying to guess passwords. In these cases, operating systems have built-in preventive measures that limit the number of times someone can incorrectly enter a password (see Table 10-3). If hackers gain access through guessing, CSA could still stop them when they try to run malicious code.

Table 10-2   *CSA Attack Mitigation*

Attack Phase	Attack Action	CSA Mitigation Engine
Probe	Scan ports	Global event correlation, firewall engine
	Guess passwords	n/a
	Ping addresses	Global event correlation, firewall engine
	Guess mail users	n/a
Penetrate	Mail attachments	Application engine
	Buffer overflows	Behavior engine
	ActiveX controls	Application engine, behavior engine
	Network installs	Application engine, behavior engine
	Compress messages	Application engine, behavior engine
	Create back doors	Application engine, behavior engine
Persist	Create new files	Application engine, behavior engine
	Modify existing files	Application engine, behavior engine
	Weaken registry settings	Application engine, behavior engine
	Install new services	Application engine, behavior engine
	Register trap doors	Application engine, behavior engine
Propagate	Mail copy of attack	Application engine, behavior engine
	Initiate Web connection	Application engine, firewall engine
	Initiate IRC communications	Firewall engine
	Initiate FTP downloads	Firewall engine
	Infect file shares	Behavior engine, firewall engine
Paralyze	Delete files	Application engine, behavior engine
	Modify files	Application engine, behavior engine
	Denial of service	Application engine, behavior engine, firewall engine
	Crash computer	Application engine, behavior engine, firewall engine
	Steal secrets	Application engine, behavior engine, firewall engine

Implementing Host Intrusion Prevention

One of the main things that you must understand when deploying CSA is that you must take care when you deploy it into your environment. Tune it according to your applications and environment. Fortunately, the process of tuning CSA has been made easy.

CSA Deployment Suggestions

You can deploy CSA effectively and safely in your environment by following a few steps. You need to run CSA and your application together in a lab to teach CSA how your applications behave, or run it in Test mode in your production network before deploying CSA.

This section contains generalized steps on how to deploy CSA. An exhaustive step-by-step deployment is beyond the scope of this book. The list of deployment steps provided is merely a high-level guideline to give you an idea of what is needed to roll out the product. For more information on deployment, refer to the Cisco website at http://www.cisco.com/go/csa.

CSA Lab Deployment

Step 1   Ensure that your hardware and software meet the minimum requirements for a CSA implementation.

Previous to version 4.5, only English (United States) language versions of operating systems are supported. CSA 4.5 supports many European and Asian languages. In addition to language support, version 4.5 supports Windows 2003, Red Hat Linux Advanced Server, and Red Hat Linux Workstation. Check the Cisco website for current language support.

Server agent for Windows requirements:

— Windows NT 4.0 Server (Service Pack 5 or later)

— Windows NT 4.0 Enterprise Server (Service Pack 5 or later)

— Windows 2000 Server (up to Service Pack 3)

— Windows 2000 Advanced Server (up to Service Pack 3)

— Single or multiple Pentium processors, 200 MHz or faster 128-MB RAM minimum

Server agent for Solaris requirements:

— Solaris 8 SPARC architecture (64-bit kernel)

— Ultra SPARC processor 500 MHz or faster

— 256-MB RAM minimum

Desktop agent requirements:

— Windows NT 4.0 Workstation (Service Pack 5 or later)

— Windows 2000 Professional (up to Service Pack 3)

— Windows XP Professional (up to Service Pack 0 or 1)

— Single or multiple Pentium processors, 200 MHz or faster

— 128-MB RAM minimum

CiscoWorks VMS with Management Center for Cisco Security Agents requirements:

— Windows 2000 Server or Advanced Server (Service Pack 1 or Service Pack 2)

— Pentium 500-MHz processor or faster

— 384-MB RAM minimum

— 2-GB disk

Step 2 Install the CSA Management Console and CiscoWorks on the workstation that will contain and control the CSA Management Console and the CSA rules.

Step 3 Create as close to a mirrored production environment as you can. Install your applications and the proper CSA agent rules on your host and server systems.

Step 4 Follow the CSA user manual to put CSA in Test mode. When CSA runs in this mode, it generates alarms and sends alarms to the CSA Management Console. However, it does not kill any processes or stop bad behavior.

Step 5 Simulate a working application environment by running your applications as they would normally run in production.

Step 6 Look at each alarm generated on the CSA Management Console.

Step 7   If an alarm is generated by your application and is expected, click the "wizard" in the event log and tell CSA to write an exception for this alarm. This action will generate rules on-the-fly and essentially teach CSA which rules are acceptable for your applications. If you have problems determining the validity of a rule, contact the Cisco Technical Assistance Center for help.

CSA Production Deployment

Now that CSA has learned what behavior is expected of your applications, you are ready to deploy CSA in your production environment:

Step 1   After you let CSA create a set of rules that will both secure your environment and allow your applications to run properly, you should deploy the CSA agents and CSA Management Console in your production environment.

Step 2   It is a good idea to still run CSA in Test mode for at least a week to ensure that no false alarms affect the operation of your business.

Step 3   After you are comfortable with your rules, use the CSA Management Console to turn CSA on in full Prevention mode.

Step 4   The polling process from the hosts will automatically download the rules in Prevention mode.

Virus Scanners and CSA: The Complete Solution

CSA is a key product in implementing full defense in depth in your business or enterprise. As stated previously, it is the last step of protection to secure your hosts and servers from all attacks. Note that Cisco recommends that CSA be run in conjunction with antivirus software. The reasons for this are twofold:

- **Additional defense in depth** — The key to a successful network defense is defense in depth. Antivirus software provides additional endpoint protection.

- **Malware cleanup** — CSA stops known viruses from doing damage and can keep unknown worms from being installed on your system. In conjunction, antivirus software cleans up known viruses by deleting them from your system.

Summary

As outlined in previous chapters, the PIX Firewall provides the first three layers of defense in depth:

* Chapter 7, "Deploying Authentication"
* Chapter 8, "Deploying Perimeter Protection"
* Chapter 9, "Deploying Network Intrusion Prevention"

These layers take several steps and mitigate many known and unknown attacks. However, in today's security environment, where valid data and protocol are used as the basis for an attack, behavior-based host intrusion prevention (CSA) is the final step in providing a complete and secure network defense.

The current attack paradigm comprises five phases:

* **Probe phase**—Finds out the components and applications in the network
* **Penetrate**—Compromises the system
* **Persist**—Installs the malware so that it can be re-executed on the devices, or configures the device so that the hacker can regain access at will
* **Propagate**—Looks for other hosts to infect
* **Paralyze**—Crashes the device, steals secrets, or takes down the network

CSA defends against this attack paradigm at all levels, providing defense in depth within the device it is protecting. It does this with three rules-based engines:

* **Behavior engine**—Stops bad behavior such as code executing off of the stack, writes to the system directory, or writes to the system registry.
* **Application engine**—Stops applications from bad behavior. For example, in general, a browser needs to access web pages, execute some scripts, and write history files and cookies to hard drives. If an application attempts to do things that it shouldn't, the application engine stops the behavior.
* **Firewall engine**—Filters traffic, rate limits during DoS attacks, and can mitigate against some probe phase behaviors.

The CSA Management Console also has a function that helps mitigate against worms, viruses, pings, and probes. The Management Console uses data provided from the agents to determine whether a host is exhibiting behavior similar to a worm or virus or is pinging or probing devices on the network. If it finds a host behaving this way, it puts that device in a global quarantine list and creates a rule that will be downloaded by hosts or servers to restrict traffic from the infected host.

A step-by-step overview is provided so that you can understand the effort necessary to deploy CSA in your business or enterprise. It's suggested that you duplicate your production environment in a lab and run CSA on the lab devices in Test mode. With CSA in Test mode, you can look at the alarms on the CSA Management Console and use a wizard to generate rules that will allow your applications to run securely and error-free.

Finally, it is recommended that CSA run with reputable antivirus software to ensure that you have additional defense in depth on the host. The antivirus software also cleans up any files that it recognizes as malware that might have been downloaded on the device via e-mail.

The remaining steps to fully deploy defense in depth in your network are covered in Chapter 11, "Deploying VPNs," and Appendix A, "Deploying Effective Security Management."

In this chapter, you learn how to deploy virtual private networks (VPNs). This chapter addresses the following topics:

- **The Importance of VPNs**—This section provides a brief description of why VPNs are important and how they can add additional security in your network.

- **Deploying VPNs**—This section explains how you can use ASDM to deploy a VPN in your network.

CHAPTER 11

Deploying VPNs

So far in Part II of this book, "Securing Network Infrastructures with ASDM," the deployment section of defense in depth is complete. This chapter covers how to leverage your existing network and extend defense in depth to users who need access to your network from remote sites.

Understanding Virtual Private Networks

In today's work environment, several classes of users are not always in the same physical location as your main computer network, including the following (to list just a few):

- People on business trips
- Remote workers
- Remote partners
- Contractors
- Remote corporate sites

Figure 11-1 shows an overview of various types of VPN users and remote access devices.

Figure 11-1 *VPN Network*

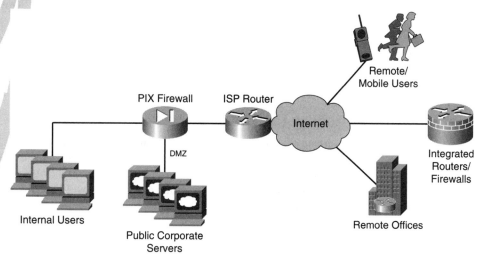

The one thing all of these people have in common (generally) is that even though they are remote, if they have access to your corporate network resources, they can be much more productive. VPN is a networking technology that enables these classes of users to do just that. When logged on to a VPN, the remote user has access to all Internet network services such as DNS, web, mail, FTP, and network applications as if they were physically on your network. They might even have an IP address in the same subnet as those users who physically are on the inside of your network.

Not only does VPN provide full access to network resources, it also provides a full set of security features that are required for remote users, including the following:

- Data encryption mitigates against traffic being stolen off of the public network.

- Tunnel and client authentication ensures that the person logging in to your network is who she claims to be.

- Data authentication ensures that the data received on both ends came from the authenticate tunnel user and hasn't been tampered with.

- "Are you there" (AYT) functionality on the client end ensures that the client PC is protected with personal firewalls or host intrusion prevention before it can log in to you network.

- Low cost, because the client can log in to a local ISP, eliminating long-distance or toll-number phone charges.

Implementing VPN Using ASDM

VPN has several different attributes that you must configure before you can establish a VPN tunnel allowing remote users to connect. Fortunately, ASDM has a built-in wizard that steps you though exactly what needs to be done to configure your ASA/PIX Security Appliance to allow the connection of VPN clients.

This section covers two steps to configure your ASA/PIX Security Appliance for VPN connectivity:

- Downloading and installing the Cisco VPN client
- Using ASDM to configure VPN on the ASA/PIX Security Appliance

Downloading and Installing the Cisco VPN Client

Cisco uses some proprietary technology in IPSec VPN, such as Dead Peer Detection, that tracks and recovers dropped VPN tunnels. Therefore, you should use only the Cisco VPN client when connecting remote users. Connectivity with other clients might work, but it's likely it will require significant configuration tweaking and that you will lose some VPN features. In this example, you use the Cisco VPN client.

CAUTION	You must install and test the VPN client on a machine other than the machine you are using for your ASDM configurations. If not, when you bring up the VPN tunnel, you will no longer be connected to your ASA/PIX Security Appliance.

To download the client, follow these steps:

Step 1 Go to Cisco.com.

Step 2 Click **Login** and enter with your Cisco username and password.

Step 3 In the left column of the web page, highlight **Technical Support** and drop down to Downloads.

Step 4 Choose **VPN Software**.

Step 5 Choose **Cisco VPN Client**.

Step 6 Choose **Download Cisco Strong Encryption Software** under Export Licensing Controls.

In this example, the operating system the author is working with is Windows 2000 Professional, so the image selected is vpnclient-win-msi-4.0.5.C-k9.exe; this might vary depending on your platform and operating system.

Step 7 Click **Yes** on the screen that verifies legal export restrictions and enter appropriate responses to reflect your VPN deployment.

Caution	The VPN client includes strong cryptography and thus is export-restricted. If you are downloading this software from a country that is not approved for VPN usage, do not click Yes on this page and terminate your installation immediately. Not doing so constitutes a violation of United States export laws.

Step 8 Click the **VPN Client Image** link.

Step 9 Enter your CCO username and password.

Step 10 Save the image to your hard drive.

You have finished with your browser and can close it if you want.

Step 11 Click the **VPN Client Installation** image.

Step 12 Create a folder on your desktop called **VPN**.

Step 13 Unzip the VPN client file into the VPN folder.

Step 14 Click **vpnclient_setup.exe** to install the VPN client.

Step 15 Click **Next** on the Welcome screen.

Step 16 Read the license agreement; if you agree, accept it and click **Next**.

Step 17 Either choose the default to install VPN in the program files directory or browse to the appropriate direct and click **Next**.

Step 18 Click **Next** at the Ready to Install prompt to start the unpacking, copying, and installing of the VPN client.

Step 19 Click **Finish** when the installation has completed; a reboot is also required for the changes to take effect.

After your system has rebooted, the VPN client is ready for configuration. First, however, you must enable the ASA/PIX Security Appliance to configure VPN connectivity.

Configure VPN on the ASA/PIX Security Appliance

Now that you have a VPN client installed on a PC, you can enable VPN service on the ASA/PIX Security Appliance.

In this example, you terminate the VPN tunnel on the outside of the ASA/PIX Security Appliance. In this case, because you have only two services (web and mail), both on the demilitarized zone (DMZ), you simply verify that VPN is working by logging on to the security appliance using the VPN client and then pinging a client on the inside interface of the ASA/PIX Security Appliance.

NOTE   You cannot ping the inside interface of the ASA/PIX Security Appliance itself from a VPN client.

Doing so successfully proves that the tunnel is working because the 192.168.1.0 network is a private address, and the ping will never succeed unless VPN has connected the VPN client as an inside user of the ASA/PIX Security Appliance:

Step 1 To start, choose **VPN Wizard** from the Wizards pull-down menu.

Step 2 You will be presented with two options, one option to connect another ASA/PIX Security Appliance or router to the VPN network and a second option to connect a remote VPN client. For this example, choose the option to connect to remote-access VPN. (See Figure 11-2.) Click **Next**.

Figure 11-2 *VPN Tunnel Type*

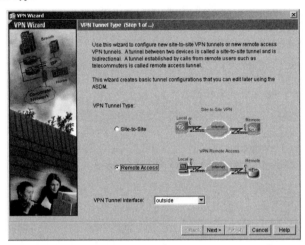

Step 3 Click the **Remote Access** option button. Doing so tells the security
appliance that you are creating a configuration for the type of VPN client
you installed on your computer. Then click **Next**.

Figure 11-3 *VPN Remote Client Type*

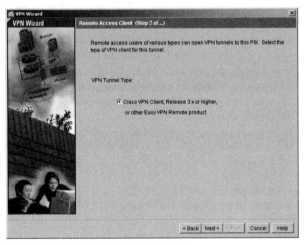

Step 4 You can enter any name you want for the tunnel group. For this example,
enter **vpntunnelgroup**. You will also be entering many of the values from
the next screens in the properties of your VPN client in the next section.

Step 5 You need to enter a preshared key for the client to authenticate the ASA/
PIX Security Appliance. Again, you need to think security best practices
and use a hard-to-guess preshared key. For this example, use the value
Qwert1234.

Step 6 You could enter a certificate here if you plan to deploy certificates in your VPN network. For more information regarding certificates, go to the technical documentation on the Cisco website at http://www.cisco.com/go/pix.

Your entries should look like those in Figure 11-4. Click **Next**.

Figure 11-4 *VPN Wizard Group Authentication*

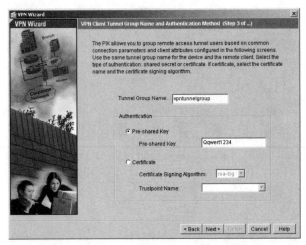

Step 7 Because in this example you use the local authentication, you need to click the **Authenticate Using the Local Authentication Database** option button, and then click **Next**. If you have an AAA server, you could elect to the use it instead for authentication. (See Figure 11-5.)

Figure 11-5 *VPN Local Authentication*

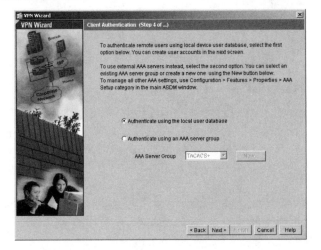

Step 8   You now need to add a user who can use the VPN client to authenticate
to the ASA/PIX Security Appliance. Enter **remote1** for the username and
qwert1234 for the password. ASDM requires you to enter this password
twice to verify that your entry is correct.

Step 9   Click **Add** to put the user into the local database.

Your screen should look like Figure 11-6.

Figure 11-6 *VPN User Information*

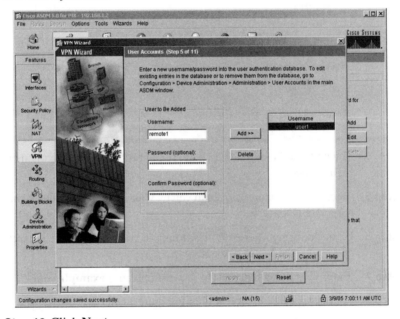

Step 10 Click **Next**.

You now need to define addresses that you are going to assign to the VPN users. Because you
want outside users to be part of the inside of your network, you must use the same subnet
you've been using for inside addresses. The valid range of private addresses on your inside
is 192.168.1.1 through 192.168.1.254. You already used part of this address range for
DHCP and inside interfaces. DHCP is using 192.168.1.100 through 192.168.1.200, and the
inside interface is 192.168.1.1. Also, you might want to have some addresses fixed so that
you can run ASDM; therefore, assume that the addresses 192.169.1.2 through 192.168.1.10
are also used. Use the range 192.168.1.50 through 192.168.99 for the addresses to be
allocated to VPN clients:

Step 1   Enter a pool name; call it **vpnpool**.

Step 2   Enter your starting address as **192.168.1.50** and the ending address as
192.168.1.99.

Step 3   Enter a subnet mask of **255.255.255.0**.

Step 4 Your entries should look like Figure 11-7. Click **Next**.

Figure 11-7 *VPN Address Allocation*

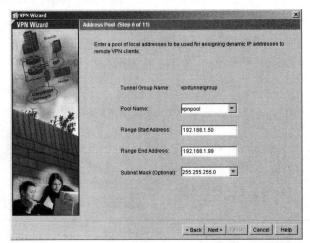

You will now be presented with the Client Attributes screen (as shown in Figure 11-8).

Step 5 Enter the DNS address given to you by your ISP or the IP address of your corporate DNS server.

Step 6 If you are using Microsoft networking in your deployment, enter the IP address for the WINS servers.

Step 7 Enter your domain name. (In this example, use **example.com**.)

Step 8 Your entries should look similar to Figure 11-8. Click **Next**.

Figure 11-8 *VPN Client Attributes*

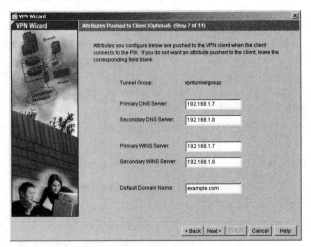

Now you are ready to enter VPN parameters.

Step 9 The first VPN screen defines how public keys (IKE) will be exchanged with your VPN client. Keys must be encrypted to mitigate possible man-in-the-middle attacks against your data. The data must also be authenticated, and you must choose a method for this encryption and authentication.

The defaults on this panel are more than adequate to provide security for a client key exchange.

Step 10 Accept the defaults by clicking **Next**.

The second VPN screen defines how encrypted data (IPSec) will be exchanged with your VPN client. Data must be encrypted to mitigate possible man-in-the-middle attacks. The data may also be authenticated to ensure that it was sourced from the VPN client and not an attacker who might have successfully launched a man-in-the-middle attack against your VPN session.

Step 11 Use 3DES as the default encryption method and use SHA as the data authentication method.

Your screen should look like Figure 11-9.

Figure 11-9 *IPSec Attributes*

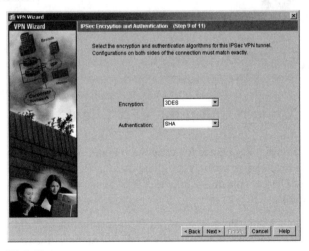

Step 12 Click **Next**.

Step 13 In the next panel, you can narrow down which addresses the VPN client can see when logged on to the ASA/PIX Security Appliance. Accept the default, which allows the VPN client to see all resources.

To find out more about filtering resources and split tunneling, again refer to Cisco.com at http://www.cisco.com/go/pix.

Step 14 Click **Next**.

Step 15 The VPN Summary panel now displays. (See Figure 11-10.) Review your entries. If you see that you made an error, use the **Back** button to go back and make corrections to your configuration. If you accept the configuration as is, click **Finish** to end the wizard.

Figure 11-10 *VPN Summary Panel*

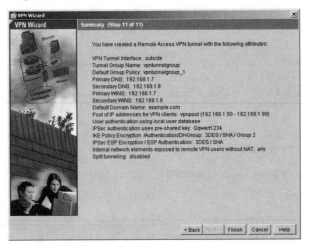

You are now ready to configure your VPN client and then log on to your ASA/PIX Security Appliance VPN.

Configure and Connect Using the VPN Client

Now that you have installed the Cisco VPN client on your PC and configured the ASA/PIX Security Appliance to accept an inbound VPN tunnel on the outside interface, you are ready to configure the VPN client on your PC and log in to the ASA/PIX Security Appliance. These steps are specific to VPN Client 4.0(5), but they should be similar in future versions:

Step 1 Launch the VPN client on your PC by navigating to **Start > Programs > Cisco Systems VPN Client > VPN Client**. Now, the first thing that you need to do is to create a connection called **ClientTest**.

Step 2 Click the **Connection Entries** pull-down and choose **New**.

Step 3 Enter a descriptive connection entry: **Remote VPN Connection**.

Step 4   Enter the outside IP address of the ASA/PIX Security Appliance of the
Host box: **199.199.199.199**.

Step 5   Click the **Authentication** tab. Enter the VPN group from your ASA/PIX
Security Appliance configuration, **vpntunnelgroup**, as the group
authentication name.

Step 6   Enter the group password you configured on the ASA/PIX Security
Appliance: **qwert1234**. Enter this twice; the second time is for
confirmation. Your entries should be similar to Figure 11-11.

Figure 11-11   *VPN Client Setup*

Step 7   Click **Save** to save the information permanently to the VPN client
properties.

Now, you need to test your VPN and verify your VPN connectivity.

Step 8   Highlight the connection you just created in your VPN client called
Remote VPN Connection and click the **Connect** icon on the
navigation bar.

Step 9   The Username and Password screen shown in Figure 11-12 displays.
Enter the credentials you created for your VPN user. The username was
remote1; the password was **qwert1234**.

Figure 11-12   *VPN Logon*

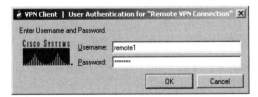

Step 10 Click **OK**.

Step 11 To verify that you have logged on to your ASA/PIX Security Appliance, double-click the **VPN client** toolbar icon. It redisplays your VPN client application.

Step 12 Click the pull-down **Status/Statistics**. You should see that the address allocated to your client is 192.168.1.50, which is the first address from the VPN client pool. (See Figure 11-13.)

Figure 11-13 *VPN Statistics*

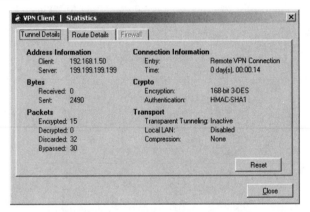

Step 13 Ping a client on the inside of the ASA/PIX Security Appliance from the Windows DOS command line of the VPN client to ensure that your connection is completed.

If you don't have a client to ping, the easiest way is to connect a separate PC in DHCP mode to the switch connecting to the inside ASA/PIX Security Appliance interface. This client will get a DHCP address of 192.168.1.100. You can then ping 192.168.1.100.

CAUTION The inside interface of the security appliance is not pingable from a VPN client.

Using the VPN Client with NAT

If a remote ISP uses network address translation (NAT) to allow connections to the Internet, this scenario will break IPSec-encrypted VPN connections.

VPN and NAT can be a tricky combination. VPN is dependent on addresses not changing. Therefore, special features are built in to the ASA/PIX Security Appliance to ensure that VPN will work if NAT is being used on the client side of the network. Take this warning seriously; it is a common scenario.

To find out whether NAT is broken, bring up the **Status > Statistics** screen on the VPN client. Do a ping to any address. If you see that the Received or Sent Packets designation is zero, you have a NAT problem, and you should take the steps outlined here to enable VPN functionality with NAT.

Configuring the ASA/PIX Security Appliance to Allow NAT for VPN

In many cases, ISPs are using NATed addresses so that they can preserve the number of IP addresses they are using. Because of the way IPSec uses addresses in envelopes and the way NAT changes those address in the middle of your connection, you need complete special configurations before these users can access your network. Follow the steps here to allow NATed VPN connectivity to your network.

On the VPN client, you make a duplicate of the existing connection and then add NAT functionality to that entry. To do so, follow these steps:

Step 1   Launch the VPN client.

Step 2   Right-click the connection you already created called **Remote VPN Connection** and choose **Duplicate**.

Step 3   Right-click the duplicate connection and choose **Modify**.

Step 4   Change the name to **Remote VPN Connection - NAT**.

Step 5   Click the **Transport** tab, and then click the **IPSec over UDP** option button. (See Figure 11-14.)

Figure 11-14   *VPN NAT Connection*

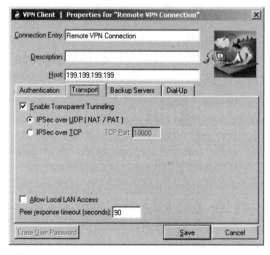

Step 6   Click **Save**.

Monitoring VPN Usage with ASDM

You can monitor the VPN client connections from three different sources:

- VPN Client | Statistics panel
- Monitor VPN statistics from ASDM
- Graph VPN statistics from ASDM

VPN Client | Statistics Panel

To view VPN statistics of a VPN client from the PC, follow these steps:

Step 1   Ensure that the client has established a VPN tunnel to the ASA/PIX
Security Appliance.

Step 2   Click the **VPN client** on the PC's toolbar.

Step 3   Choose **Statistics** from the Status pull-down menu.

This displays the panel shown in Figure 11-13.

This panel displays the IP addresses of your client, packets in and out, connect information,
and encryption protocol information.

Monitor VPN Statistics from ASDM

To view the VPN tunnel information from the ASA/PIX Security Appliance, you need to
view two ASDM sections:

- Monitor VPN Statistics
- Monitor VPN Connection Graphs

The first option, Monitor VPN Statistics, is the more powerful of the two. For all tunnels
terminating on the ASA/PIX Security Appliance, you can view the following:

- Username of the connection
- Tunnel group name of the connection
- IP address information
- Protocol encryption information
- Login time duration

By clicking **Details**, you can see the same information just mentioned as well as the
following:

- Bytes in and bytes out
- Full session information, including IKE parameters and ports used

- Access lists applied to the sessions
- IKE and IPSec parameters

In addition to showing VPN statistics, the VPN Sessions panel enables you to perform some management of the VPN sessions. Various buttons on this panel enable you to control the VPN connections, as follows:

- Log out a VPN tunnel
- Ping a client with an established tunnel
- Log out a tunnel by username, IP address, tunnel group, or protocol

Figure 11-15 show the Sessions Panel.

Figure 11-15 *VPN Statistics Session Panel*

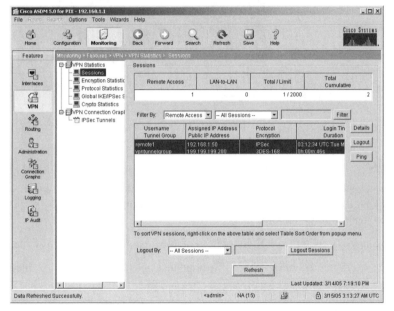

You can graph VPN tunnel statistics by navigating to **Monitor > Features > VPN > VPN Statistics > IPSec Tunnels**.

Step 1   Click the two entries in the Graph panel, **IPSec Active Tunnels** and **IKE Active Tunnels**.

Step 2   Click **Add**.

Step 3   Click **Show Graphs**.

This view shows you the number of active tunnels and is updated every 10 seconds. (See Figure 11-16.)

Figure 11-16 *VPN Session Graph Panel*

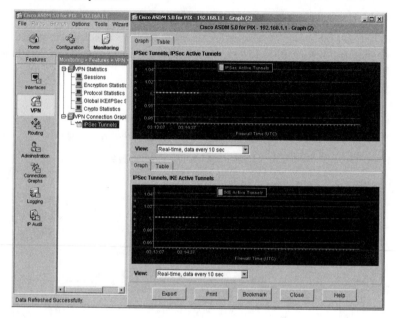

Summary

This chapter explained how to deploy IPsec VPNs on the security appliance and how to monitor those sessions. It included client configuration as well as ASA/PIX Security Appliance configuration using ASDM.

You have now completed all the steps to deploy defense in depth in your network. You have

- Configured your initial security appliance and connected it to the Internet (Chapter 5).
- Added a web and a mail server (Chapter 6).
- Deployed authentication to the ASA/PIX Security Appliance and authenticated connections to web services (Chapter 7).
- Deployed perimeter protection (Chapter 8).
- Deployed intrusion detection (Chapter 9).
- Deployed host intrusion prevention (Chapter 10).

In this chapter, you deployed VPN on your ASA/PIX Security Appliance. VPN enables employees and partners to work remotely and have complete secure access to your internal network. VPNs have the following security attributes:

- User sessions are authenticated with usernames and passwords.
- Tunnels are authenticated with secret preshared keys.

- Data is encrypted so that it cannot be sniffed off of the network.
- Data is authenticated using a private key so that you know the data came from the trusted client that authenticated on your network.
- Networking dialup costs are reduced because your remote users can dial local ISPs to connect with VPN, reducing long-distance and toll-charged phone costs.

You used ASDM to configured VPN tunnels and to monitor and control the tunnels.

VPN monitor statistics gave you all the information the ASA/PIX Security Appliance has about VPN tunnels, including the following:

- Number of tunnels
- Username of the connection
- Tunnel group name of the connection
- IP address information
- Protocol encryption information
- Login time duration
- Bytes in and bytes out
- Full session information, including IKE parameters and ports used
- Access lists applied to the sessions
- IKE and IPSec parameters

In additional to viewing statistics, the monitor control panel also conveniently gives you substantial control over your VPN tunnels. It enables you to

- Log out a VPN tunnel.
- Ping a client with an established tunnel.
- Log out a tunnel by username, IP address, tunnel group, or protocol.

PART III

Appendixes

This appendix provides a short summary of security best practices for you to use when deploying the ASA/PIX Security Appliance in your network.

This appendix addresses the following topics:

- **Layer 2 Best Practices**—Guidelines on how to mitigate network sniffing and other Layer 2 attacks in your network.
- **Authentication Best Practices**—Guidelines on how to strengthen you authentication profile.
- **Perimeter Best Practices**—Guidelines on how to apply access rules in your network.
- **Intrusion Prevention Best Practices**—Guidelines on applying intrusion prevention software.
- **Host Intrusion Prevention Best Practices**—Guidelines on effective management of host intrusion prevention.
- **VPN Best Practices**—Guidelines for strengthening your VPN deployment.
- **Event Logging Best Practices**—Guidelines on how to deploy event logging in your network.

Deploying Effective Security Management

Congratulations! If you have followed the steps outlined in this book, the layers of defense in depth should be effectively deployed.

This appendix highlights some of the best practices that have been discussed in previous chapters as well as some additional best practices that you can implement to improve the security posture of your network. Many of the concepts presented in this appendix are covered in detail in the white paper titled "SAFE: A Security Blueprint for Enterprise Networks" located on the Cisco website at http://www.cisco.com/go/safe.

This appendix is a summary by design. The hope is that you can go directly to any topic and immediately find best practice information for any security technology addressed in the previous chapters.

Layer 2 Best Practices

Layer 2 (network switching) is beyond of the scope of this book and, therefore, has not been addressed in great detail. However, it is very important to the deployment of your network from both an architectural and a security standpoint.

From a physical standpoint, Layer 2 is generally implemented by a network switch. Switches are used to connect devices on the network. For example, on the inside of your network, you might have 20 PCs. To connect those PCs to each other and then to the Internet, you need to plug them into a switch. The switch is the glue that connects all the network wire.

From a security standpoint, a switch should keep each device on the network from seeing data going to or from another device. By default, switches do just that—they prevent one device from seeing the packets destined for another device. Unfortunately, switches might be misconfigured or compromised by a Layer 2 attack. If a switch is misconfigured, it could allow traffic for one or all PCs to be seen by other systems on the network.

You might be asking yourself how a hacker can gain access to your inside network to compromise a Layer 2 switch with all of this security that you put in place. The answer is simple. A hacker could be

- Someone in your company already on the network
- A trusted vendor

- Someone who walked into your office posing as a vendor
- Someone who bypassed your physical security and plugged into your network
- A hacker who compromised any inside host in your network by using a directed attack, a worm, a Trojan, or a web or e-mail virus

If your switch is compromised, a hacker could easily see all the data that goes across your network, including the following:

- Confidential e-mail
- Usernames and passwords
- Device configurations
- Customer data
- Database queries on web data
- Chat data
- Employee data
- Company patents or confidential projects
- Financial information

Essentially, a hacker can "own" your network and own your corporate and customer information if Layer 2 is compromised.

You need to ensure that all Layer 2 devices on your network are locked down. It is recommended that you read the document titled "SAFE:L2 Application Note" located at http://www.cisco.com/go/safe. If you follow these best practices, you will ensure that the security posture of your switches is such that a hacker would have a difficult time getting access.

Authentication Best Practices

The method used for authentication in this book is local security appliance database authentication, which is an excellent way to demonstrate the configuration capabilities of ASDM and the ASA/PIX Security Appliance. Chapter 7, "Deploying Authentication," mentioned several times that there are some advantages to authenticating with a AAA server. The Cisco AAA server is called Cisco Access Control Server (or Cisco ACS).

AAA offers not only authentication, but also authorization and accounting. Authentication validates username and password credentials before allowing user, and sometimes device, access. Authorization is the control of what users can do after they have been authenticated to a device. Accounting keeps track of how long a person has been logged on to a device and, if authorization is being used, can even track what a user did while he had access to the device. These functions can prove helpful if you need to track changes on devices in your networks.

One topic that wasn't discussed is one-time password authentication (OTP), which is available via AAA. OTP allows a user to log on to a device only once per password. Under this technology, passwords are tokens that are generated via token cards or token software that runs on a PC. This password method is among the best because it doesn't matter whether a password is sniffed on the network; it's only good for one attempt in 30 or 60 seconds, depending on the token vendor.

The other thing mentioned several times in this book is the format for usernames and passwords. It's very important to use hard-to-guess usernames and passwords. Several "excellent" freeware password-cracking tools are available on the Internet. These tools usually start guessing usernames and passwords using words from dictionaries and then going into sequential algorithms. If someone gains a copy of your Microsoft password database or your UNIX or Linux password file, he will usually run these files through his password crackers and be able to obtain several passwords in a matter of hours if best practice naming has not been followed. Therefore, you should always use passwords (and usernames if you can do it) that have a combination of the following attributes:

- At least eight characters (ten preferably)
- Uppercase characters
- Lowercase characters
- Numerals
- Special characters

By following these guidelines, you exponentially increase the amount of time it takes a password cracker to decode your passwords.

Another thing you want to do with passwords is change them often. This is a policy decision for each administrator. Changing passwords frequently, such as once every 60 days, is a good policy.

AAA is also capable of expiring passwords at user-defined intervals and enforcing policy such as password length so that users cannot choose the length of their own password.

A best practice that many administrators are using is running their own password crackers against their password databases and notifying users if their password is easily guessed.

An effective way to mitigate brute-force or dictionary password attacks is to enforce password lockouts, which disable (or lock an account) after five failed attempts.

Perimeter Best Practices

The three golden rules for defining access rules on your firewall are as follows: Enforce a restrictive policy, only allow traffic "required" for your company to run, and deny all other traffic. If you are being asked to allow new traffic through your firewall, err on the side of caution. Deny the request until you do research and understand the potential security impact of allowing the request.

This rule is enforced by default in the ASA/PIX Security Appliance. It comes configured to not let any traffic in from the outside, except as a response to traffic that has been requested from the inside. When you generate access lists, if the requirement is to have web traffic to a web server, make sure you write your access list that way. In other words, only allow traffic to the IP address of the web server and don't allow HTTP traffic in to your entire network.

Look closely at customer access service policy rules that you can deploy. The functionality given to you by ASDM and the ASA/PIX Security Appliance to deploy your own service policies rules is powerful. Look at them often and get an understanding for how they might be able to increase the security posture of your network. For example, you might notice that an Internet vulnerability has just come out that exploits your FTP server but a patch is not ready. The vulnerability uses the FTP command **APPE** to append a Trojan to a system file. You could easily go into the ASDM Service Policy panel and write a policy that drops packets that contain the FTP **APPE** command. If you ever need help or advice on deploying policies such as these, contact the Cisco Technical Assistance Center or your local Cisco sales team. They have security engineers available 24/7 to help with any type of question.

There was no discussion in this book about using the ASA/PIX Security Appliance without network address translation (NAT). This is possible now with ASA/PIX version 7, but it is not generally recommended. NAT keeps hackers from seeing real inside addresses on your network, and the less a hacker knows about your network, the higher security posture you maintain.

Vulnerability scanning is another good way to help ensure that you have the strongest possible security posture. A vulnerability scan is easily accomplished for free by running a program such as Nessus (http://www.nessus.org) to scan the outside of your firewall. It will report to you all the ports that are open in your firewall and all the possible vulnerabilities associated with those ports. From the output of this report, you can make sure that you have all application patches and hot fixes current on your systems. It can also tell you whether you have ports open on your firewall that you didn't know about.

You should run vulnerability scans at least once a month on your network. However, on top of that, you should also have a professional security organization come in at least once every year or once every two years and do what's called a *security posture analysis* on your system. This is an in-depth scan that you can't actually do with off-the-shelf products. The Cisco Security Posture Assessment (SPA) team has found that upward of 60 percent of all networks have vulnerabilities that can be exploited from the Internet and more than 90 percent of networks can be exploited if a hacker makes his way to the inside.

Intrusion Prevention Best Practices

The best practices for deploying intrusion prevention in this environment are limited. The inspection point is at the perimeter of the network, and the ASA/PIX Security Appliance has 51 signatures to protect you. These signatures are narrowed down to the attacks that are still common on the Internet and are easily recognizable by the firewall.

The ASA 5500 family of security appliances can run the full IPS 5.0 operating system, which by default contains more than 1500 signatures and also provides protocol misuse protection.

The reports from these attacks could become very handy for you at some point. Many administrators use these reports to justify to their management that security threats are real and that attacks are launched against your network all the time. As a result, these reports can be used, if necessary, as a tool to justify return on investment to purchase a full-blown intrusion prevention system that has several hundred signatures and can be more effective at mitigating network and host attacks.

If you want to learn more about IPS and IPS best practices, read the white paper titled "SAFE: IDS Deployment, Tuning, and Logging in Depth," located on the Cisco SAFE web page. This page is specifically for larger intrusion detection system deployment, but it does contain a lot of information that might prove helpful if you need to learn more about IPS deployment.

Host Intrusion Prevention Best Practices

As stated in Chapter 10, "Deploying Host Intrusion Prevention," host intrusion prevention (CSA) is the last line of defense in a computer attack. The perimeter can do everything it's designed to do, and do it correctly, but there are still day-zero attacks that use valid traffic that can exploit your hosts and servers. Therefore, host intrusion prevention should be viewed as equally important as perimeter security devices.

Remember that host intrusion prevention might stop processes and programs that are acting badly. Therefore, be sure that you have given CSA a chance to tell the difference between good and bad device behavior. Therefore, it is important to deploy CSA correctly. You *must* put your applications in a lab with CSA and run them in Test mode before rolling CSA into production. It's even a good idea to continue running CSA in Test mode for a few weeks in production to ensure that you don't run into any unforeseen problems. After you have completed these steps, CSA should effectively stop any computer attack it encounters.

VPN Best Practices

VPN is quite self-explanatory as it relates to the security appliance deployment in Chapter 11, "Deploying VPNs." You could address a few minor points to increase your security posture.

Clients that come in as VPN connections should be a great concern for you as an administrator. These clients have generally been in many insecure environments that attract viruses, worms, Trojans, adware, and spyware. An average PC, connected to a large Internet service provider (ISP) without a firewall or host intrusion prevention, will likely be infected in less then 30 minutes.

Here's a list of environments where malicious code is easily picked up, many times without any indication to the user:

- Home PC with the kids downloading games
- Home PC with no perimeter protection
- Home PC with no firewall protection
- Home PC with outdated or no antivirus protection
- Home PC with everyday browsing
- Laptop in wireless hotspots such as airports, coffee shops, and Internet cafés

Almost every VPN client that logs on to your firewall will fall into one, some, or all these categories. Each category is dangerous from a security perspective. The bottom line is that VPN clients need to be looked at as insecure machines, not because the users can't be trusted but rather because they have been exposed to many different Internet dangers. A best practice that should be taken seriously is to ensure that these PCs have a policy enforced that says they *cannot* log on to a system unless they are running a personal firewall and host intrusion prevention software. This is referred to as "are you there" (AYT) functionality. The Cisco VPN client can currently enforce firewall AYT policy and, in early 2005, will support AYT functionality for the Cisco Security Agent. It is in your best interest to deploy this technology to protect your company and its network assets.

NOTE   AYT technology ensures that the security posture of a PC is adequate before letting the PC on your network. Another technology that enforces this technology and is cost free (if you have Cisco networking gear) is called *Network Admission Control* (NAC). To find out more about NAC, refer to http://www.cisco.com/go/nac.

You also need to keep careful control over VPN secret keys. Visualize the scenario in which you give the same secret key to every employee in the company for VPN access and one of the employees gets fired. Of course, the first thing you do is take the fired employee's username and password out of the database. However, because the ex-employee's PC still has the secret key, and the viable fact that he probably knows usernames of other people in the company, it might not be too difficult for the ex-employee to use someone else's username and launch a brute-force password attack against your VPN deployment. You can mitigate this risk in a few ways:

- Have a plan and process in place to change and distribute VPN preshared keys at frequent intervals, or change the key when someone is terminated.

- Force frequent password changes.

- Use the feature AAA, which will disable an account after a certain number of log failures.

- Watch your login failure logs. If you find many failures for one user, that might represent a brute-force password attack, and you would want to disable that user and issue a new username to him.

Another best practice to deploy with VPN is keepalives. You can use keepalives to try to determine whether a remote client is still active, and you can use keepalives to tear down a connection if it's determined that the client is no longer active. Keepalives are on by default in the ASA/PIX Security Appliance VPN deployment. You can modify or view the settings by navigating to **Configuration > Features > VPN General > Tunnel Group > IPSec**.

Event Logging Best Practices

Event log management and response might be one of the most neglected areas of security management. Many security managers rely on users or security bulletins from operating system and application vendors to decide when it's time to take action on a possible security compromise. By the time these announcements have hit the Internet, it's usually too late for administrators to react. Assets have already taken a hit, and damage has already been done.

NOTE This fact, by the way, is the number one reason you should have CSA installed on all your systems. Customers who had CSA deployed during all the largest attacks, including Code Red, Nimda, Sasser, and Slammer, suffered no downtime at all.

The problem to be solved in this section is how to become proactive in searching out logs to recognize early signs that your network might be the target of an attack or that an attack might be in progress.

ASA/PIX Security Appliance messages aren't going to be your best source to determine whether your network assets are under attack. CSA logs are the best source for that. It's recommended that, along with CSA, you get a software package called *Event Monitor*. Event Monitor consolidates all your CSA alarms in a hierarchal interface, much like a spreadsheet. All like events are sorted together, and you can expand the event to a detailed level. By using this tool, you can recognize whether a new attack is underway because you will likely see groupings of the same error messages with different destination IP addresses. In most cases, these events give you enough information to understand whether you can do anything to help stop the attack at the perimeter. With new features in CSA 4.5, if the CSA Management Center senses multiple "like" messages, it assumes a worm or mutating virus is in the network and generates a rule to quarantine the infected hosts.

Remember, defense in depth is all about layers of defense.

Here is a simple example of how you could have manually used the CSA logging information to increase your layers of defense when Slammer hit.

CSA protected the hosts and servers by recognizing that a buffer overflow took place in the SQL process and that malicious code was attempting to run from the overflowed buffer. Because SQL uses UDP port 1433, security administrators could have done the following to increase the security posture of their environment:

- Security administrators could have written a custom CSA rule to stop SQL (UDP/1433) traffic on machines that don't rely on UDP 1433.

- Security administrators could have written access rules stopping UDP/1433 traffic on the perimeter.

- If the traffic was coming from a single source, security administrators could have written access rules stopping traffic from that source. CSA 4.5 does this automatically.

ASA/PIX Security Appliance syslogs tend to be more focused on functions of the firewall. The security appliance syslog has seven different severities or classes of syslog messages, as follows:

- Alert messages, Severity 1
- Critical messages, Severity 2
- Error messages, Severity 3
- Warning messages, Severity 4
- Notification messages, Severity 5
- Informational messages, Severity 6
- Debugging messages, Severity 7

Table A-1 classifies ASA/PIX Security Appliance syslog messages and provides a description for each class.

| NOTE | You can find all syslog messages and the proper responses in the ASA/PIX Security Appliance technical documentation at http://www.cisco.com/go/pix or http://www.cisco.com/go/asdm. |

Table A-1   *ASA/PIX Syslog Message Classes*

Message Classes	Description
Alert	These messages indicate that action has been taken by the security appliance to resolve a problem or that action needs to be taken by the administrator because of an interface failure, unit standby failure, or bad cables. An administrator should always follow up on an alert message.
Critical	These messages indicate that traffic has been blocked or dropped, that spoofed traffic has been detected, or that flags are invalid in traffic. An administrator should usually follow up on critical messages.
Error	These error messages are specific to security appliance resources such as xlate failures and translation slot failures. An administrator should always follow up on error messages.
Warning	These messages are generally warnings about connection problems. Many of these problems might be cleared up by the protocols on either end, but an administrator might have to follow up on these warning messages.
Notification	These messages are a mix of notifications of what a security appliance logged-in user is doing on the machine and some messages about Java and ActiveX blocking. An administrator should look at these messages to ensure that unauthorized changes are not being made to the security appliance.
Informational	These messages describe connections being built and torn down through the security appliance. In most cases, these messages don't need to be audited by an administrator unless users report that they are having problems with specific connections or services.
Debugging	These messages are mostly related to IPSec. An administrator uses these messages when bringing up an IPSec tunnel for the first time. For the other debug messages, refer to the Security Appliance technical documentation on the Cisco website.

ASA/PIX Version 7 Advanced Features

ASA/PIX version 7 is a major release of what was previously known as the PIX operating system. ASA is a new class of devices that now share the operating system with the PIX Security Appliance. Several major enhancements add to the functionality of the already robust PIX feature set. Some of the features, such as IPv6, are included to support emerging network implementations. However, most features are to help to increase network security and protect network assets.

To be consistent with the format of this book, the features are listed by how they fit into the defense in depth layers:

- Authentication enhancements
- Perimeter protection enhancements
- Intrusion prevention enhancements
- Security management
- VPN enhancements
- General security appliance enhancements

Authentication Enhancements

The enhancements for authentication have all been in the area of authentication, authorization, and accounting (AAA) support and include the following:

- Simultaneous RADIUS accounting servers
- Authentication and accounting for management

Simultaneous RADIUS Accounting Servers

ASA/PIX version 7 has a new feature that allows you to send RADIUS accounting data to more than one server at a time. This feature ensures that if a RADIUS server does goes down, you still have complete accounting records on the machine that has remained working.

You configure this feature through the ASDM panel, as follows:

Configuration > Features > Properties > AAA Setup > AAA Server Groups > Add

Authentication and Accounting for Management

ASA/PIX version 7 has enhanced its generation of accounting records and its authentication capabilities. The ASA/PIX Security Appliance now reports and authenticates administrative sessions and includes the configuration changes made during those sessions. In addition, accounting records are now generated for console sessions as well as serial connections. Console sessions could include ASDM and web access, whereas serial includes activity from the physical serial console port. Similar records are also generated in syslog.

You configure the feature through the ASDM panel, as follows:

Configuration > Features > Device Administration > Administration > AAA Access > Accounting

Configuration > Features > Device Administration > Administration > AAA Access > Authentication

Perimeter Protection Enhancements

ASA/PIX version 7 offers six new features related to perimeter protection. All of the features are enhancements to access control lists (called *access rules* in ASDM):

- Time-based access rules
- Granular outbound access rules
- Transparent firewall
- Access rules for Ethernet types (used for Layer 2 transparent firewall support)
- Selectively enable and disable control of access rules
- IP fragment re-assembly

Time-Based Enabled Access Control Lists

ASA/PIX version 7 allows you the flexibility to control the time, day, and month that access rules will be enforced. You can use this feature to enforce access such as ensuring that your network can be accessed only during business hours, not after hours or weekends. This enforcement helps to mitigate some attacks because many hackers won't attempt to break into systems during hours they think that administrators might be viewing logs.

You configure this feature through various ASDM panels.

You can first create the time range using the following panel:

Configuration > Features > Security Policy > Building Blocks > Time Ranges

Then apply them to security policies and access rules using the following panels:

Configuration > Features > Security Policy > Access Rules > Edit > Time Range
Configuration > Features > Security Policy > Access Rules > Add > Time Range

Granular Outbound Access Rules

ASA/PIX version 7 now allows more control over access rules by adding functions to control whether the ACLs are applied inbound or outbound on a selected interface.

This feature allows you to contain possible malicious traffic that might be sourced from the inside of your network by unsuspecting users who might have been infected by an e-mail virus or an attack against a vulnerable user application such as a web browser or desktop service.

This feature can be configured through the ASDM panel using either of the following operations:

Configuration > Features > Security Policy > Access Rules > Add
Configuration > Features > Security Policy > Access Rules > Edit

Transparent Firewalls

This new ASA/PIX version 7 feature enables you to create a security appliance that acts like a network bridge and is transparent to the rest of the network. With this feature enabled, the ASA/PIX Security Appliance operates as a Layer 2 device and makes the appliance invisible to hackers who might be running tools to "discover" all your network devices before they begin an attack. This feature is not configurable from ASDM and, therefore, is not covered in this book. Refer to your ASA/PIX version 7 operating system documentation or go to http://www.cisco.com/go/pix for more information.

Access Control Lists Enforcing Ethernet Types

ASA/PIX version 7 now enables you to filter ethertypes that traverse the security appliance. This functionality ensures that only IP traffic framed in the correct ethertype format transverses the security appliance. This function is used to support a new feature called *transparent firewalls* (see previous paragraph) and can be configured using the following ASDM panel:

Configuration > Features > Security Policy > Ethertype Rules

Enabling and Disabling of Access Control Lists

ASA/PIX version 7 now gives you the flexibility to enable or disable access lists with a single click. This flexibility can save you substantial time (for example, when you just need to add a rule to troubleshoot). Allowing ICMP through the security appliance is not something you want to do as a best practice. However, you could configure the rule, leave it disabled, and then, if you need the rule for a few minutes for troubleshooting, you would just go into ASDM and click **Enable**, run your test, and then again disable it immediately.

You configure this feature through the Access Rules panel by clicking the **Enable** check box.

IP Fragment Re-Assembly

ASA/PIX version 7 has new capabilities to recognize and respond to IPv4 and IPv6 fragmented packets. These packets are subject to the same filtering as all security appliance traffic and then put into a queue for fragmentation assembly. If the fragments are valid packets, they are forwarded to their destination. If the assembled packets aren't completed and don't match protocol specifications, it is assumed that they are either erroneous or part of an attack and are subsequently dropped.

This is a significant security feature because attackers try to use fragmentation in many different ways to subvert security appliance security. You will also see this technology referred to as *traffic normalization*.

This feature is turned on by default and can be controlled through the ASDM panel:

Configuration > Features > Properties > Advanced > Fragment

Intrusion Prevention Enhancements

The new service policy rules can actually fall into the category of perimeter protection or intrusion prevention. In the ASA/PIX Security Appliance, intrusion prevention is thought of in two ways:

- **Signature protection**—Protection based on signature matches with an associated action such as drop, alarm, and reset.

- **Application firewall**—Protection based on protocol compliance and optionally user configuration. Protocol compliance stops malicious software that tries to use HTTP as a tunneling protocol to pass other data besides web traffic through your security device. You are also given the option to write your own customer rules to enforce security features such as blocking file attachments and URI size overloading.

The following list displays the network service policy enhancements to ASA/PIX version 7. In many cases, the features are Cisco proprietary and cannot be disclosed. The protocols inspections that aren't Cisco proprietary are described in the following sections:

- ICMP inspection
- HTTP deep packet inspection
- FTP command filtering
- Configurable firewall inspections
- ESMTP command filtering
- H.323 T.38 inspection
- H.323 GKRCS inspection
- TCP pools for URL filtering
- SIP IM support inspection
- GTP inspection
- SunRPC inspection
- MGCP command filtering
- CTIQBE inspection
- Domain Name Services inspection and command filtering
- ILS inspection
- NetBIOS inspection
- Point-to-point Tunneling Protocol inspection
- Remote Shell inspection
- RTSP inspection
- SKINNY inspection
- Simple Network Management Protocol (SNMP) command filtering
- SQLNet inspection
- Trivial File Transfer Protocol inspection
- X-Display Management Protocol inspection

ICMP Inspection

This new feature of ASA/PIX version 7 allows stateful return of ICMP packets. If an ICMP packet request is sourced from the inside network, the ASA/PIX keeps a state (even though ICMP is stateless) and allows the ICMP reply traffic back into the inside network of the ASA/PIX. In previous versions of the ASA/PIX Security Appliance, the reply traffic was blocked unless specifically allowed by an access list.

HTTP Deep Packet Inspection

This feature ensures that HTTP is being used as designed for web access and not malicious applications or intent such as illegal file sharing, spyware, adware, unencrypted instant messaging, URL buffer-overflow attempts, and the tunneling of confidential data.

This new ASA/PIX version 7 enhancement allows very granular filtering based on the content of an HTTP request. ASA/PIX version 7 can decide to drop or report packets depending on how you have configured the filtering option. Those choices include the following:

- Enforce RFC compliancy for HTTP
- Enforce permitted MIME types
- Configure the minimum and maximum size of different fields of the HTTP packet
- Enforce the content type in the response message to be what is configured in the message's Accept Type field
- Filtering of HTTP messages on valid HTTP keywords
- Enforce maximum and minimum header lengths and URLs

You configure all of these features through the ASDM panel, as follows:

Configuration > Features > Security Policies > Service Policy Rules > Add
Configuration > Features > Security Policies > Service Policy Rules > Edit

FTP Command Filtering

This new 344868ASA/PIX version 7 feature allows inspection on FTP protocol commands. The passing of these commands can be allowed or disallowed based on your configurations and requirements. Syslog messages can be generated to notify you if these commands are attempted after you have configured your security appliance to block the commands. This feature helps you to track down users or software with malicious intent.

Configurable Security Appliance Inspections

This ASA/PIX version 7 enhanced feature allows grouping of inspection commands. The group can then subsequently be applied to various rules within the ASA/PIX version 7 operating system.

ESMTP Command Filtering

Previous inspections of SMTP are augmented to support the same Extended Simple Mail Protocol.

TCP Pools for URL Filtering

The ASA/PIX version 7 inspection enhancement controls the reuse of URL filtering requests and improves the overall handling efficiency of URL filtering requests.

SIP IM Inspection

This new ASA/PIX version 7 feature adds inspection support for instant messaging of the RTC client for Windows Messenger v4.7.0105.

SunRPC Inspection

This new ASA/PIX version 7 feature allows you granular control over which RPC services will be allowed through SunRPC-style connections traversing the ASA/PIX Security Appliance.

MGCP Command Filtering

This enhanced ASA/PIX version 7 feature for MGCP provides support of network address translation (NAT) for the existing MGCP inspection. Original source addresses are embedded in the payload of the packet, which might potentially break NAT. This inspection ensures that the appropriate addresses are written to the address headers of these packets.

Domain Name Services Command Filtering

This new ASA/PIX version 7 feature enables you to control certain aspects of the DNS protocol such as the maximum length of a DNS packet so that hackers can't exploit or overflow buffers on DNS servers using malformed or oversized packets.

Simple Network Management Protocol Command Filtering

This new ASA/PIX version 7 feature enables you to configure and control which version of SNMP that you are allowing into your network. This feature helps you to keep attackers from using unauthorized versions of SNMP to exploit your network.

Security Management

Several major enhancements assist you in managing the ASA/PIX version 7 operating system, including the following:

- ASDM 5.0
- Modular policy framework

- Online image updates
- Auto-update
- SSH2
- Multiple boot images and configuration files
- Syslog TCP transport

ASDM 5.0

ASDM 5.0 is a new and fully functional GUI that enables you to control all aspects of configuration and monitoring for the ASA/PIX version 7 operating system. ASDM uses HTTPS encrypted sessions to mitigate chances that a hacker would be able to steal usernames, passwords, or configurations off of the network and enables you to configure virtually all of the new ASA/PIX version 7 operating system enhancements.

Modular Policy Framework

This is a new feature of ASA/PIX version 7, enabling you to create groups of services or classify different aspects of the operating system. The modular policy framework allows individual traffic flows between hosts or networks to be defined, and quality of service (QoS), application inspection, and connection limits can then be applied separately to each flow.

Online Image Upgrades

This new feature enables you to use ASDM to upgrade the ASDM and ASA/PIX version 7 images from the PC that is running ASDM. You can navigate to the images and select the location in Flash memory where the images are to be copied.

You can see this feature by clicking the **Tools** pull-down menu and choosing **Upload Image from Local PC**.

Auto-Update

This new feature was part of the PIX VMS management suite and was ported to ASDM 5.0 and ASA/PIX version 7. It enables you to schedule automatic updates for your ASA/PIX operating system.

The auto-update feature simplifies the process and scheduling of updates to your ASA/PIX security appliances. It enables you to easily select the images to be updated and to schedule the dates and times that the update will occur.

You can see this feature in ASDM by navigating to the following panel:

Configuration > Features > Properties > Auto Update

SSH2

This is a new feature of ASA/PIX version 7 that enables you to manage your ASA/PIX Security Appliance in CLI mode with a secure encrypted command-line utility. There were many vulnerabilities with SSH1. SSH2 addresses those problems, resulting in a much more secure management environment.

You can see this feature in ASDM by navigating to the following panel:

> **Configuration > Features > Device Administration > Administration > Secure Shell**

Multiple Boot Images

This new feature of ASA/PIX version 7 enables you to select the priority and specify up to four operating system images to boot from Flash memory or a TFTP server.

You can see this feature in ASDM by navigating to the following panel:

> **Configuration > Features > Device Administration > Administration > bootimage_config**

SYSLOG TCP Transport

This new ASA/PIX version 7 feature supports the sending of syslog messages using TCP messages that keep track of connection state and provide a reliable transport mechanism. The ASA/PIX Security Appliance keeps trying to send messages if the TCP syslog server becomes unavailable. This ensures that syslog messages are not lost.

You can see this feature in ASDM by navigating to the following panel:

> **Configuration > Features > Properties > Logging > Syslog Servers**

Then, choose the **Add** or **Edit** dialog boxes.

VPN Enhancements

VPN enhancements for ASA/PIX version 7 include the following, in summary:

- Filter clients by operating system and version
- IKE DoS protection
- Client-friendly reboot
- Same interface packet turnaround (a.k.a. traffic U-turn on an interface)
- "Are you there" functionality for popular personal firewalls and CSA

Filter Clients by OS

This new ASA/PIX version 7 enhancement enables you to limit the clients that can connect to your system by operating system and version, which means you can ensure that clients connecting to you network have security patches in place to satisfy your host security policy.

You can see this feature in ASDM by navigating to the following panel:

> **Configuration > Features > VPN > Group Policy > Add/Edit > IPSec > Client Access Rules**

IKE DoS Protection

This feature disables the sending of SCSI Parallel Interface (SPI) messages in the clear, reducing the possibility that these messages can be intercepted and used as a denial-of-service (DoS) attack against the security appliance.

Client-Friendly Reboot

This new ASA/PIX version 7 feature waits until all VPN clients have terminated before rebooting the ASA/PIX.

You can see this feature in ASDM by navigating to the following panel:

> **Configuration > Features > VPN > IKE > Global Parameters**

Same Interface Packet Turnaround

This new ASA/PIX version 7 feature allows VPN clients terminating on the same interface to talk to each other, essentially creating hub-and-spoke secure client communication.

Previous operating systems versions would not let you reroute VPN traffic out the same interface. This resulted in you needing to have another device on the inside of your security appliance and required complex configuration and rerouting back to the outside of your network. With this new feature, this is handled automatically for you.

You can see this feature in ASDM by navigating to the following panel:

> **Configuration > Features > VPN > General > VPN System Options**

"Are You There" Functionality for Popular Firewalls and CSA

This new ASA/PIX version 7 feature enables you to configure the security appliance to require that a client connecting via a VPN tunnel must have certain security software installed before connectivity is established. This requirement is especially critical for VPN clients because they are coming into your network from the outside where they can easily pick up worms, viruses, and other malicious software.

General Security Appliance Enhancements

- Same security level communications
- No NAT functionality
- VPN stateful failover
- Interoperability with IOS CA server
- Asymmetric routing
- OSPF neighbor
- PIM-Sparse mode
- Ping enhancements
- 4096-bit RSA Key support
- Policing
- Logging enhancements
- Virtual firewall support

Details for these general new features and enhancements are defined in the sections that follow.

Same Security Level Communications

This new ASA/PIX version 7 feature enables you to set more than one interface to the same security level. This enables two-way traffic flow between these interfaces, similar to a router.

You configure this feature at the following ASDM panel:

Configuration > Features > Interfaces

No NAT Functionality

This new ASA/PIX version 7 feature eliminates the requirement that NAT must be configured for traffic to traverse the security appliance.

You can see this feature in ASDM by navigating to the following panel:

Configuration > Features > NAT

VPN Stateful Failover

This new ASA/PIX version 7 allows VPN state to be updated between the active and the secondary failover ASA/PIX. If the primary ASA/PIX goes down, VPN sessions continue uninterrupted because the state has been maintained between the two failover boxes.

You can see this feature in ASDM by navigating to the following panel:

> **Configuration > Features > Properties > Failover**

Interoperability with IOS CA Server

This new ASA/PIX version 7 feature allows the ASA/PIX Security Appliance to generate and receive certificate requests for the Cisco IOS CERT server.

Asymmetric Routing

This new ASA/PIX version 7 features enables stateful asymmetric routing during failover. It is used only with active/active failover, which is not included in ASDM and not covered in this book.

OSPF Neighbor

This new ASA/PIX version 7 feature allows the recognition of Open Shortest Path First (OSPF) neighbors across a VPN tunnel. Some caveats apply: The OSPF neighbor can be only one hop away and neighbors must belong to the same subnet.

PIM-Sparse Mode

The new ASA/PIX version 7 feature allows an ASA/PIX version 7 PIM-Sparse mode to scale through the ASA/PIX Security Appliance.

Ping Enhancements

The new ASA/PIX version 7 feature adds arguments to the **ping** command, enabling you to use ping extended options that have also been deployed in Cisco IOS 12.3. This includes, in alphabetic order, the following:

- Data pattern
- Datagram size
- DF bit

- Repeat count
- Timeout interval
- Verbose output
- Sweep range of sizes

4096-Bit RSA Key Support

This new ASA/PIX version 7 feature allows support for 4k-bit RSA keys.

Policing

This new ASA/PIX version 7 feature supports two queues for QoS support:

- Low latency queue (LLQ)
- Best effort queue

QoS enables you to define which traffic will have precedence as it traverses the security appliance. For example, you might want your IP telephony traffic to be processed before your web browsing traffic, resulting in clear voice communication.

You configure QoS from the ASDM panel, as follows:

> **Configuration > Service > Service Policy**

Logging

This ASA/PIX version 7 enhancement includes legacy support for syslog formats used in previous ASA/PIX versions. It also includes support for the new syslog format called EMBLEM.

You configure syslog from the following ASDM panels:

> **Configuration > Features > Properties > Logging > Logging Setup**
> **Monitoring > Logging > Live Log**

Virtual Firewall Support

This ASA/PIX version 7 enhancement provides you with the features to support several different security appliance contexts within a single ASA/PIX Security Appliance. This provides businesses an easy way to consolidate multiple security appliances into a single physical appliance.

ASA/PIX Version 7 and ASDM Software Recovery

In the unlikely event that the ASA/PIX Security Appliance will no longer boot because of hardware or software malfunction, you can take certain steps to easily reinstall the software on your security appliance.

If these procedures don't work for some reason, you should immediately contact the Cisco Technical Assistance Center for help in the recovery process. Refer to the Cisco website at http://www.cisco.com/go/support.

You need to do four things before you can reinstall the ASA/PIX version 7 operating system:

Step 1 Download the ASA/PIX version 7 operating system and ASDM software from Cisco.com.

Step 2 Prepare your PC for the version 7 upgrade. Install a TFTP server on your PC and configure your PC so that you can recover the ASA/PIX operating system.

Step 3 Download ASA/PIX version 7 to your security appliance.

Step 4 Download ASDM to your security appliance.

Obtaining the ASA/PIX Version 7 and ASDM Software

To obtain a version of the ASA/PIX version 7 operating system, follow these steps:

Step 1 Log on to Cisco.com using a valid username and password.

Step 2 Navigate to Technical Support and then Downloads.

Step 3 When you are on the download pages, navigate to Cisco Secure Software and then Cisco Secure PIX Firewall Software.

Note   Occasionally, Cisco changes the look of its website, so these steps might vary depending on when you download the software.

Step 4 Proceed to the location marked Download PIX Firewall Software. On this page, you see the binary image for the PIX version 7 operating system.

Step 5 Click the image name. You will be prompted to open or save the image. Click **Save** and put the images in a safe location on your PC; the file will later be transferred to the home directory of your TFTP server. If you have a TFTP server on your system already, you can save the PIX file directly into the home directory of the TFTP server. Carefully read and adhere to the warnings and restrictions that refer to federal law and shipping secure software to restricted countries.

Step 6 Repeat this procedure for the ASDM software.

Prepare Your PC for an ASA/PIX Upgrade

To recover your ASA/PIX Security Appliance with version 7, you must have a PC with a TFTP server, and you must configure you network interface card to allow connectivity to the security appliance.

You can install any number of free TFTP servers from the Internet on your PC. Any implementation of TFTP should work for this download.

NOTE Your PC can be either a Windows- or Linux-based machine. For this book, Windows was used as the primary operating system so that is what the examples show.

Before you can transfer the software from your PC to the ASA/PIX Security Appliance, you must establish a network connection between the two. This connection requires configuration on the PC as well as configuration on the appliance.

If you already know how to do this procedure of connecting the two machines, use the following steps only as a reference. If you have no experience in doing this, however, you can follow the instructions step by step and to move the file from the TFTP server to the ASA/PIX Security Appliance:

Step 1 Install the TFTP software on your PC and ensure that the ASA/PIX version 7 binary and ASDM file are in the TFTP default directory. This procedure was described previously.

Step 2 Configure the properties of the network card on your PC so that it can communicate with the security appliance. Set the following parameters: IP address **192.168.1.2**, subnet mask **255.255.255.0**, default gateway **192.168.1.1**.

Step 3 Make sure that the ASA/PIX version 7 binary and ASDM 5.0 software are in the download directory for your TFTP server, and then launch the server.

Your PC should now be prepared to copy the ASA/PIX operating system and ASDM software.

Preparing ASA/PIX Security Appliance for Software Recovery

You must now put the ASA/PIX Security Appliance in a mode so that you can configure it to use its TFTP download functions:

Step 1   You must be first connect to the PIX via the console port. To do so, use a serial cable from your PC to the security appliance console port and use a terminal emulator such as HyperTerminal.

Step 2   Set the HyperTerminal properties to use your PC serial port, the same as the parameters illustrated in Figure C-1.

Figure C-1   *HyperTerminal Communication Settings*

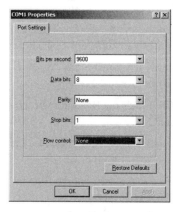

After you establish console connectivity, you must reboot your ASA/PIX Security Appliance by using the power switch. When the following output is displayed, press the **Esc** key on your keyboard.

```
Cisco Secure PIX Firewall BIOS (4.2) #6: Mon Aug 27 15:09:54 PDT 2001
Platform PIX-515e
Flash=E28F640J3 @ 0x3000000
Use BREAK or ESC to interrupt flash boot.
Use SPACE to begin flash boot immediately.
Reading 1921536 bytes of image from flash.
```

After you enter the Monitor mode on the security appliance, you are ready to install the version 7 operating system and will see the following on your screen:

```
Use BREAK or ESC to interrupt flash boot.
Use SPACE to begin flash boot immediately.
Flash boot interrupted.
0: i8255X @ PCI(bus:0 dev:13 irq:11)
1: i8255X @ PCI(bus:0 dev:14 irq:10)
monitor>
```

Now, you must complete the following steps to prepare the ASA/PIX
Security Appliance to install the version 7 software:

Step 3   Plug a crossover Ethernet cable between the Ethernet 0 port on your
security appliance and the networking card on your PC.

Step 4   Enter the following commands one at a time at the monitor prompt:

(a)   Initialize Ethernet zero on your security appliance to
prepare for the download:

```
monitor> int 0
0: i8255X @ PCI(bus:0 dev:13 irq:11)
1: i8255X @ PCI(bus:0 dev:14 irq:10)
Ethernet auto negotiation timed out.
Ethernet port 0 initialized.
```

(b)   Configure the security appliance to know the IP address of
your PC, which is the TFTP server:

```
monitor> server 192.168.1.2
server 192.168.1.2
```

(c)   Configure the IP address of the security appliance Ethernet
port:

```
monitor> address 192.168.1.1
address 192.168.1.1
```

(d)   Define the name of the file that is to be uploaded from the
PC's TFTP server. This should be the ASA/PIX version 7
image. In the example, you use **pix70.bin**, although Cisco
might change this naming convention at any time:

```
monitor> file pix70.bin
file pix70.bin
```

(e)   Wait 5 to 10 seconds to ensure that the security appliance
driver has bound to the hardware interface, and then verify
that you have network connectivity between the appliance
and your PC using the **ping** command:

```
monitor> ping 192.168.1.2
Sending 5, 100-byte 0x1b03 ICMP Echoes to 192.168.1.2,
timeout is 4 seconds:
!!!!!
Success rate is 100 percent (5/5)
```

After pings are successful between the ASA/PIX Security Appliance and
your PC, you are ready to start the procedure to upgrade to ASA/PIX
version 7 and ASDM.

Recovering the ASA/PIX to Version 7

The following tasks have been completed:

- Your PC has the ASA/PIX and ASDM software.

- TFTP is running on your PC.

- Your PC is connected physically to the security appliance.

- The ASA/PIX Security Appliance is configured to access the PC's TFTP server.

You are ready to start the download procedure. A word of caution: Some steps have been highlighted for you that are critical in this process. If these steps are not followed, you might need to restart the download process from the beginning:

Step 1   Enter the following command to start the download procedure:

```
monitor> tftp..........
```

The dots indicate the download is in process. You can also check the log on your TFTP server to ensure that data is being transferred.

Step 2   At this point, the ASA/PIX Security Appliance should boot automatically. You will see the ASA/PIX prompt come up on your screen. Enter the command **show version** to verify that version 7.0.x is installed. You should see a line on the show version that indicates that 7.0.x is on your machine:

```
PIX (7.0) #0: Wed Aug 11 01:28:06 MDT 2004
Hardware:   PIX-515E, 64 MB RAM, CPU Pentium II 431 MHz
Flash E28F128J3 @ 0xfff00000, 16MB
BIOS Flash unknown @ 0x0, 0KB
 0: Ext: Ethernet0            : media index  0: irq 10
 1: Ext: Ethernet1            : media index  1: irq 11
License Features for this Platform:
Maximum Physical Interfaces : 6
Maximum VLANs               : 25
Inside Hosts                : Unlimited
Failover                    : Enabled
VPN-DES                     : Enabled
VPN-3DES-AES                : Enabled
Failover standby only       : Disabled
Cut-through Proxy           : Enabled
```

Step 3   As a final step, you must update your **boot** command to point at your new ASA/PIX version 7 image and then save the configuration to memory. Enter the following series of commands:

```
pixfirewall# conf t

pixfirewall(config)# boot system flash:/pix70.bin

pixfirewall(config)# wr mem
```

At this point, your ASA/PIX Security Appliance should be fully operational.

If your configuration is lost, you might need to paste or restore it from backup. If you do need to paste the configuration, you must first remove the enable password and then reset it after you restore the configuration. Because the password is encrypted when it is cut and pasted, if you don't remove the password line before pasting, your new password will be an impossible-to-remember hash.

Installing ASDM 5.0 on the ASA/PIX Security Appliance

After installing and verifying the ASA/PIX version 7 operating system, you need to install ASDM 5.0. The process is similar; you just use different filenames. The following steps define the ASDM download procedures.

It might be possible that even though you had to recover the ASA/PIX operating system that ASDM is still working. Before you start this procedure, after you have pasted your configuration, try to access the ASA/PIX Security Appliance using your web browser. If ASDM works, you can skip the remainder of this appendix:

Step 1 Use the **ping** command to ensure that you still have connectivity between your PC and the ASA/PIX Security Appliance: **ping 192.168.1.2**. If you don't have connectivity, you might need to reconfigure your PC and your security appliance to establish a communication path. If you followed this procedure step by step, however, you should be fine.

Step 2 Now, you are ready to download the ASDM software. Enter the following command on the ASA/PIX Security Appliance in Enable mode:

```
copy tftp://192.168.1.2/asdm50.bin flash:
```

You, should see exclamation marks displayed on your screen indicating that the file is in the process of downloading.

Note   Note again that the filename for the ASDM software might be different than in the previous command.

When prompted for the output filename, you must use **asdm.bin** to be consistent with the rest of this book.

Step 3 After the ASDM download is complete, you must configure the ASA/PIX Security Appliance to identify the image name for ASDM. In Enable mode on the security appliance, enter the following command:

```
asdm image asdm.bin
```

If you have a saved configuration that you pasted into the security appliance, you won't need to enter the preceding command.

Step 4   To enable ASDM to run, you must first enable the web user interface with the following command:

```
http server enable
```

If you have a saved configuration that you pasted into the security appliance, you won't need to enter the preceding command.

Step 5   After the HTTP server is started, you must add a command that tells the ASA/PIX Security Appliance what IP address it can access an ASDM session from. To enable your PC to administer your PIX, enter the following command:

```
http 192.168.1.2 255.255.255.255 inside
```

This will allow only access for the PC that has the 192.168.1.2 IP address. If you have a saved configuration that you pasted into the security appliance, you won't need to enter the preceding command.

Step 6   After you complete this process, you might need to reset your interface address to match the IP addressing scheme of your network.

Step 7   Enter the **write mem** command to save the configuration in the Flash memory of your ASA/PIX Security Appliance.

You have now completed the process of restoring the ASA/PIX version 7 operating system and the ASDM 5.0 PIX management utility.

INDEX

K–L

M

N

O–P

R

W-X-Y-Z

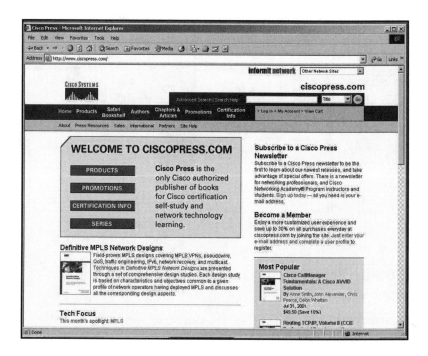

Cisco Systems

Cisco Press

3 STEPS TO LEARNING

STEP 1

First-Step

STEP 2

Fundamentals

STEP 3

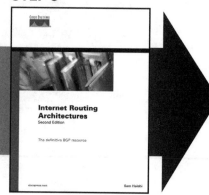

Networking Technology Guides

STEP 1   **First-Step**—Benefit from easy-to-grasp explanations. No experience required!

STEP 2   **Fundamentals**—Understand the purpose, application, and management of technology.

STEP 3   **Networking Technology Guides**—Gain the knowledge to master the challenge of the network.

NETWORK BUSINESS SERIES

The Network Business series helps professionals tackle the business issues surrounding the network. Whether you are a seasoned IT professional or a business manager with minimal technical expertise, this series will help you understand the business case for technologies.

Justify Your Network Investment.

Look for Cisco Press titles at your favorite bookseller today.

Visit **www.ciscopress.com/series** for details on each of these book series.